Reconfiguring Class, Gender, Ethnicity and Ethics in Chinese Internet Culture

New information technologies have, to an unprecedented degree, come to reshape human relations, identities and communities both online and offline. As Internet narratives including online fiction, poetry and films reflect and represent ambivalent politics in China, the Chinese state wishes to enable the formidable soft power of this new medium whilst at the same time handling the ideological uncertainties it inevitably entails.

This book investigates the ways in which class, gender, ethnicity and ethics are reconfigured, complicated and enriched by the closely intertwined online and offline realities in China. It combs through a wide range of theories on Internet culture, intellectual history, and literary, film, and cultural studies, and explores a variety of online cultural materials, including digitized spoofing, microblog fictions, micro-films, online fictions, web dramas, photographs, flash mobs, popular literature and films. These materials have played an important role in shaping the contemporary cultural scene, but have so far received little critical attention. Here, the authors demonstrate how Chinese Internet culture has provided a means to intervene in the otherwise monolithic narratives of identity and community.

Offering an important contribution to the rapidly growing field of Internet studies, this book will also be of interest to students and scholars of Chinese culture, literary and film studies, media and communication studies, and Chinese society.

Haomin Gong is Assistant Professor of Chinese at Case Western Reserve University in Cleveland, USA.

Xin Yang is Associate Professor of Chinese at Macalester College in St. Paul, Minnesota, USA.

Routledge Contemporary China

For a full list of titles in this series, please visit www.routledge.com

Reconfiguring Class, Gender, Ethnicity and Ethics in Chinese Internet Culture

Haomin Gong and Xin Yang

Routledge
Taylor & Francis Group
LONDON AND NEW YORK

First published 2017 by Routledge

2 Park Square, Milton Park, Abingdon, Oxfordshire OX14 4RN
711 Third Avenue, New York, NY 10017

Routledge is an imprint of the Taylor & Francis Group, an informa business

First issued in paperback 2018

British Library Cataloguing-in-Publication Data
A catalogue record for this book is available from the British Library

Library of Congress Cataloging-in-Publication Data
A catalog record for this book has been requested

ISBN: 978-1-138-95153-2 (hbk)
ISBN: 978-1-138-35161-5 (pbk)

Typeset in Times New Roman
by Apex CoVantage, LLC

Contents

Figures

Acknowledgements

This book marked a new stage of our decade-long academic collaboration and friendship. We began collaborating on a variety of projects as colleagues at the College of William and Mary in 2006. Our mutual interest in Chinese Internet literature and culture led us on this exciting and rewarding journey of collaborative research. After our brief meeting in Williamsburg, we took academic positions at different institutions but were able to take advantage of the Internet and collaborative software, both of which have facilitated remote collaboration. When we look back on this experience, it seems only felicitous that we employed these methods to carry out research on the culture of the Internet.

Numerous colleagues and mentors have given us much-needed feedback, comments, and suggestions on our ongoing project. Jin Feng and Heather Inwood have shared their insights on Chinese Internet culture. Wendy Larson, Sheldon Lu, Xiaomei Chen, Michelle Yeh, Tze-lan Sang, Maram Epstein, Jiayan Mi, Satoko Suzuki, Ping Wang, Peter Jianhua Yang, James Laine, Jingqi Fu, Charles Musgrove and Yanfang Tang have been encouraging and guiding us since the beginning stage of our careers. Geng Song, Bo Zhu, and Bin Yang shared many thoughtful conversations which sparkled inspiration and new ideas. Rebecca Lawrence at Routledge has been very patient with us, working diligently at each stage of our writing. Our editors Cristina Garafola and Richard Stack have meticulously reviewed our manuscript.

This project also has received funding from the W. P. Jones Faculty Development Fund, the Baker-Nord Center for the Humanities, the ACES+ (Academic Careers in Engineering & Science) Initiative at Case Western Reserve University, and the Wallace International Travel Fund at Macalester College. Senior capstone seminars on Cyber China conducted at Macalester College also played an important role in the project. Our conversation with college students on various topics surrounding Internet culture gave us inspiration to think about Chinese Internet culture from multiple perspectives. Our respective home departments, the Department of Modern Languages and Literature at Case Western Reserve University and the Department of Asian Languages and Cultures at Macalester College, have been extremely generous in mentoring us.

An early version of Chapter 1, "Digitized Parody: The Politics of *Egao* in Contemporary China," was published in *China Information* 24, no. 1 (2010): 3–26.

An early version of Chapter 2, "Circulating Smallness: The Dialectics of Micro-narrative," was published as "Circulating Smallness on Weibo: The Dialectics of Microfiction" in *Frontiers of Literary Studies in China* 8, no. 1 (2014): 181–202. We thank both publishers for granting us permission to reprint them in this book.

Last but not the least, we would like to thank our families and beloved ones. Haomin has no words to express the debt he owes to his parents, whose love has been an invaluable asset in his life; to his wife Lina Dai, without whose unremitting support and love this book would have been impossible; and to their daughter Stephanie, who has brought endless joy that lights his life. Xin dedicates the book to her parents, brothers, and sister in China, for their unfading love and support; to her husband Zhongming Chen, for his unending love, patience, and wisdom; and to their daughter Mindy Chen, who has bought so much joy and magic energy to her life.

Introduction

Cyberspace, heterotopia, and postsocialism in China

On December 16–18, 2015, a much hyped World Internet Conference was held in Wuzhen, a small scenic town in Zhejiang Province in China. Permanently set in Wuzhen, this was the second of the annual World Internet Conferences that Beijing had organized and orchestrated, unmistakably showing the Chinese government's ambition and determination to play a more visible role in the promising though challenging world of the Internet.

The Chinese Internet has experienced exponential growth since it was first connected to the world Internet in 1994. In the past decade or so, this growth has been especially eye-catching, as the Internet permeated almost every corner of Chinese society and almost every aspect of people's everyday lives. Through optical fibers China seems, optimists believe, to be finally seamlessly connected to and merged into the increasingly globalized world; but the reality shows that that is not yet entirely the case. During the few days when the World Internet Conference was held, the small town of Wuzhen, with a special technological setup, was open to the outside world without any restrictions that an ordinary Internet connection in China would encounter. This was indeed an "extra-ordinary" space and time, blessed as it was by the special event, not unlike the situation in many other such events, that had international involvement and aimed at achieving global impacts. In accordance with this international spirit, the apparently encouraging words of "freedom and order" that the Chinese President Xi Jinping highlighted in his opening speech, however, only reminded the attendees, and those who were not allowed to attend the Conference, of the imposition of "order" and transience of freedom on the Chinese Internet (Makinen, Yang and Li 2015). Not unlike many other things in China, the Internet in China indeed has its own "Chinese Characteristics."

With the breakneck development of the Chinese Internet, studies of the Chinese Internet have also grown at a rapid rate in recent years, and it has become one of the most dynamic fields in China studies. In English scholarship on the subject, a growing number of articles and book-length studies are published every year. Yet, despite the momentum and dynamics it has gathered, English scholarship on the Internet in China seems to be dominated by scholars' preoccupation with issues raised within the disciplines of political science, sociology, and communication, with comparatively fewer studies conducted in the fields of literature, art, and culture. This is clearly shown in any bibliography of studies of the Chinese Internet.[1] Moreover, among the existing studies there is a tendency to overemphasize the potential that the Internet may have in causing *social* and *political* changes in Chinese society, while less attention has been paid to its *literary* and *cultural* impacts. As David Kurt Herold (2011: 5–15) observes, current academic studies of the Chinese Internet basically fall into four major approaches, namely, taking the Chinese Internet respectively as a space of "control and resistance," "a tool for interaction and organization," "a driver for progress and development," and "new media." Except for the last approach, which occasionally touches upon Chinese Internet's cultural relevance, the other three mostly regard the Internet in China as a socio-political arena which is, perhaps and hopefully, capable of changes.

This "wishful" prospect, further still, is a product, exemplified in the case of studies on the Chinese Internet, of an inveterate bias in the West, which sees a third world country such as China as a particular area that awaits liberation from the universal West. As Herold (2015: 22) writes in another place:

> Academic research on the Internet in China appears determined to assign the Internet the role of promoting democracy in China, or as James Leibold phrased it, "mainstream analysis in the West continues to stress its revolutionary potential in China. . . . A perverse kind of 'digital Orientalism' . . . prevents us in the West from asking the same sort of difficult questions about the internet's impact in China that we have long asked ourselves." While nobody would seriously argue that the main purpose of the Internet in Europe or America is the provision of support for democracy, this appears to be the consensus among researchers of the Chinese Internet, which may be based more on wishful thinking than on data about Internet use in China.

This "digital Orientalism," indeed a problematic trend, conforms to a condescending and discriminating gesture prevalent in area studies, a fertile field of studies that emphasizes the particularity and alternativeness, as opposed to the universality of the West, of a case in a non-Western area. This mindset, as has been proved in intellectual history time and again, is harmful to both the research and the researched. In addition, all of these approaches, Herold (2015: 5–15) argues, are to different degrees "offline-centered" and need to be complemented by studies that take the Chinese Internet, borrowing Jürgen Habermas' highly influential theory, as a unique *online* space of the public sphere.

In recent years scholars have grown more aware of this problem and often reflect on their own positions in their research. For instance, Guobin Yang (2009b) emphasizes the importance of "emotions" in his studies of political activism facilitated by the Internet. In his introductory article on the Chinese Internet to the special issue that he edited for *China Information*, Yang (2014: 136; our emphasis) points out that people's understanding of the Chinese Internet's "multidimensional character, its diverse forms and actors, and the complex and fluid dynamics of contestation surrounding it, remains limited," and ascribes this problem to a tendency to focus on technology at the expense of *meaning and people*, and partly to a bias towards sweeping and dichotomous analytical categories, such as state vs. netizens, politics vs. entertainment, and authoritarianism vs. democracy. One of the perniciously appealing ways of sensationalizing the Chinese Internet falls under this either/or dichotomy.

In fact, Michel Hockx (2005: 671–2) has observed this lack of attention to *people* in his earlier studies of the Chinese Internet. English-language scholarship of the Chinese Internet, he claims, has given disproportionate attention to the issues such as state control, civil liberties, and e-economics, while research on cultural production is almost absent. Jin Feng (2013: 7) echoes Hockx observation and further identifies, in the existing Chinese-language research on the subject, the problem of over-theorization at the expense of textual analysis. On top of that, she also points out the unfortunate lack in any effort by Chinese scholars in employing the "categories of class and gender" in their analyses, two main categories that Feng focuses on in her pioneer studies of Chinese web romance literature. We agree with Feng, and we would also like to add, in addition to class and gender, that the categories of ethnicity and ethics, which loom large on the Chinese Internet, are also largely insufficiently explored in current studies of the Chinese Internet. These four categories of class, gender, ethnicity, and ethics are the focus of this study of online literature and culture in China.

A turn to studies of literature and culture in studies of the Chinese Internet, in our view, is a constructive approach much to be welcomed, one which will surely complicate and enrich people's understanding of the Chinese Internet at large. This is because, as the few recently published books have shown, Internet literature and culture in China has been a tremendously dynamic site, on which negotiations and contests among different powers through the mediation of the technology of the Internet, and those between human beings and the Internet in their interactions, are most vigorously manifested. The transformative and restructuring power of the Internet to human society and lives can be more productively construed in Internet literature and culture with the latter's attention to *human* engagement with the technology.

In recent years it has been encouraging to see the publication of a few excellent book-length studies of the cultural and literary aspects of the Chinese Internet, each contributing to this burgeoning field in its own way. Jin Feng's (2013: 4) *Romancing the Internet: Producing and Consuming Chinese Web Romance* examines the specific genre of web romance fiction, and investigates the ways in which women writers and readers paradoxically both defy and embrace "patriarchal ideologies and societal norms at the same time," by "recycl[ing] textual and visual elements from popular culture to imagine an ideal masculinity and construct their own gender identity vis-à-vis this 'other'." Heather Inwood's (2014) *Verse Going Viral: China's New Media Scenes* focuses on the writing, circulation, and consumption of Internet poetry in China, unraveling a paradox surrounding this writing, that is, the traditionally viewed "high-brow" cultural form of poetry is simultaneously marginalized, precisely because of its elitism, in this age of prevailing commercialization and consumerism, and yet also brought to an unlikely flourishing, thanks to interactive opportunities provided by the Internet and other new media.

Michel Hockx's recent monograph, *Internet Literature in China*, deserves special attention. This much expected work is a comprehensive survey of Chinese Internet literature based on the author's decade-long research of the subject. By situating the Chinese Internet writing within China's postsocialist condition, Hockx presents a dynamic scene in which web-based literary creations reshape and transform not only the production, circulation, and consumption of online literature, but also its forms and aesthetics. A trailblazing work indeed, *Internet Literature in China*, however, focuses rather exclusively on what may be called high and serious literature, while popular literature or genre fiction, a significant component of online writings, is mostly off his radar. This rather "elitist" approach to the subject is quite understandable because, as Hockx (2015: 6–7) makes clear in the opening pages, this work is intended for a Western readership who are unfamiliar with Chinese Internet literature; therefore, for the sake of an easy acceptance by Western readers, whose views of Internet literature are largely shaped by a mainstream understanding that Internet literature is the body of writings that engage closely with the *mediality* of the Internet, and explore new possibilities provided by the Internet in their experimentations, Hockx's strategy of writing proves to be effective.

On the other hand, however, as many critics have noted, Chinese Internet literature presents unique features that are, in many ways, in sharp contrast with those in the West. This is not another claim of exceptionalism in the Chinese case, but, as Guobin Yang (2014: 136) observes, "The Internet in China has taken on such distinctly Chinese characteristics that it may now be called the Chinese Internet in the same way as we call China's literature 'Chinese literature' or China's politics 'Chinese politics'." For one thing, Internet literature in China mostly refers to any form of writing on the Internet, and the predominant form of such writings, despite Hockx' fervent discussions of the more experimental cases, are "traditional" works, by Western standards, without much experimentation with the mediality of the Internet. It is in fact these more conventional popular literary works that are the main subject of studies of Chinese literature in much of Chinese-language scholarship (Shao 2015a, Zhejiang 2015). While we agree that the experimental works that Hockx investigates constitute an important part of Chinese Internet literature, we believe it is those popular writings that are more revealing of the specific postsocialist condition under which they are produced and consumed.

Besides the works mentioned above, Paola Voci's *China on Video: Smaller-Screen Realities*, although not particularly dealing with the Internet per se, shows a high degree of thematic relevance to the topic of our exploration. This book investigates the video and the mini-film exclusively produced for and consumed on smaller screens in China, an increasingly prevalent form of filmmaking and consumption only made possible by and prospering on the Internet. Voci (2010, back cover) argues that though such smaller-screen videos may seem "insignificant" in terms of "production costs, distribution size, profit gains, intellectual or artistic ambitions," their "lightness," however, demonstrates an "alternative way of seeing and understanding the world."

These studies, although vigorous in their own terms, can arguably be further complemented by an investigation that focuses on literary and cultural phenomena, including verbal, textual, audio-visual, and many other forms of expression specifically shaped by the Internet, and addresses the issues of class, gender, ethnicity, and ethics among other things, issues that loom large and constitute the most important dimensions of the culture on the Chinese Internet. This form of investigation is precisely what the present book aims to carry out. The reason why we focus on these issues refashioned on the Internet is mainly because current studies of Internet culture, we find, are largely dominated by explorations of the *technologicality* and *mediality* of the Internet, and the "new" cultures that emerge as the result of the advent of the Internet as a new technology and medium;[2] but the "new" cultures that are viewed and sensed from a *humanist* perspective have only just begun to attract some critical attention. We believe a specific investigation of class, gender, ethnicity, and ethics – aspects that are integral parts of human lives – refashioned in Internet literature and culture, is able to provide us with a vantage point, from which we can gain a more intimate and nuanced understanding of the relationship between human beings and the Internet, and avoid the dichotomistic views of the Chinese Internet that Herold and Guobin Yang describe above.

Further, this examination, characterized as it is by the spirit of multiplicity and complexity, is marked by an emphasis on close reading and textual studies carried out within a broader examination of the larger sociocultural context. Only by so doing, we echo many critics' concern: can an understanding of the Internet culture become more grounded and informed?

Cyberspace, neoliberalism, and postsocialism

Chinese Internet culture began to flourish as Internet access became increasingly available in China in the late 1990s, coinciding with a large-scale expansion of the postsocialist condition in the country. Or, perhaps it is no coincidence that the two emerged at the same time. Michel Hockx has keenly pointed out the relationship, for instance, between Chinese Internet literature and postsocialism. Thus he writes,

> . . . the postsocialist condition is nowhere more recognizable than on the Internet, a mixed, messy space where the socialist publishing system has been left far behind, but residual socialism lingers through novel regulation systems and continuing censorship; where commercialism is rampant, but where there is plenty of room for independent expression and creativity; and where genuinely novel forms of communication and interaction are integrated with artistic and political ideals constantly and on a daily basis.
>
> (Hockx 2015: 17–18)

Mapping the development of the term *postsocialism* in China studies and combing through its disparate implications in a variety of discussions, Hockx suggests that the highly mixed space of the Chinese Internet is directly or indirectly informed by the increasingly diversified postsocialist condition. While this observation is insightful, Hockx fails to acknowledge the role that neoliberalism plays in the formation of Internet culture in postsocialist China. Neoliberalism, in fact, is both implicitly embedded in the development of the Internet and an integral part of the forming of the postsocialist condition in China, under which the Internet increasingly becomes a restructuring force. An examination of the relationship among cyberspace, neoliberalism, and postsocialism will yield some new understandings of literary and cultural expressions on the Internet.

Critics have noted that the Internet, along with other information technologies, for all its unprecedented power made accessible to individuals in the vast network of communication, has for a long time been taken, or imagined, as a utopian technology of counterculture, a culture, it was hoped, that would, through a countering of "an unfeeling bureaucracy, a calculating, mechanical form of social organization that had brought humankind to the edge of nuclear annihilation" (Turner 2006: 237), lead to an ideal of individual freedom and collective harmony. This techno-utopian social vision was largely justified by the Cold War fear of communism, corporate capitalism, and nuclear wars in the US; and, as it continued to be modeled by technological development and cultural changes, this techno-utopianism gradually formed into a discursive structure of flexible and networked sociability, through which the American public understood self and society. However, this vision, it turns out, was based on a decisively ideological shift in the political and cultural valence of information technologies, and witnessed a neoliberalist turn in the years of its development.

Fred Turner in his well researched book, *From Counterculture to Cyberculture* (2006), analyzes in detail the process in which, as the book title indicates, a counterculture based on personal computers and the Internet metamorphizes into a mainstream cyberculture that has become a norm of today's sociability. He describes the way in which computers and the Internet were, in the initial stage of the metamorphosis, informed by Norbert Wiener's cybernetics and other information theories, and thus imagined as an emblem of counterculture; and he continues to summarize the technologies' following evolutions thus:

> Thanks in no small part to [Steward] Brand's work at the Whole Earth Catalog and later at *Rolling Stone*, desktop computers had come to be seen as "personal" technology. In keeping with the New Communalist ethos of tool use, they promised to transform individual consciousness and society at large. Thanks to the citizens of the WELL [Whole Earth 'Lectronic Link], computer-mediated communication had been reimagined in terms of disembodied, communal harmony and renamed virtual community. Cyberspace itself had been reconfigured as an electronic frontier. Finally, in the 1990s, the social and professional networks of the Global Business Network and *Wired* seemed to suggest that a new, networked form of economic life was

emerging. Because of computer technologies, their example implied, it was finally becoming possible to move through life not in hierarchical bureaucratic towers, but as members of flexible, temporary, and culturally congenial tribes.

(Turner 2006: 237–8)

One critical moment in this evolution, Turner believes, was an ideological metamorphosis that turned the military-industrial-academic technocracy backed by government sponsorship, a system that people of the 1960s had sought to undermine, into a techno-optimism that they embraced. As Manuel Castells (2010: 45) also observes, "The creation and development of the Internet in the last three decades on the twentieth century resulted from a unique blending of military strategy, big science cooperation, technological entrepreneurship, and countercultural innovation." Cybernetics, with its claim of an ideal(istic) homeostasis of decentralization, democracy, and wholeness, realized by inextricably connected information, played a decisive role in this "countercultural innovation," as people came to seek in this originally militarily-industrially-academically oriented information theory new rhetorics for self-expressivity and communal collectivity. One key in this ideological metamorphosis was information technologies being taken as *tools*, tools that could be, and, indeed in the opinion of the New Communal experimentalists, had been, transformed for individual and collective reformation rather than their original military purposes.

Another significant ideological shift was the gradual yet decisive neoliberalization of information technologies in the 1980s. While the first information technology revolution in the 1970s was "technologically induced rather than socially determined," Castells remarks (2010: 60), the one in the 1980s, however, was particularly figured by the social ethos of neoliberalism. Castells (2010: 60) continues to explain that, once the second information technology revolution

came into existence as a system, . . . its development and applications, and ultimately its content, were decisively shaped by the historical context in which it expanded. Indeed, by the 1980s, capitalism (specifically, major corporations and governments of the club of G-7 countries) did undertake a substantial process of economic and organizational restructuring, in which new information technology played a fundamental role and was decisively shaped by the role it played.

The simultaneous emergence of the Reagan/Thatcher mold of neoliberalism and the information technology revolution in the West in the 1980s is by no means a coincidence. The neoliberalist market-utopianism and the cybercultural techno-utopianism share many ideals in common, such as organizational decentralization, systemic deregulation, structural flattening, atomic individualism, unconstrained communication, automated control systems, and so on. In fact, neoliberals did make use of many of the ideas and ideologies of the cyberculture, or the *cybermyth*, as many would call it, repackaging them into a set of technological wonders, and thus justifying neoliberal practices with them (Wang 2014: 29).

Many "public intellectuals" in this process stood up and promoted the utopic vision of computers and the Internet in neoliberal terms. For instance, Nicholas Negroponte (1995) famously declares that being digital can "flatten organizations, globalize society, decentralize control, and help harmonize people." This remark is echoed by Thomas L. Friedman's (2005) equally vociferous claim that "the world is flat," which in turn is heralded by similarly optimistic yet much earlier visions, such as Alvin Toffler's (1980) information age, "third wave" society. Toffler's book *The Third Wave*, in fact, played a special role in China's reform and neoliberal turn, as it became an instant bestseller in China once it was translated in the mid-1980s, and as a result tremendously fueled Chinese public imagination of the imminent, Westernized future of a networked society.

Kevin Kelly (1995: 25–6), one of the most active and influential promoters of new techno-neoliberal rhetorics, has a well-known saying that is perhaps most representative of the euphoric ethos of the time:

> The Net icon has no center – it is a bunch of dots connected to other dots – a cobweb of arrows pouring into each other, squirming together like a nest of snakes, the restless image fading at indeterminate edges. The Net is the archetype – always the same picture – displayed to represent all circuits, all intelligence, all interdependence, all things economic and social and ecological, all communications, all democracy, all groups, all large systems.

This conspiracy, if it can be so called, between neoliberalism and information technology evolution is achieved, as Wang Weijia (2014: 30) sees it, through a series of ideological exchanges: on a macroscopic level, neoliberalists painted a utopian picture of a world of ultimate freedom and co-prosperity arrived at through implementation of information technologies; on a microscopic level, they proposed an ideal mode of production characterized by a flexible, decentralized, and networked way of work that depends on and is informed by information technologies; and finally, they constructed a digitalized world as the only prospect for the transformation and future of capitalism.

These ideological exchanges are realized, Wang (2014: 33–6) continues to explain, through a reliance on four rhetorics. First, the "biological rhetoric" metaphorizes new information technologies into the force of "nature," which follows a "universal" law. This metaphorization, along with the one that rhapsodizes capitalism, particularly neoliberal capitalism, as appealing to "commonsense" intuitions, desires, and values, constructs a myth in which information technologies and neoliberal capitalism form a mutually informed couple, self-legitimated by a claimed discourse of nature and universalism (Dawkins 1976, Kelly 1995, 2002, Negroponte 1995, Rothschild 1990). Second, the rhetoric of the "end of history" (Fukuyama 1992), a much debated neoliberal allegation, validates and is validated by the prevailing techno- and market-utopianism. Yet, the moment when people are "blessed" with the increasing compression of time and space also marks the time when technological divides and socioeconomic gaps are becoming increasingly wide. Third, the rhetoric of the "outlaw area," first proposed by Richard Buckminster Fuller in the 1960s (Tomkins 1966) and made popular by William Gibson's 1984 science fiction *Neuromancer*, has been taken by counterculturalists as an area where experiments on a holistic self and a harmonious virtual community can be carried out. Similar to the neoliberal utopia in which complex, socioeconomic issues are reduced to a simple freedom in the market, the cybermyth of an outlaw area likewise ideologically simplifies such issues into mere participation in a cultivation of consciousness and community through technological explorations. Both therefore foreclose any real political endeavor in tackling those issues.[3] And fourth, "authoritarian populism," an ideology that Stuart Hall (1988: 123–46) believes has played a key role in the rise of neoliberalism in the West, finds its counterpart in the process of the explosion of the Internet. If neoliberalism intriguingly, and successfully, fashions political and economic elites into representatives and benefactors of public interests, cybermyth similarly portrays techno-elites as true inheritors of the counterculturalists, and makes believe that "netizens" play the role of fully enfranchised citizens.

Needless to say, just as neoliberalism is by no means the *natural* end of socioeconomic development which its proponents paint it to be, but is instead an ideological construct (Duggan 2003, Wang 2003), cyberculture is no more than a specific product, instead of a natural and universal outcome, of the social, political, and cultural condition of neoliberal capitalism. Critics have already questioned the ideological underpinnings of cyberculture and neoliberalism. For instance, Castells (2010) points out that the so-called logic of the network is only an extension of capitalist logic. Vincent Mosco (2004: 68), similarly linking the myth of cyberspace to capitalism, also remarks,

> Today, we are more prone to hear the voices of myth – the voices of Fukuyama, Negroponte, Dyson, and others who display a new history (or unhistory) based on a vision of capitalism triumphant and transcendent, launched a friction-free adventure into cyberspace (and every other form of space) by the power of new communication and information technologies.

Thus, Wang Weijia (2014: 27) rightly declares, the myth of cyberspace is "more a product of social development than that of new information technologies."

This is also true with the case in China. By the time the Internet emerged as one of the fastest-growing technologies in the mid-1990, China had already been on the neoliberal track for more than a decade. Deng Xiaoping launched the Reform and Opening-up policy in 1978, which marked the beginning of the market-oriented economic reforms that are still in place today. "China's neoliberal policies began in earnest in 1984," Robin Visser writes (2010: 92). Although these policies faced increasing questions and challenges, mainly from the New Left, as neoliberalism at large did globally in the 1990s, in China they continued to play a major part in shaping contemporary economic and social cultures.

The Internet, upon its introduction to China, immediately formed an ecology that was on the one hand similar to its Western counterpart, but on the other shaped by the specific postsocialist condition in China.[4] For one thing, while Chinese Internet has tremendously freed netizens from constraints imposed by the traditional bureaucratic, hierarchical social structure, it is also largely controlled by the authoritarian Party-state. (This will become clear in the case studies in the following chapters.) Indeed, the Internet culture in China did not experience the ideological metamorphosis "from counterculture to cyberculture" which its Western counterpart had gone through, mainly because the Internet and other information technologies developed in, or migrated to, China against a very different sociocultural background. These technologies, for an ordinary Chinese user, have no history of being transformed from being products of the military-academic-industrial technocracy, to personal tools for experimenting with individual expressions and communal harmony under the condition of anti-bureaucracy, anti-hierarchy social movements. In other words, they had skipped their "formative" stage of development, and were presented to Chinese users upon their arrival almost immediately as "personal" technologies that would soon hugely free the latter up. These utopian ideals euphorically resonated with the then still largely prevailing neoliberal ethos in China, and together they greatly fueled Chinese netizens' imaginations of a democratic, heterarchical, flexible, networked, and, most importantly, free society made possible by the advent of the neoliberal turn, a significant part of the postsocialist condition, and information technologies.[5]

Yet, just as questions of class, gender, ethnicity, and ethics are largely masked by neoliberal rhetorics and in the forming of new politico-economic elites, these questions are also mostly obscured in the myth of cyberspace, which tends instead to turn toward rhetorics of empowering the individual and constructing the virtual community (Turner 2006: 97–100). An overemphasis on the utopian *disembodied* intimacy in the virtual community that flourishes in cyberspace only leads to an overlooking of netizens' *embodied* lives that inevitably rely on material supports. This oversight of materiality and sociality of the cyberspace is paralleled by an active obscuring of "the material and technical infrastructures on which both the Internet and the lives of the digital generation depend," and it, in Turner's view (2006: 260, 262), contributes to the failure of countercultural technological experiments due mainly to people's lack of attention to politics. Mihaela Kelemen and Warren Smith (2001: 370) also specifically criticize libertarian rhetorics surrounding the virtual community, arguing that "cyberlibertarians have misunderstood what community is by placing too much emphasis on a disembodied individual," and "cyberlibertarian rhetoric is a far cry from the everyday practices that are being constructed and reproduced via the Internet." They bring to the fore the *sociality* of cyberspace interactions, and expect the Internet to "open up a new space where human 'will to live' is expressed in a social and embodied fashion." Thus, David Kurt Herold (2011, 2015) especially emphasizes the importance of teasing out interactions of online and offline spaces in studies of the Internet. Peter Marolt (2015: 15) echoes him by pointing out the urgency of bringing back to the map an investigation of politics in a specific sociohistorical context:

> The new politics is not less place-based or a-historical, but rather the opposite. It consists of richer hybrid places, permeated with meanings created by knowledgeable individual agents who find themselves in specific places and times that provide the context for their own authorial idiosyncrasies.

Therefore, a vigorous interrogation of the questions of class, gender, ethnicity, and ethics, under the specific postsocialist condition in China, in Internet culture is much needed. We strongly believe that a study of the Internet is, in the last analysis, a study of human beings, not technologies. The Internet has been, at an accelerating rate, restructuring relationships among people of different ages, colors, genders, ethnicities, classes, educational backgrounds, political orientations, economic statuses, and so on, both in the virtual cyberspace and the real sociohistorical space. These relationships need to be put under scrutiny in the concreteness and complexity of human lives. As Jack Linchuan Qiu (2006: 106) observes in his study of the Chinese working class' relations with the Internet, the reason why the Internet has made the process of restructuring contemporary society and culture possible is because of the specific microstructure of power, such as companies and schools (or the so-called street corner society), upon which social functions of technologies depend. In other words, it is the specific social and cultural structures in reality, in Qiu's view, that determine the way in which the Internet, in return, restructures online and offline social and cultural spaces, but not vice versa. Thus, an exploration of the way in which specific aspects of these structures, namely, class, gender, ethnicity, ethics, etc., shape and are shaped by the Internet, a dynamically interactive process indeed, will offer us some new insights into Chinese Internet culture that is powerfully transformative and rapidly transforming.

Chinese Internet literature and culture prove to be a fertile ground for such an investigation. Conflicts of values best exemplified in Internet literature and culture, the cultural critic Wei Yingjie (2008: 105) claims, is a mirror of Chinese culture at large in modern transformation. In a way, Chinese Internet culture and literature are not simply a reflection of this transformation, but also a corrective that bears much agency.

Cyberspace as a heterotopia

Our discussion of the complicated relation of cyberspace, neoliberalism, and postsocialism above has revealed that cyberspace is a contested site in which the multifarious reality is reflected. While utopia is not the best term to conceptualize Internet culture, we find Michel Foucault's idea of *heterotopia* extremely helpful in understanding the flourishing verbal, visual, and audio texts produced, circulated, and consumed in cyberspace, and by extension, at the crossroads of the virtual and the real. In his influential article "Of Other Spaces," Foucault (1986:

23, a piece based on a lecture given in 1967) writes, "In any case I believe that the anxiety of our era has to do fundamentally with space, no doubt a great deal more than with time." This claim on the anxiety of the 1960s, which is echoed by David Harvey's (1973, 2000, 2006) criticism of late capitalism, is also extremely applicable to the social condition in the new millennium, as cyberspace has simultaneously imposed multiple challenges on and offered many opportunities to existing spaces, turning "reality" into a slippery term. Foucault's theory of heterotopia, by which the philosopher attempts to address the spatial complexity in the West in the 1960s, in a way also offers insights into the new challenges and opportunities that cyberspace brings to contemporary China.

Indeed, heterotopia is a richly loaded term. Literally it means an other place – "hetero-," meaning other and different, is a prefix opposite to "homo-," meaning the same, and "topia" refers to place. Foucault uses the term to designate spaces outside everyday life. He maps out six principles of heterotopia: (1) every culture creates heterotopias; (2) an existing heterotopia can function in more than one fashion; (3) a heterotopic space can juxtapose multiple spaces in one; (4) a heterotopia can link "heterochronies," merging pieces of time; (5) heterotopias "presuppose a system of opening and closing that both isolates them and makes them penetrable"; and (6) any hyperopia is intricately related to other spaces (Foucault 1986: 24–7). More specifically, a heterotopia can be a hospital, a prison, a boarding school, a vacation place, or any space that exists apart from the "normal" workings of society. It can also be a museum or a festival which merges different times and spaces, represented by artifacts from different eras and locations, in a single space. It exists in a cemetery, as the cemetery connects to other spaces (such as family and village), and its meaning has changed from the sacred to the symbolic illness. It is also found in a boat, for another example, whose mobility brings difference to the otherwise highly regulated social routine. Heterotopic spaces, according to Foucault (1986: 24), are "counter-sites, a kind of effectively enacted utopia in which the real sites, all the other real sites that can be found within the culture, are simultaneously represented, contested, and inverted."

The idea of heterotopia has been constructively employed in studies of Internet culture. Robin Rymarczuk and Maarten Derksen (2014), for instance, study Facebook as a heterotopia in a creative way. They see Facebook as "a system of opening and closing," since it requires logging in and signing out. Facebook embraces "a different kind of time," as it records our timeline and traces into our past. It breaks down the barrier between the private and the public, reality and illusion, as we display our private life for (controlled) public views. Indeed, not only Facebook or other social media, but the online space in general, are heterotopic.

Before we discuss Chinese online space in the theoretical framework of heterotopia, two other closely related concepts need to be examined. First, in his book *The Power of the Internet in China: Citizen Activism Online*, Guobin Yang (2009a) identifies forms of "utopian realism," which is embodied in images of freedom, home, and justice, in almost all online communities in China, such as Chinese-language forums and BBS (Bulletin Board System). He reads utopian realism as a critique of the present condition and a yearning for a better world, and believes it plays a more important role than any practical and utilitarian engagement in Chinese netizens' pursuit of their imagined power, empowerment, and senses of belonging in the 2000s. This utopian spirit is also embedded in Chinese Internet literature and culture, as exemplified in claims such as "literary revolution" (Shao 2015b: 143) and "from subculture to mainstream culture" (Zhuang 2014),[6] and constitutes an important aspect of cyberspace. Various groups found on Chinese social media such as Weibo, WeChat, and QQ, for example, are hailed for their breaking of geographical boundaries, and for providing a new public means to expose, publicize, and address social injustice, corruption, and the dark corners of the society. On the personal level, people tend to use these new media to project their positive sides and to construct rosier images of themselves. Both convey a strong sense of utopianism, which may find its counterpart on Facebook (Zhao, Grasmuck, and Martin 2008: 1816–36).

Second, the online space is also a real, physical, and technology-enabled object that shapes the way people relate to the world and other people around them. William Mitchell's (1999) idea of an "e-topia" highlights the role technologies play in the construction of cyberspace. Mitchell argues that the digital network is a new urban *infrastructure*, just like railroads, highways, electric power supplies, and telephone networks, and that the virtual space is part of urban design. Online banking, e-commerce, and cyber dating all prove what Mitchell predicted in 1999. Presidential campaigns on Twitter in the US and official Weibo and WeChat accounts that Chinese state and local agencies have created and managed also show that the online reality is becoming part of ideological platforms. Online engagements with reality have indeed presented its pragmatic power, which has increasing impacts on offline spaces. Even forms of playful online self-presentations are an integrated part of self-formation, according to Shanyang Zhao's (2005: 387–405) research on the digital self in social media, as the digital self and the Internet play an increasingly important role in affecting a person's self-development.

While cyberspace is both utopian and e-topian in nature in different ways, heterotopia is a better term to characterize this online space. If utopia means something ideal yet unattainable, heterotopia is concrete, real, and tangible, an "enacted utopia," as Foucault (1986: 24) terms it. If e-topia captures the practical function of cyberspace, heterotopia undoubtedly characterizes part of the online fantasy that is beyond the real. Foucault's (1986: 24) use of the metaphor of a mirror is extremely pertinent in our discussion of the multilayered reality online:

> The mirror is, after all, a utopia, since it is a placeless place. In the mirror, I see myself there where I am not, in an unreal, virtual space that opens up behind the surface; I am over there, there where I am not, a sort of shadow that gives my own visibility to myself, that enables me to see myself there where I am absent: such is the utopia of the mirror. But it is also a heterotopia in so far as the mirror does exist in reality, where it exerts a sort of counteraction on the position that I occupy. From the standpoint of the mirror I discover my absence from the place where I am since I see myself over there. Starting

from this gaze that is, as it were, directed toward me, from the ground of this virtual space that is on the other side of the glass, I come back toward myself; I begin again to direct my eyes toward myself and to reconstitute myself there where I am. The mirror functions as a heterotopia in this respect: It makes this place that I occupy at the moment when I look at myself in the glass at once absolutely real, connected with all the space that surrounds it, and absolutely unreal, since in order to be perceived it has to pass through this virtual point which is over there.

The metaphor of the mirror appropriately captures the features of technology-enabled online space. On the one hand, online reality can be utopias, as the online space enables a fantasized, aestheticized, and idealized reality through selected displays of texts and images; on the other hand, the virtual reality is also a reality – an increasingly important one – that people face almost everywhere and every day. In this sense, cyberspace, by merging different spaces – both the real and the unreal – becomes a new entity.

Foucault's heterotopia is border-crossing and heterogeneous. It represents, reflects, and also subverts our highly regulated norms, disrupting the continuity and normality of common everyday places. The online space is heterotopic also because it destabilizes borders on many fronts: borders between the real and the imaginary, the public and the private, the fantastic and the realistic. The Internet can be a space outside the norm, at least at the beginning stage of its emergence, and it is at the same time also a new norm of life, as technologies have already become an integral part of our everyday reality. It simultaneously represents and subverts many aspects of our regulated life. Taking daily communication as an example, people tend to send text messages to each other via social media, while they physically have their friends by their side. The norm of "communication" is thus revised and remodeled. Cyberspace, for another example, can also merge different spaces, such as public squares, banks, shopping malls, and cinemas, creating new meanings for such places and eventually becoming a new space itself. This online space, David Der-wei Wang (2011) claims, is a heterotopia that *zhainan* or *zhainü* (homebodies) are infatuated with. These people shut themselves at home and make the online world become their only meaningful location. The online space, at this moment, disrupts the daily routine whilst becoming a new everyday lifestyle.

In terms of literary studies, David Der-wei Wang (2011) uses the concept of heterotopia to discuss Chinese science fiction, including Liu Cixin's *The Three-Body Problem* (*Santi*) and Han Song's *Subway* (*Ditie*). These writings, in Wang's view, have challenged the boundaries among sense, rationality, perception, and habitual thinking, disturbing our perception of reality and fantasy, and providing a new way of thinking about the problematic world in which we find ourselves. Shao Yanjun (2012) also employs the concept of heterotopia in her studies of online fiction, especially online writings on fantasy, time-travel, and other surreal subjects.[7] In Shao's opinion, the prevalent presence of fantastical, supernatural, and unrealistic elements in Chinese online fiction is a manifestation of the structural transformation of the overall literary system, from one modeled on and governed by the socialist political system, to a more market-oriented one. These elements fill the vacuum left by the increasing irrelevance of grand narratives characteristic of socialist writings, or are taken as defiance of the predominance of the latter. They are, however, also deeply rooted in reality, as Shao (2012: 14) writes, "an iron house is unbreakable, or there is no better way after the iron house is demolished. Why can't people just have some daydreaming (*yiyin*)?" Such fiction is obviously fantasy, yet it also projects real desires, anxieties, and subconscious mentalities of people in contemporary China.

In our investigation of online configurations of class, gender, ethnicity, and ethics, we especially attend to the multiple layers of heterotopia. We explore the Internet as a heterotopia, as it blurs different boundaries, disrupts many norms, and yet creates new models. One such example is the intermediacy of online and offline narratives crossing the borders of new and conventional media in cases such as adaptations of online texts into films or TV dramas. We also study the heterotopic-ness of literary and cultural texts and see how their fictional contents imply the imagined that derive from real emotions and mentalities in everyday lives.

Foucault in his essay implies that a heterotopia could function as political intervention. Seeing a boat as a heterotopia, Foucault (1986: 27) believes it offers both hope and differences. Otherwise, "in civilizations without boats, dreams dry up, espionage takes the place of adventure, and the police take the place of pirates." Written during the Cold War era, Foucault's essay does not lack any specific references. The online configuration of class, gender, ethnicity, and ethics, in our investigation, however, is a far more complicated process. The online verbal and visual texts do offer alternative voices, different concepts, and avant-garde attitudes, which all challenge conventional mainstream ideas. Nevertheless, the official and the traditional narratives also find their way to exercise their impact. In our reading of the literary and cultural texts, we constantly encounter paradoxes and dilemmas, which demonstrates the contestation of multiple social players and heterotopic nature of the space and texts.

Structure of the book

With the increasing computerization, digitization, and Internet-ization in our society, new information technologies have, to an unprecedented degree, come to reshape human relations and identities – be they class, gender, ethnic or ethnical identities – both online and offline. As those technologies are becoming growingly "personalized," individuals seem to be (imaginatively) empowered, and their sense of self is thus reimagined and reconstructed, apparently endowed with more flexibility and agency. This process of reconfiguration is enacted through a systemic transformation of mechanisms of cultural production and consumption on the large-scale, and personal empowerment on the individual scale, as for many people, these technologies play the role of a form of prosthesis, extending people's physical abilities and, most importantly, consciousness. Yet, the postsocialist condition that is, in part, shaped by information technologies via the neoliberal turn, also determines ways in which this reconfiguration is implemented. Arguably, online identity construction may be more complex than that during the time when the Internet was not present, since, as Rob Cover (2012, 2015) shows, in this age of ubiquitous digital and networked media and communication, digital users play a more extensive role, by ways of creative, manipulative, and interactive user-generated content online, in (re)fashioning their representations of selves on different platforms. Our book studies this refashioning of online identity embodied in representative literary and cultural phenomena on the Chinese Internet.

The first two chapters examine the technologically, economically, and commercially stratified society reflected in *egao* (digitized and online spoofing) and micro-narratives. In our investigation of the *egao* phenomenon in Chapter 1, we particularly look at the case of the young netizen Hu Ge's digitized video spoofing the high-profile blockbuster film *The Promise* (2005) produced by the established "Fifth Generation" director Chen Kaige. Hu Ge's spoof video, "A Bloody Case Caused by a Steamed Bun," exhibits his creativity in manipulating a variety of audio-visual resources, dexterity in editing digital materials, and cynicism towards the establishment in his humorous satires, all highly characteristic of the burgeoning *egao* culture arguably initiated by this video. For all of these characteristics, as well as for the controversial lawsuit Chen Kaige filed against Hu Ge following the viral circulation of the video and the nationwide debates about the Chen–Hu clash extensively covered in various media, this case, for many, marks the first milestone in the development of the *egao* phenomenon in China. A specific study of this case, as we do in this chapter, may yield some understanding of the *egao* phenomenon in general.

Chapter 2 is a study of the creation of a variety of micro-narratives prevalent on the Chinese Internet, including microfiction, micro-films, and literary apps. We examine specifically pieces from the Sina Microfiction Contests, Chen Peng's *The Life of Eiliko Chen in Beijing* (*Eilikochen de jingdu shenghuo ji*), Wen Huajian's *Love in the Age of Microblogging* (*Weibo shiqi de aiqing*), the first microblog novel in China; micro-films on the disturbing role cell phones play in affecting human relations; and Han Han's literary app "ONE·*yige*" and the stories it enables. These textual, audio-visual, and technology-enabled micro-narratives exemplify different ways in which common netizens take advantage of communicative, interactive, and digital technologies made handy to them, and narrate their micro-ness against the grain of grand narratives that mark the postsocialist developmentalism.

Both the *egao* phenomenon and micro-narrative creations destabilize traditional understandings of class that are gradually becoming irrelevant. Boundaries are blurred between the subcultural and the mainstream, the masses and the elites, the individual and the communal, the (post)modern and the traditional, the global and the local, as well as technological connectedness and physical com-partmentalization. Such endeavors disclose the increasing social stratification and class consolidation and meanwhile critique the very forces that socially divide and restructure people.

Chapter 3 explores the imagination of gender in online popular fiction and dra-mas. We focus on online/offline, cross-media *constructed-ness* of gendered imagi-nation by reading web fiction and dramas. The constructed-ness of the gendered fantasy and desire is at many levels: first finished by the online writer and then revised by the online reader. When the fiction crosses the media boundaries, gen-dered desire continues to be revised and remodeled, reflecting the negotiation and contestation of different ideologies and mentalities in different spaces: the virtual and the real, the playful and the political, the market and the official. Such imag-ing of gender nevertheless provides alternative ways of identifying masculinity, femininity, and sexuality.

Chapter 4 investigates problematics of self-representation of ethnic identity online. While ethnicity has always been a highly contested issue in modern Chi-nese history, the Internet further complicates reconstruction and representation of ethnic identity online and offline, as the ethnic is inevitably crisscrossed with not only the local, the national, and the global but also the virtual, as the result of restructuring both real- and cyber-spaces. In this chapter we analyze online writings by the well-known dissident Tibetan woman writer Woeser, the wedding photos of a young Tibetan couple that have gone viral on the Chinese Internet, and the flash mob performance of singing a popular Cantonese song in Tibetan. These three cases reveal in different ways ethnic groups' new attempts, in this age of the Internet, in negotiating their identities within the hegemonic Mandarin culture dominated by the Han ethnicity in China.

Chapter 5 interrogates ethical problems of Chinese Internet culture through an examination of literary and cinematic representations of the so-called Human Flesh Search Engine (*renrou sousuo*, hereafter RRSS) phenomenon. While morality has consistently been a philosophy of government in Chinese history, and it is also claimed to be carried over, though not unproblematically, into the Party-state's management of the Internet (Hockx 2015: 12), the Internet, how-ever, seems to be only governed by, for a large number of common netizens, a spirit of ultra-freedom never seen anywhere else or at any other time. RRSS is arguably a most telling embodiment of this sentiment of ultra-freedom, a senti-ment that obviously comes out of a misuse, or abuse, of the (hyper)connectivity granted by the Internet. The populist ethos, as well as the nihilistic or even cha-otic situation brought about as a result of an act of the RRSS, poses challenges not only to the legal system in China, but also to the overall ethics in Chinese cyberspace.

The five cases studied in this book, all of them in many ways hot topics regard-ing the Internet in contemporary China, do not simply showcase what is conven-tionally deemed as "politics of resistance," politics, in the case of the Internet in China, that are modeled in the constant contention between the authorities and

netizens (Yang 2009a, 2014). But, rather, they bring back into our consciousness the political awareness that still looms large in the enormously diversified
relationships among traditional establishments, netizens, and new socioeconomic
elites, but is at risk of going obsolete or unfashionable as a result of neoliberal
depoliticization.

Further, these cases also demonstrate a growing trend of self-reflection, albeit
to different degrees, on (sub)cultures on the Internet, the subjects who have created them, and the sociocultural condition under which they develop. This sense
of self-reflectivity, in our view, has lent an even more dynamic power and critical
lens to the rapidly growing Internet culture, as an ability of self-reflection, a sense
of self-consciousness, in a way, marks a growing complexity in our approaches
to the information technology of the Internet, which we are increasingly unable
to do without. While much of the reconfiguration we study is still going on, and
much of its political valence thus remains yet to be seen; nevertheless, we are
cautiously hopeful that, with this growing sense self-reflectivity, the cyberspace
in China will be a site, perhaps a most dynamic one, where more constructive
cultures will emerge.

Notes

1 Just to name a few among the numerous publications every year: many address issues
such as online civil society and empowerment (Tai 2006, Zheng 2008), citizen activism and online nationalism (Jiang 2011, Lagerkvist 2010, Yang 2009a), and politics in
online society and communities (Herold and Marolt 2011, Marolt and Herold 2015).
Scholars also paid some attention to the relation of the Internet and identity formation
(Bax 2014, Liu 2011) and sexual politics (Jacobs 2012). The few monographs published so far includes Feng (2013), Hockx (2015), and Inwood (2014).
2 Marshall McLuhan's theories on new media has been very influential and attracted a
great many followers in China since they were introduced to Chinese intellectuals and
the public in the 1990s. In a recent study of Chinese Internet literature, for example,
Shao Yanjun (2015b: 113–14) specifically uses McLuhan's ideas of "electronic inter-
dependence," "a unity of sensibility and of thought and feeling," "tribal base," and so
on as a framework, and explains the way in which canonization of Chinese Internet
literature is based primarily on literary works' embodiment of "Internet-ness."
3 Turner (2006: 262) concludes his book in a serious reflection:

> as the short life of the New Communalist movement suggests, information and
> information technologies will never allow us to fully escape the demands of our
> bodies, our institutions, and the times in which we find ourselves. . . . Only by
> helping us meet that fundamentally political challenge can information technology
> fulfill its countercultural promise.

4 Although Michel Hockx (2005) finds connections between the literary communities
of the Republican period (1911–1949) and contemporary cyber literary communities,
it remains the case that Internet literature and culture, without doubt, are rooted in the
specific social and cultural condition of a postsocialist China.
5 For studies of neoliberalism in China, see David Harvey's (2005) influential book,
A Brief History of Neoliberalism, Chapter Five, "Neoliberalism 'with Chinese Characteristics'," and Robin Visser's (2010) well researched book, *Cities Surround the
Countryside: Urban Aesthetics in Postsocialist China*, Chapter Two, "Theorizing the
Postsocialist City: Cultural Politics of Urban Aesthetics."

6 Criticisms of the low quality of Internet literature and culture also abound. See, for instance, Kong (2005).

7 According to Shao Yanjun (2012), political participation, the dream of the rise of a grand nation, and the question of true love can all be put into practice when protagonists travel back to the past or to a non-existent outer space. Not necessarily a utopia, the imagined world is not a perfect world where dreams can be granted and ideals achieved. Instead, the fictional world is still a highly institutionalized space in which an individual, instead of changing the world, changes the way they do things in accordance with their own better interests.

Bibliography

Bax, Trent. (2014). *Youth and Internet Addiction in China*. New York: Routledge.

Castells, Manuel. (2010). *The Rise of the Network Society*. 2nd ed. Chichester, West Sussex and Malden, MA: Wiley-Blackwell.

Cover, Rob. (2012). "Performing and Undoing Identity Online: Social Networking, Identity Theories and the Incompatibility of Online Profiles and Friendship Regimes." *Convergence: The International Journal of Research into New Media Technologies* 18, no. 2: 177–93.

———. (2015). *Digital Identities: Creating and Communicating the Online Self*. Los Angeles: Elsevier.

Dawkins, Richard. (1976). *The Selfish Gene*. New York: Oxford University Press.

Duggan, Lisa. (2003). *The Twilight of Equality? Neoliberalism, Cultural Politics, and the Attack on Democracy*. Boston, MA: Beacon Press.

Feng, Jin. (2013). *Romancing the Internet: Producing and Consuming Chinese Web Romance*. Leiden and Boston, MA: Brill.

Foucault, Michel. (1986). "Of Other Spaces." Trans. Jay Miskowiec. *Diacritics* 16, no. 1: 22–7.

Friedman, Thomas L. (2005). *The World Is Flat: A Brief History of the Twenty-First Century*. New York: Farrar, Straus and Giroux.

Fukuyama, Francis. (1992). *The End of History and the Last Man*. New York: Free Press.

Hall, Stuart. (1988). *The Hard Road to Renewal: Thatcherism and the Crisis of the Left*. London and New York: Verso.

Harvey, David. (1973). *Social Justice and the City*. London: Edward Arnold.

———. (2000). *Spaces of Hope*. Berkeley, CA: University of California Press.

———. (2005). *A Brief History of Neoliberalism*. Oxford, England and New York: Oxford University Press.

———. (2006). *Spaces of Global Capitalism: Towards a Theory of Uneven Geographical Development*. London and New York: Verso.

Herold, David Kurt. (2011). "Introduction—Noise, Spectacle, Politics: Carnival in Chinese Cyberspace." In *Online Society in China: Creating, Celebrating, and Instrumentalising the Online Carnival*, edited by David Kurt Herold and Peter Marolt, 1–19. Abingdon and New York: Routledge.

———. (2015). "Users, Not Netizens: Spaces and Practices on the Chinese Internet." In *China Online: Locating Society in Online Spaces*, edited by Peter Marolt and David Kurt Herold, 20–30. London and New York: Routledge.

Herold, David Kurt, and Peter Marolt, eds. (2011). *Online Society in China: Creating, Celebrating, and Instrumentalising the Online Carnival*. Abingdon and New York: Routledge.

Hockx, Michel. (2005). "Virtual Chinese Literature: A Comparative Case Study of Online Poetry Communities." *The China Quarterly* 183: 670–91.

——. (2015). *Internet Literature in China*. New York: Columbia University Press.

Inwood, Heather. (2014). *Verse Going Viral: China's New Media Scenes*. Seattle: University of Washington Press.

Jacobs, Katrien. (2012). *People's Pornography: Sex and Surveillance on the Chinese Internet*. Bristol and Chicago, IL: Intellect.

Jiang, Ying. (2012). *Cyber-Nationalism in China: Challenging Western Media Portrayals of Internet Censorship in China*. Adelaide: The University of Adelaide Press.

Kelemen, Mihaela, and Warren Smith. (2001). "Community and Its 'Virtual' Promises: A Critique of Cyberlibertarian Rhetoric." *Information, Communication & Society* 4, no. 3: 370–87.

Kelly, Kevin. (1995). *Out of Control: The New Biology of Machines, Social Systems, and the Economic World*. Reading, MA: Addison-Wesley.

——. (2002). "God Is the Machine." *Wired* 10, no. 12. http://www.wired.com/2002/12/holytech/. Last accessed August 31, 2016.

Kong, Shuyu. (2005). *Consuming Literature: Best Sellers and the Commercialization of Literary Production in Contemporary China*. Stanford, CA: Stanford University Press.

Lagerkvist, Johan. (2010). *After the Internet, Before Democracy: Competing Norms in Chinese Media and Society*. Bern and New York: Peter Lang.

Liu, Fengshu. (2011). *Urban Youth in China: Modernity, the Internet and the Self*. New York: Routledge.

Makinen, Julie, Yingzhi Yang, and Alexandra Li. (2015). "'Freedom Requires Strict Order': China Preps for Second World Internet Conference." *Los Angeles Times*, December 15. http://www.latimes.com/world/asia/la-fg-china-internet-20151215-story.html. Last accessed August 31, 2016.

Marolt, Peter. (2015). "Grounding Online Spaces." In *China Online: Locating Society in Online Spaces*, edited by Peter Marolt and David Kurt Herold, 3–19. London and New York: Routledge.

Marolt, Peter, and David Kurt Herold, eds. (2015). *China Online: Locating Society in Online Spaces*. London and New York: Routledge.

Mitchell, William J. (1999). *E-Topia: Urban Life, Jim—But Not as We Know It*. Cambridge, MA: MIT Press.

Mosco, Vincent. (2004). *The Digital Sublime: Myth, Power, and Cyberspace*. Cambridge, MA: MIT Press.

Negroponte, Nicholas. (1995). "Being Digital – A Book (P)review." *Wired* 3, no. 02. http://www.wired.com/1995/02/negroponte-27/. Last accessed August 31, 2016.

Qiu, Jack Linchuan. (2006). "Cong xinxi zhongceng dao xinxi zhongjian" (From the information have-less to the information mainstay). *Ershiyi shiji* 97: 101–10.

——. (2009). *Working-Class Network Society: Communication Technology and the Information Have-Less in Urban China*. Cambridge, MA: MIT Press.

Rothschild, Michael L. (1990). *Bionomics: The Inevitability of Capitalism*. New York: Henry Holt and Company.

Rymarczuk, Robin, and Maarten Derksen. (2014). "Different Spaces: Exploring Facebook as Heterotopia." *First Monday* 19, no. 6. June 2. http://firstmonday.org/ojs/index.php/fm/article/view/5006/4091#author. Last accessed August 31, 2016.

Shao Yanjun. (2012). "Zai 'yituobang' li goujian 'geren linglei xuanze'huanxiang kongjian: wangluo wenxue de yishi xingtai gongneng zhi yizhong" (Constructing a fantasy space of 'individual, alternative choice' in a heterotopia: One of the ideological functions of Internet literature). *Wenyi yanjiu* 4: 16–25.

——. (2015a). *Wangluo shidai de wenxue yindu* (*Literary crossing in the age of the Internet*). Guilin: Guangxi shifan daxue chubanshe.

——. (2015b). "Wangluo wenxue de 'wangluo xing' yu 'jingdian xing'" (The Internet and classical qualities of Internet literature). *Journal of Beijing University (Philosophy and Social Sciences)* 52, no. 1: 143–52.

Tai, Zixue. (2006). *The Internet in China: Cyberspace and Civil Society*. New York: Routledge.

Toffler, Alvin. (1980). *The Third Wave*. New York: Morrow.

Tomkins, Kevin. (1966). "In the Outlaw Area: Profile of R. Buckminster Fuller." *The New Yorker*, January 8. http://www.newyorker.com/magazine/1966/01/08/in-the-outlaw-area. Last accessed August 31, 2016.

Turner, Fred. (2006). *From Counterculture to Cyberculture: Stewart Brand, the Whole Earth Network, and the Rise of Digital Utopianism*. Chicago: University of Chicago Press.

Visser, Robin. (2010). *Cities Surround the Countryside: Urban Aesthetics in Postsocialist China*. Durham, NC: Duke University Press.

Voci, Paola. (2010). *China on Video: Smaller-Screen Realities*. London and New York: Routledge.

Wang, David Der-wei. (2011) "Wutuobang, etuobang, yituobang: cong Lu Xun dao Liu Cixin" (Utopia, dystopia, heterotopias: from Lu Xun to Liu Cixin). *Wenyibao*, July 11.

Wang, Hui. (2003). *China's New Order: Society, Politics, and Economy in Transition*. Edited by Theodore Huters. Cambridge, MA: Harvard University Press.

Wang Weijia. (2014). "Dian xinziyou zhuyi: saibo misi de lishi yu zhengzhi" (Dot-neoliberalism: history and politics of cybermyth) *Jingji daokan* 6: 25–36.

Wei, Yingjie. (2008). "'Life Politics' Promotes Modern Progress: On the Chinese Internet's Conflict of Values." *Art Today: Cultural Conflicts in China* (special issue): 102–8.

Yang, Guobin. (2009a). *The Power of the Internet in China: Citizen Activism Online*. New York: Columbia University Press.

——. (2009b). "Beiqing yu xixue: wangluo shijian zhong de qinggan dongyuan" (Of sympathy and play: Emotional mobilization in online collective action). *Chuanbo yu shehui xuekan* 9: 39–66.

——. (2014). "Political Contestation in Chinese Digital Spaces: Deepening the Critical Inquiry." *China Information* 28, no. 2: 135–44.

Zhao, Shanyang. (2005). "The Digital Self: Telecopresent of Others as a Looking Glass through which Individuals form Their Identity which is Different from Their Offline Ones." *Symbolic Interaction* 28, no. 3: 387–405.

Zhao, Shanyang, Sherri Grasmuck, and Jason Martin. (2008). "Identity Construction on Facebook: Digital Empowerment in Anchored Relationships." *Computers in Human Behavior* 24, no. 5: 1816–36.

Zhejiang Writers Association, and Zhejiang Internet Writers Association, eds. (2015). *Huayu wangluo wenxue yanjiu* (*A study of Chinese language Internet literature*). Hangzhou: Zhejiang wenyi chubanshe.

Zheng, Yongnian. (2008). *Technological Empowerment: The Internet, State, and Society in China*. Stanford, CA: Stanford University Press.

Zhuang Yong. (2014). "Wangluo wenxue de 'zhuliu hua': cong shidai fengxiangbiao dao chuangzuo jizhi pingjing" (Internet literature goes mainstream: from the benchmark of a time to a bottleneck in the production mechanism). *Wenxue bao*, June 5: 020.

1 Digitized parody

The politics of *egao* in contemporary China

In early 2006, a 20-minute video entitled "A Bloody Case Caused by a Steamed Bun" *Yige mantou yinfa de xue'an* (一个馒头引发的血案, hereafter "A Bloody Case") became one of the most popular online video clips in China.[1] The video was a spoof of the 2005 blockbuster *The Promise* (*Wuji* 无极), by the world-renowned director Chen Kaige (陈凯歌). This hilarious video immediately won acclaim from netizens, spawning a flood of similar spoofs. With its rapid spread, a special subculture, coined *egao* (恶搞), emerged, which began to reshape the ecology of the Internet landscape.

This chapter investigates the complex politics involved in the *egao* phenomenon and its dialectic position between negotiation of the cultural space linking individual playfulness in virtual reality and communal transgression in social reality. To be more specific, it explores specific features of *egao*, the sociocultural condition under which it emerged, and the political ramification and significance of the destabilization of social structure caused by it, which coincides with the large-scale restructuring of classes taking place in postsocialist China. We believe that *egao*, as a new parodic practice in contemporary China, is a site where issues of power struggle, class reconsolidation, social stratification, (online) community formation, and cultural intervention, along with the transformative power of digital technologies, intersect. Through an analysis of Hu Ge's (胡戈) "A Bloody Case," we argue that *egao* provides an alternative locus of power, permitting the transgressing of existing social and cultural hierarchies, and precipitates the emergence of a group of young, technology-savvy, economically and socially marginalized, subculture-oriented, and politically inactive netizens. Satiric and ludicrous in nature, *egao* playfully subverts a range of authoritative discourses, be they political, commercial, or cultural ones, and provides a vehicle for both comic criticism and emotional catharsis, yet sometimes generates moral controversies. As a form of cultural expression of the new digital generation, it also offers insight into the collective attitudes of the new tribe, if not class, of netizens towards the larger social condition and transformation.

To examine *egao* as a new technology-enabled cultural intervention, this study situates *egao* both within the general paradigm of the parodic and the specific sociocultural context of contemporary China. Our critical exploration starts off from a definition of *egao* within these two frames, and then examines how the advances of new digital technologies reshape the phenomenon in its format and sociality. This, in turn, leads to a historical investigation of the specific social situations in which the *egao* culture took shape, and to a formal analysis of its distinctive discursive features. In all, this exploration, we hope, sheds some lights on the class reconsolidation as a result of the advent of the Internet in particular, and the overall social transition to the postsocialist condition at large.

Defining *egao*

What is *egao*? There have been many attempts to define it. The official newspaper *Guangming Daily Guangming ribao* (光明日报) characterizes *egao* as "a popular online strategy, in the form of language, picture, and animation, which comically subverts and deconstructs the so-called normal" (Chen, Zhang, and He 2007: 24). The English-language newspaper *China Daily*, a mouthpiece of the Party-state, defines *egao* in a more complicated way:

> *Egao* is a popular subculture that deconstructs serious themes to entertain people with comedy effects. . . . The two characters "*e*" meaning "evil" and "*gao*" meaning "work" combine to describe a subculture that is characterized by humor, revelry, subversion, grass-root spontaneity, defiance of authority, mass participation and multi-media high-tech.
>
> (Huang 2006)

These definitions from official media capture some characteristics of *egao*, such as its subversiveness of authority. However, they also demonstrate certain ideological ambiguities and uneasiness, for instance, in interpreting *egao* as something detrimental to the establishment.

Egao has also attracted scholarly attention in English. Yongming Zhou and Daria Berg have addressed, respectively, in conference papers on *egao*, the carnivalesque and iconoclastic nature of the genre. Both affirm *egao*'s function as a new avenue for individual(istic) expression of Chinese netizens. Particularly, Berg (2008) approaches the issue from the sociological perspective and focuses mainly on the democratizing role played by the development of the Internet in China in shaping the *egao* phenomenon. Through a political-cultural approach, Zhou (2008) also sees *egao* as a liberating cultural practice of the individuals against "established norms and values," though at the same time constrained by "general control mechanisms in China." These pioneer studies of *egao* provide insightful overviews of the cultural phenomenon and open the ways for further discussion. Later studies of *egao* provides further information on the phenomenon and complicates our understanding. Discussions of them are on the way.

　In our study, we see *egao* first and foremost as a form of parody, with a level of inevitable comic and satiric effects.[2] Like other parodic practices, *egao* usually imitates the parodied texts, or blatantly transplants parts or all of them into an entirely different text or context. By so doing, they create ironic incongruity that triggers humor and laughter and form varying kinds of polemical relationships with the texts and/or matters that they satirize.[3] Secondly, *egao* is a particular form of parody that is specifically shaped by the sociohistorical junction of contemporary China.[4] Contemporary cultural conditions in China determine the discursive emergence of the *egao* culture, which is to say, both its forms and the politics involved. It can thus serve as a locus for unraveling the underlying cultural, social, and political agendas.

To begin with, it is necessary to note that parody is an age-old cultural phenomenon around the world. One can trace it back as far as ancient Greece. It has existed throughout the course of human history in various forms. Scholarly studies of parody are abundant. For example, the French theorist Gérard Genette (1997) delimits parody by carefully studying the formal relationships between the "hypotext" and "hypertext." Parody is differentiated from the related forms of pastiche, travesty, skit, transposition, burlesque, and forgery by its standing as a direct textual transformation (rather than an indirect imitation) in a playful (rather than a satirical) manner.[5] Margaret A. Rose (1979, 1993) offers comprehensive analyses of the history of theories and practices of parody from ancient to contemporary times. She views parody as a self-reflective practice, which not only challenges authority but also creates a new text by mirroring itself.[6] Linda Hutcheon (1985), on the other hand, focuses on parodic practices in the twentieth century. She also views parody as a metatext that simultaneously critiques and creates. But she refuses to see parody simply in a polemical relationship with the hypotext.[7] Simon Dentith (2000: 9) offers a rather inclusive definition of parody, which refers to "any cultural practice which provides a relatively polemical allusive imitation of another cultural production or practice." Dan Harris (2000: 6, original emphasis) defines parody as

> the process of recontextualizing a target or source text through the transformation of its textual (and contextual) elements, thus creating a *new* text. This conversion – through the resulting oscillation between similarity to and difference from the target – creates a level of ironic incongruity with an inevitable satiric impulse.

In view of the disparate definitions of parody and the disputes among critics on the attributes of parody, Dentith (2000: 22 and passim) thinks that a more fruitful approach to the politics involved is through an investigation of its historicity. It is only through investigations of specific situations in which certain forms of parody are demonstrated that we can have a better understanding of them. In the case of *egao*, we also believe that an exploration of the social and cultural scene in contemporary China will produce more insights into *egao* as a special form of parody. Specifically, we will look into the role digital technologies and the technology-enabled cultural form and content play in the postsocialist condition of China.

Digital technologies, alternative space, and netizens

For the emergence of the parodic form of *egao*, one important social determinant was the advent of digital technologies in China at the turn of the twenty-first century. Digital technologies, especially the technologies of digital processing and the Internet, became widely accessible to common Chinese people, particularly to the young, urban generation. *Egao*, in a sense, is a cultural product of these digital technologies.

First, *egao* products are predominantly made by individuals using digital technologies. The availability of these technologies to the masses and spoofsters' knowledge of and skills in textual, audio, and video editing are prerequisites for the *egao* culture. Most *egao* videos are produced entirely by using digital technologies on personal computers. On the one hand, these technologies offer the *egao* culture some unique textual features rarely seen previously. In twentieth-century China, practices of parody could be found in every decade.[8] However, special effects created by digital technologies, especially in the audio and visual aspects, are totally new to Chinese people, a point on which we will elaborate when we discuss "A Bloody Case." On the other hand, individual access to these technologies, previously only available to a small group, greatly shapes the contextual features of *egao*. Most manifestly, it makes individual participation and creation in the field of audio-visual processing possible and brings grassroots street wisdom and popular voices into an area hitherto the exclusive province of specialists and elitists.

Second, the virtual world of the Internet is the space where *egao* takes shape, spreads, and flourishes. Many studies have been done on the development of the Internet in Chinese society. Scholars have paid special attention to such issues as democratization, liberalization, public space, civil society, and state control in regard to the rapid growth of the Internet in contemporary China.[9] For *egao*, the Internet offers a space other than that of traditional media for individual expression, and it provides an imagined empowerment for netizens, who can, for the first time, intervene in the formation of an institutionalized narrative. This space – which does not simply refer to the physical cyberspace but also to the social space created thereby – is marked by a rising level of social tolerance and freedom and, simultaneously, an increasing level of constraint.[10] Virtual reality inevitably produces a new sense of temporal and spatial relationships among participants of *egao* practices.

The Internet plays a catalytic role in the formation of new social groups in contemporary China. With respect to *egao*, we see a paradoxical process of social formation modeled by the decentralized and instantaneous features of the Internet: on the one hand, *egao* is a highly individual activity, but on the other, the collection of spoofsters is an "imagined community" (Anderson 1991).[11] These spoofsters share many characteristics in terms of demography and social behavior. A predominant portion of the spoofsters, as well as other *egao* participants, are young netizens, most of whom live in urban areas. Another fact provides additional support for this hypothesis. In 2006, when a larger number of *egao* works appeared, the population of Chinese netizens just reached a new high of 137 million, 82.5 percent of whom were aged below thirty-five, and the majority of whom lived in cities rather than in the countryside; yet 72.4 percent had an income of less than RMB 2,000 (approximately US$250) per month, which was not considered high in China then (CNNIC 2007: 30, 47, 50).[12] In addition, these spoofsters and other *egao* participants are familiar with digital technologies to varying degrees. As most of them belong to the younger generation, they are open to new technologies and ideas. Spoofsters also have their own spaces: BBS (Bulletin Board System), blogs, and video-sharing platforms on various websites, including China's portal websites Sina.com and Sohu.com, where they exchange their ideas, share their experiences, and disseminate their products. New digital technologies provide the means through which such interactions take place, and thus help form communities and a new class that eventually exert social impacts.

"Post-" society, social stratification, age of irony

Besides technological transformation, the "post-" condition of China, social (re)stratification, and the attitude of irony have also played a vital role in the emergence of the *egao* culture.

When exploring the question of the contours of "particular social and historical situations in which parody is especially likely to flourish," Dentith (2000: 28–32) proposes two main criteria: (1) parody is more likely to flourish in "open" societies or social situations than in "closed" ones; and (2) strong stratification within a society is also very likely to produce parody. For the first criterion, by "open" societies, Dentith means societies characterized by "a sense of cultural belatedness" rather than by "cultural confidence." For him, the various "post-" societies belong to this category, because in them "there is pervasive consciousness of a past which is still strongly present, though the value of that inheritance is deeply contested." Fredric Jameson (1991: 1–54) views pastiche as a dominant cultural form of postmodernism.[13] Hutcheon (1989: 93) also maintains that "parody – often called ironic quotation, pastiche, appropriation, or intertextuality – is usually considered central to postmodernism, both by its detractors and its defenders." In the case of *egao*, contemporary Chinese society has been described in several "post-" coinages: postmodern, post-New Era, post-revolutionary, post-Reform, and postsocialist. To varying degrees, these terms indicate a sense of complicated linkages to their predecessors and therefore a lack of affirmativeness of their own cultures.[14] This seems to conform to Dentith's first claim. However, this claim reeks of generality and needs to be critically substantiated by specific studies of contemporary Chinese society with respect to *egao*.[15]

As for the second criterion of social stratification, it is closely relevant to the *egao* culture, for the appearance of *egao* coincides with the process of the large-scale social (re)stratification in contemporary China. This process has been accelerated by the advent of rampant commercialization since the 1990s (Liang 1998, Lu 2002, 2004). A new social unevenness has created prevalent social discontent, which provides a basis for the emergence of *egao* as an avenue for satirical expression on social inequalities that are caused by class differences.[16] *Egao*, viewed from this perspective, is about power relationships in contemporary China. As Ella Shohat (1991: 238) tells us,

> Parody is especially appropriate for the discussion of "center" and "margins" since – due to its historical critical marginalization, as well as its capacity for appropriating and critically transforming existing discourses – parody becomes a means of renewal and demystification, a way of laughing away outmoded forms of thinking.

Similar statements are also made about laughter and humor, a prominent part of *egao*.[17]

In this vein, many studies have drawn upon Bakhtinian conceptions of the carnivalesque and explored the subversive power of parody (Bakhtin 1984a, 1984b, Stam 1989). Although Bakhtin's theory of "carnival," which is a remarkable critical work in the theorization of parody, is broached in his study of the specific historical situation of the Early Modern period in Europe, it is still a powerful weapon against the establishment in cultural conditions where an authority prohibits other voices. In the specific case of *egao*, the two studies by Zhou and Berg mentioned previously also regard the carnivalesque feature in *egao* as an effective challenge to authority.

However, in *egao*, the conception of the "carnivalesque" is not always applicable. First, the carnival is usually in a collective form. But unlike many satirical arts in the West, as Zhou (2008) sees it, *egao* is usually an "individual" act that does not have any clear political agenda and cannot turn into any activism. Still, community formation as a result of shared experience is an important part of *egao*. Second, the primary target of the carnival is usually authoritarian officialdom. Indeed, many *egao* works satirize officialdom and the establishment. However, it sometimes also makes fun of innocent subjects, which is foreign to the Bakhtinian account of the carnivalesque.[18] The "*e*" in *egao* implies two meanings: "naughtiness" as in *ezuoju* (恶作剧), and "evil" as in its definition in official media. Both implications are applicable in *egao* practices and this sometimes brings up controversy over the limit of what can be spoofed in *egao*. For each parodic form in any specific condition there are always sacred words. For *egao*, a phenomenon that is still developing, sacred words of one work may become targets of satire in another.[19] This is a battleground of different ideological forces, not only between authorities and *egao* practitioners, but also among the practitioners themselves.

Despite the very disruptive power of parody and laughter recognized by many critics (Boskin 1997, Cixous 1981, Finney 1994, Rea 2015), we should also be aware of their cathartic effect (Mulkay 1988, Parkin 1997, Pfister 2002a, Reichl and Stein 2005). *Egao* is sometimes simply for fun and functions as a vent for pent-up emotions. As we will demonstrate later, it serves as a channel for both spoofsters and audiences to vent their disappointments, express their dissatisfactions, and ease their anxieties. In creating and consuming *egao* texts, audiences find playful relief in the virtual world.

The last social condition we would like to examine is what Harris calls the "age of irony," in which the originally subversive parody becomes canonized (at least in the genre of film). Harris's (2000: 1–4) claim is advanced upon the observation that there has been an increasing level of cultural irony in the US since the mid-1970s, and he characterizes it as the culture's state of "ironic supersaturation." Does China in the late 2000s have a similar social situation? A quick answer to this question is: "No." For, unlike the US, contemporary China is not "an era where postmodern activity has become more the norm than any sort of alternative practice" (Harris 2000: 1). However, on the other hand, we have witnessed an increasing level of cultural irony in China since the 1990s. In talking about the politics of laughter in folk culture in contemporary China, the Beijing-based scholar Liu Xiaobo (刘晓波) (2006) takes Hu Ge's *egao* as a representative form and traces the "*egao* spirit" back to Wang Shuo's (王朔) novels of "hooliganism" popular in the late 1980s and '90s. He maintains that this *egao* spirit has been prevalent among the masses ever since that period, yet in various forms, which include: Cui Jian's (崔健) rock 'n' roll, beauty writers and their "lower body" writing, the remaking of the "Red Classics" *Hongse jingdian* (红色经典) into TV dramas, and Liu Di's (刘荻) political parody online.[20] Judging from the continuity and prevalence of these parodic practices, we may say that a spirit of cultural irony has been on the rise over the past two decades, at least among the grassroots population.[21]

This statement leads to the issue of *egao*'s attributes as an emerging discourse, specifically, the question of the rise of *egao* as a new expressive and narrative mode against the accumulating spirit of irony in China. *Egao* is an emerging cultural mode shaped by the rising cultural irony in contemporary China and is in turn shaping the latter's cultural scene. Historically speaking, the accumulating cultural irony in Chinese society over the past two decades prepared for the discursive appearance of the *egao* culture in 2006, during which process Hu Ge's *egao* video was regarded as the event that marked the emergence of *egao*. Conversely, once *egao* became a discursive sign, those preparatory events that preceded it were then renamed from the perspective of *egao*. Combined, these processes constitute *egao* as a distinctive narrative mode that has fully earned its discursive standing.

Constructive discourse: spoofsters and audiences

The discursive standing of *egao* can be further revealed in the formation of constructive communities of spoofsters and their audience and in the resulting interactive relationships so formed. Because parody is fundamentally an imitative form of cultural practice, it is typically seen as being nonconstructive or even "parasitic" (Dane 1988: 5, Kiremidjian 1969: 231–2). This seems to be especially the case with *egao*, which does not simply imitate the parodied texts, but more often transplants the latter directly into a new text and context. This heavy reliance on hypotexts triggers theoretical and practical questions in the fields of both culture and law.

Many theorists have taken a different view with regard to the "constructiveness" of the parodic (Rose 1979). Dentith (2000: 189) sees parody as simultaneously destructive and constructive: "Parody creates new utterances out of the utterances that it seeks to mock," and "it preserves as much as it destroys – or rather, it preserves in the moment that it destroys – and thus the parasite becomes the occasion for itself to act as host."[22] This is particularly applicable to the *egao* phenomenon, for the moment spoofsters imitate and transplant hypotexts into new texts and contexts, they are also, playfully and self-reflexively, creating new comments both on the target hypotexts and on the world.

Stanley Fish (1980) tells us that the construction of the meanings of a text is largely the work of "interpretive communities" who share "interpretive strategies." In responding to Terry Caesar's questions – "Is it possible to have parodic attitudes where there is no parody? Is it possible to have parody where there is not the formal character of the thing parodied?" – Harris (2000: 7) answers: "a parodic viewing strategy" is possible among the audience.

In the *egao* culture, such communities actively participate in making the meaning of *egao* productions. Hutcheon (1985: 93) argues that readers are active "cocreators" of the parodic text. Joseph A. Dane (1988: 10) also points out that a given reader may, in fact, "read any text as a parody." It is clear that the meaning of *egao* productions relies not only on both a shared familiarity with the hypotext and a shared attitude toward the hypertext, but also on the interactive relationships between the initial producer and the audience. The audience's active decoding directly contributes to the construction of *egao*. Thus the comic and satiric effect of *egao* is a distinctively cooperative work of the spoofsters and their audiences.

"A Bloody Case Caused by a Steamed Bun"

Hu Ge's video "A Bloody Case Caused by a Steamed Bun" is the first, and by far the most famous, work of *egao*. The video grew out of Hu's disappointment with Chen Kaige's film *The Promise*, which he had seen in December 2005. It took Hu about ten days to complete his parody on his personal computer. He shared the video with his friends and, unexpectedly, at the beginning of 2006, the video became one of the hottest hits on the Internet (Wang 2006).

The Promise tells a complex story of love, freedom, and destiny in an allegorical fashion. Queen Qingcheng (倾城) (Cecilia Cheung [张柏芝]), formerly a poor slave girl, now possesses everything most women would desire – beauty, wealth, and the special favor of the king. But in exchange for her current prestigious status she is cursed never to have true love. The film opens with Duke Wuhuan (无欢) (Nicholas Tse [谢霆锋]) besieging the Kingdom and demanding Qingcheng. Coming to her rescue are General Guangming (光明) (Sanada Hiroyuki [真田广之]) and Slave Kunlun (昆仑) (Jang Dong-Gun [张东健]), who both fall in love with her. But at the same time they also fall into providential dilemmas that prevent them from actually loving her. This nasty trick turns out to be the combined work of Manshen (满神) (Chen Hong [陈红]), the Goddess of Destiny, who determines everyone's fate, and Wuhuan, who has been plotting revenge on

Qingcheng. His desire for vengeance originates from his childhood: as a child he was traumatized by Qingcheng, who cheated him out of a steamed bun, and this, he believes, has turned him into a narrow-minded, cold-blooded killer. The film ends in a dramatic fight, with Kunlun and Qingcheng surviving Wuhuan's crazy vengeance and breaking the curses placed on both of them.

Hu Ge's *egao* video, sending up the over-the-top premises of Chen's film, resets the story, which supposedly takes place in some remote historical epoch, in the context of a modern TV program, "China Crime Report" *Zhongguo fazhi baodao* (中国法治报道), hosted by a stony-faced anchor on the state-run China Central TV (CCTV). In the program, the TV anchorman is investigating the 2005 murder case of Manager Wang ("the king"), who ran a recreation company. Wang was killed in a fight with his wife Zhang Qingcheng, and Captain Sanada of the City Inspection Team is the main suspect. The negotiation expert Chen Manshen finds out that the real criminal is Zhang Kunlun, but when the policeman Lang is sent to arrest him, feelings between the two grow. In the following court trial, Xie Wuhuan stands up as a witness, and all the parties involved in the murder case – Qingcheng, Kunlun, and Sanada – are found guilty. Wuhuan is given the privilege of carrying out the execution, which is broadcast live. The execution ends in a fight leading to the death of Wuhuan and Sanada and the union of Kunlun and Qingcheng. The investigation reveals the mystery step by step in a suspenseful fashion as such a program usually does, during which everything in the original film is given a present-day, worldly spin. The deliberately blurred boundary of past and present, the imaginary and the real, sets up a background for the new narrative Hu intends to create.

Obviously, Chen's film *The Promise* is the main target of Hu's *egao*. The film took Chen three years to make and cost an unprecedented RMB 300 million (about US$40 million). It also topped the Chinese box office, with revenues of around RMB 220 million (about US$30 million) (Box Office Mojo 2006). However, despite Chen's huge reputation, the substantial investment, the all-star cast, the lush cinematography, and Chen's high-profile promotion in the media, the film received mixed reviews. Some people praised the film for its "oriental charms" and its deep "humanistic spirit." Chen Kaige had, in their view, told an elegant story of "love, friendship, desire, and fear." In contrast, some audiences were very critical of the film and claimed that it was "empty, confusing, and mindless." One netizen commented sarcastically: "If time could really go back as it does in *The Promise*, I would immediately return my ticket."[23]

Most of those who openly supported Chen Kaige were well-established figures, such as film directors, actors, and professional reviewers, and their praise was expressed through interviews and film reviews in established media groups such as Sina.com, and on their official online pages.[24] Those who criticized the film included both celebrities and common netizens, but the latter contributed a significant portion of the negative views and their criticisms inundated various BBS, discussion forums, and blogs.

The audience's preferences implied, of course, a cultural stratification directly related to the broader social stratification of contemporary China, which can be seen in the differentiation of the social groups of technology-savvy youngsters and well-established elites. Supporters of *The Promise* identified with a kind of elite taste for the allegorical, mythical, and even educational, which Chen had tried to achieve. Detractors, however, read these as pretentious and empty. These stratified responses, which included attacks on elitism, and which were, of course, greatly facilitated by advances in digital technology, formed the background for the emergence of the new culture of *egao*. Access to the digital realm further distinguished different social and cultural groups, especially that of the "digital youth" and "conventional elite" when *egao* became an online trend, and leads to the formation of a tribe of young netizens (Zhu 2006b: 28–9).

"Digital youth" here mainly refers to netizens such as the spoofsters and participants of *egao* who actively produce and consume *egao* products online. These people are usually young urbanites who love digital technology, and for whom the Internet is a major resource and living space. In this case, Hu Ge's hobby-turned-profession is that of a freelance computer music producer and online musical device seller. He produced all his *egao* videos with his own editing software and these videos were spontaneously duplicated and disseminated across the Internet by millions of netizens.

When "A Bloody Case" first emerged in cyberspace, it immediately attracted the attention of netizens and caused a sensation in discussion forums, BBS, and blogs. For instance, on www.tianya.cn, one of the most popular Chinese bulletin boards, almost all netizens there expressed their admiration of Hu Ge's ridiculing of Chen Kaige's film. Netizens used words such as "awesome," "hilarious," and "genius" to comment on Hu. One posting goes: "This is awesome! It really cracks me up. 'A Bloody Case' is really the essence of *The Promise*. This is real entertainment at the grassroots' level."[25] Hu's fans even formed various "steamed bun groups." These young digital enthusiasts identified with Hu's jokes, appreciated his punch lines, recognized the cultural notes, and shared his playful satire. To help other people better understand the *egao* clip, some netizens even transcribed the lines and mock commercials, listing the sources of the music Hu used in "A Bloody Case" and posting them online. When Chen Kaige threatened to sue Hu Ge, netizens arranged a large-scale online sign-up in support of Hu (Guo 2006).

Conventional elites, on the other hand, include people in support of Chen's elitist approach in this case and against spoofsters' violation of the established norms. For them, denigration of *The Promise* only revealed disrespect for serious art and degradation of cultural taste. *Egao* not only exposed cultural and moral degeneracy but also violated intellectual property rights (Yang 2006). "A Bloody Case" almost brought Hu Ge a lawsuit from Chen Kaige for copyright infringement.[26] The case remains unresolved and the legal questions involved remain to be addressed by experts in law. While most netizens stood by Hu, these conventional elites were on Chen's side. The film reviewer Cheng Qingsong (2006), for example, voiced his full support of Chen's reaction. He claimed that Chen, as a citizen, has his right to seek justice by legal means. However, this proposed lawsuit only increased Hu Ge's popularity and won him more sympathy and admiration. "A Bloody Case" was consecrated as an *egao* classic.

This confrontation certainly highlights the tension between the establishment and the grassroots, usually at the margins, as well as the miscommunication between the euphoric digital youth, who want to have fun and be cool, and the conventional elites, who view *egao* from a far more serious perspective. This tension bespeaks a social divide and restratification caused by different approaches to this Internet subculture of *egao*.

Digital technology and parodic effect

A significant part of the satirical and ludicrous effects in "A Bloody Case" comes from the spoofster's innovative employment of digital technologies. In parody, such effects are usually achieved through "recontextualization" and by "treating a low subject with mocking dignity" and, conversely, "handl[ing] serious situations in a trivial manner" (Harris 2000: 6, Gehring 1999: 3). In "A Bloody Case," much of the recontextualization is realized through the means of digitalized audio-video editing. This can be immediately noticed from the opening scene, where Hu transplants images, video clips, and sound effects from disparate sources into a new text and creates a hilarious mixture by means of incongruous juxtaposition. The video opens with a trailer/preview taking the format of the "China Crime Report," but the content of the report is from *The Promise*, and the background music is from the US blockbuster *The Matrix*. The voice-over, dubbed by Hu Ge himself, introduces the "murder case," based on *The Promise*:

> A small steamed bun led to a bloody murder. A supposedly innocent child had his personality distorted because of a trivial event. What made him so fragile? A policeman was summoned to arrest the suspect, but never fulfilled his responsibility. Why was this? The murder case was complicated. The truth was not revealed until the last minute. Welcome to the 2005 special edition of China Crime Report "A Bloody Case Caused by a Steamed Bun."

Following this, the scene cuts to a typical image of "China Crime Report": an anchorman sits in front of the camera with a "China Crime Report" sign behind him and the CCTV logo in the upper left corner. In announcing the allegory-turned-mundane murder case, Hu's dubbing imitates the standardized tone, language, and style of an anchorman in the official media. As the narrative unfolds, it is accompanied by electronic fast-beat music from a foreign science fiction thriller. This merging of the three different sectors transgresses spatial and temporal borders of different cultures.

There are many places throughout the video where Hu deliberately mismatches the image and sound in order to create a sense of comic absurdity. For example, in the scene where the policeman (Lang) reconciles with the criminal (Kunlun), while the pictures are directly cut from *The Promise*, the music is from popular love songs (Zheng Jun's [郑钧] "Cinderella" *Hui guniang* [灰姑娘] and Zhang Yu's [张宇] "The Fault Caused by the Moon" *Yueliang rede huo* [月亮惹的祸]). This turns the sense of friendship and ethnic bond into an implicit sense of homosexual love.[27] The final scene where Kunlun and Qingcheng break their curses and live happily ever after in *The Promise* is accompanied by the revolutionary song of "Ode to Red Plum" *Hongmei zan* (红梅赞). With the aid of computer media software, Hu Ge succeeds in transplanting the cultural products that audiences are familiar with and fusing them in a comic framework, creating a new visual text with new meanings. As the new text oscillates between familiarity and unfamiliarity among audiences, it creates a playful discrepancy, achieving a mixed effect of catharsis and criticism.

Targets of subversion and transgression

The primary target of Hu's *egao* video is Chen's elitism, shown in the film's grand narrative and style. This is clearly exhibited in Hu's overall high-profile-debunking fashion in which he restructures the plot and in the allegory-turned-triviality that populates the video. The symbolic names Chen gives to the characters are such examples. The names are a significant part of his allegorical design. For instance, the name of Qingcheng has specific allusion to the classical phrase *qingguo qingcheng* (倾国倾城, literally, "toppling kingdoms and towns"), a phrase that describes a stunning beauty (and is also indicative of the idea of a *femme fatale*), which originated in the famous story of the Han Emperor Liu Che (刘彻) (156–87 BCE). In the same way, all the other character names indicate the symbolic role the characters play in the allegory. However, in his *egao* video, Hu purposely mixes the actors' names with the characters' and therefore churns out extremely quotidian ones that give a satirical effect through the ultra incongruity in them. In the case of Qingcheng, the actress Cecilia Cheung's surname "Zhang" (Mandarin pronunciation of "Cheung") is yoked with the character name and makes the ludicrous "Zhang Qingcheng." The same happens to all the other character names: Xie Wuhuan, Chen Manshen, Zhang Kunlun, and so on. This act tremendously deflates the allegorical ambience created in the film.

Moreover, the naming itself, the combination of the surname of the actors and actresses with their fictional roles, also exaggerates the effect of the blurring of the boundaries between the world on screen and the world in reality, and lays bare the tricky relationship between the two that had been taken advantage of, for commercial purposes, throughout the production and exhibition of *The Promise*. This very commercial orientation that underlies the elitist myth that Chen creates is certainly another main target of Hu's *egao*. Besides the substantive investment, excessively refined production, and bombarding promotional maneuvers, Chen also takes advantage of the popular genre of costume drama, featuring swordplay, oriental mysticism, exoticism, and sentimentalism, aiming rather explicitly at the Oscars and the international film market. Moreover, the quite enviable lineup of superstars from across East Asia – Hong Kong's heartthrob couple Nicholas Tse and Cecilia Cheung, Japanese celebrity Sanada Hiroyuki, and Korean idol Jang Dong-Gun – is an effective promotional strategy by constantly being a hot topic surrounding the filmmaking. In Hu's video, Chen's commercial approaches are seized on and made fun of. The grandiose palace that Chen invested substantially in for visual effect becomes no more than a strangely shaped and poorly located entertainment club named "Circle within a Circle" that verges on bankruptcy. In this way, the sublimity, grandness, and mythicality fabricated by Chen are transformed into vulgarity and destitution. This transformation effects a vigorous transgression of linguistic, generic, and cultural boundaries, as well as of that between the real and the fictional.

Embedded in satirizing the hypotexts are also references to many prevalent social issues close to the audience. As the story unfolds, the catalyst of the murder turns out to be a contract dispute between the boss and his migrant sex worker in a nightclub. Such disputes are widespread in contemporary China due to the inadequacy of a regulatory mechanism. Audiences can certainly recognize the satirical account of the underground porn industry, back pay for migrant workers, the interrogation systems of the police, and the education of young children.[28] Hu's satirical edge also points at the phenomenon of ubiquitous commercials in TV programs by imitatively chopping his own video in parts with some deliberately awkward mock advertisements, generating viewers' identification in a comic way. All the social problems are narrated in the intentionally misplaced contexts, symbolizing the absurdity of the reality as well as of the hypotext.

One place that may best illustrate the critical edge of Hu's *egao* lies in his spoof of General Guangming (literally, "Illumination"), played by the Japanese actor Sanada. In "A Bloody Case," the general is turned into "Little Captain Sanada." Hu Ge explains his identity in this way:

> Little Captain Sanada is Japanese. He came to China determined to express his sincere apologies to the Chinese people. In 2004, as a city inspector, he single-handedly smashed the headquarters of unlicensed street peddlers. . . . What kind of spirit is this that makes a foreigner selflessly adopt the grand cause of the Chinese people as his own?

Sanada's new title (captain) and profession (city inspector) invoke several layers of irony. First and foremost, it is a conspicuous reference to Japanese militarism during the Sino-Japanese War (1937–1945). Sanada's "unselfish spirit of internationalism," as solemnly announced by the anchorman, is ironic in its historical context and hilarious as the "internationalism" is his new job as a city inspector in China. Second, it brings to light a long-term social issue: the notorious confrontation between the bullying city inspectors and powerless street peddlers. Third, the last sentence – "What kind of spirit is this that makes a foreigner selflessly adopt the grand cause of Chinese people as his own?" – is a verbatim quotation from one of Mao Zedong's (1977: 337–8) best-known articles, "In Memory of Norman Bethune," published in 1939. This sentence still sounds familiar to many Chinese today, evoking their historical memories and reminding them of the ideological preaching of socialism. An ironic and playful tone becomes explicit in this juxtaposition of the once most sacred sentence of the revolutionary era with the profane entertainment endeavor of the current reform era. More importantly, Hu mocks Chen Kaige's employment of transnationality, which is represented in the use of established actors and actresses from the region, as a profitable means of attracting a pan-Asian audience. The satirical effect comes not only from the extreme incongruity between the glorious and the vulgar, but also from that between the roles in different contexts – the real, the imaginary, and the stereotypical.

Self-reflexive playfulness

Another fact about *egao* that deserves our attention is that, despite its subversiveness, *egao* involves a strong sense of playfulness. "A Bloody Case," as Hu claimed in several interviews, came about from the initial thought of "having some fun" and experimenting with the possibilities of digital technology because of his disappointment with the film *The Promise* (Wang 2006). In addition, at the beginning of many of Hu's *egao* videos, including "A Bloody Case" and "The Empire of the Spring Festival Transportation" *Chunyun diguo* (春运帝国), the following lines appear: "The clip you will see is the product of my self-entertainment. The content is purely fabricated. It is for individual entertainment only and dissemination is forbidden." These lines are an obvious parody of the warning against copyright infringement that always appears at the beginning of copyrighted intellectual products. For the group of people who are somewhat used to pirate products, copyright protection is another target for their *egao*.[29] Moreover, the line also asserts the *egao* product's own right as a new text and highlights one important characteristic of *egao*: the self-entertainment-oriented and individual-based creation and consumption.

For Hu, *egao* serves as a channel to vent his dissatisfaction with the established norms (the film, the social problems, etc.). As audiences laugh along, they identify with the critiques and laugh off their feelings of discontent as well. In a way, *egao* serves simultaneously as a means for critical expression and for emotional catharsis. The playfulness is a significant attribute of *egao*, but it may go awry and border on moral irresponsibility if it mindlessly makes fun of something that hardly deserves satirical judgment. This mentality of individuality and playfulness coexists with grassroots collectivity and social effectiveness. Though initially made for fun, "A Bloody Case" became increasingly political as it involved a great many people, social groups, and institutions who contributed to its discursive signification. Such consequences are, of course, way beyond anything Hu Ge had originally expected, yet this is the paradox of the *egao* culture in the age of digital technologies, which atomizes people and yet links them together at once.

Nevertheless, this kind of individual creativity and satirical laughter does not go without self-questioning. Toward the end of "A Bloody Case," the people involved in the murder case, Zhang Qingcheng, Zhang Kunlun, and Captain Sanada, are brought together and are about to be punished by Xie Wuhuan. Wuhuan takes out a steamed bun, shows it to Qingcheng, and accuses her of cheating him over a steamed bun twenty years previously. Then Hu Ge inserts a flashback, in the form of a black-and-white video recording, and takes the audience back to the scene when Qingcheng took away Wuhuan's steamed bun and ate it, thus traumatizing him. The scene then cuts back to the execution, and shows a freeze-framed close-up of the steamed bun Wuhuan is holding, accompanied by the voice-over: "Attention please, Xie Wuhuan's steamed bun has come from nowhere. . . . The steamed bun was eaten twenty years ago. Where did Wuhuan's steamed bun come from?" Then Wuhuan utters the words, in a painful tone, dubbed by Hu Ge himself again, "As for this question, I don't know either. Everything is arranged by the director."

Hu's playful judgment, through the mouth of Wuhuan, gives the much-needed self-reflexivity of *egao*, which not only deconstructs the grand narrative of Chen Kaige's seemingly sublime allegorical cinema but also affirms the fictional status of both the hypotext and the *egao* video. At this point, Hu's *egao* becomes a multimedia criticism of Chen's film, challenging Chen's authority as the director of the film: in spite of the film's mythical, allegorical, and epical gesture, everything is no more than the director's arbitrary fabrication. Moreover, by so doing, Hu also self-reflexively announces his own status as the "author" of his own products. Obviously, they are nothing other than authorial/arbitrary fabrications, and thus they are susceptible to further deconstruction. In this way, Hu reconfigured the author(ity).

From counterculture to cyberculture?

The *egao* discourse is still developing in many ways and involving more people. When Hu Ge was "authorized" as the founding father of *egao* by his fans, and therefore accumulated cultural capital – he was the focus of media attention, a celebrity who attracted a great many interviews, and he was even invited by local TV stations to participate in producing TV programs – spoofs on Hu himself soon came out. An eight-minute *egao* video, "Yi ge mantou yinfa de mafan" (The trouble caused by a steamed bun), was edited by anonymous netizens who satirically narrate the trouble that Hu Ge, as a celebrity now, got himself into.[30] In the same format, the spoofsters took video clips from Hu Ge's "A Bloody Case," Hong Kong comedy films, and TV entertainment shows, and made them into an *egao*. They playfully commented on the confrontation between Chen and Hu. In the meantime, another *egao* of "A Bloody Case," a song entitled "Jixiang san bao mantou ban" (Three treasures of luck – the steamed bun version), was widely disseminated on the Internet.[31] The music was from the popular song *Jixiang san bao* (Three treasures of luck), which was filled with familial joyfulness; but the lyrics were satirically changed to make fun of the Chen–Hu disputes. In this way, audiences have played an active role in appreciating, disseminating, enriching, and recreating the meaning of *egao* text, and challenging new "authorities" established in the process of spoofing itself.

As a grassroots (sub)culture, *egao* initially emerged on the Internet as an individualized, playfully subversive expressive mode; yet the rapid growth and increasing popularity of *egao* also caught the attention of political institutions and the commercial mainstream. On the one hand, the established institutions tried to regulate *egao* through legal means (Meng 2009). Bothered by the increasing numbers of *egao* clips, the State Administration for Radio, Film and Television (SARFT) planned to announce new regulations on online videos and required the authors of *egao* to apply for a permit, but this plan never came into effect.

Guangming ribao (Guangming daily) also organized a workshop, invited experts from the media and universities, and discussed how to prevent *egao*. The participants analyzed *egao* from the perspectives of morality, law, and culture, and called for a stop to the *egao* trend (Guangming wang 2006). The State Copyright Bureau also announced further moves to regulate *egao* with legal mechanisms. As a result, many spoofsters began to show willingness to cooperate with the establishment. For instance, in 2008 Hu Ge produced two video clips in accordance with mainstream propaganda, singing praise of the state-engineered disaster relief efforts after the Sichuan earthquake. This act, in Paola Voci's (2010: 114) view, marked Hu Ge's transformation from a subcultural techno-geek to a mainstream model citizen promoting social cohesion and engagement. Party-state actions to control *egao* have regulated or tamed the "chaotic" online practice in some way, but they have also further contributed to publicizing and enriching the *egao* discourse.

On the other hand, the commercial mainstream also attempted to cash in on this widely popular format. Immediate invitations of Hu Ge to interviews and commercial programs, as well as massive media coverage of his works and the Chen–Hu dispute, pushed the grassroots netizen to a status of a celebrity, and tellingly demonstrated the power of capital. Hu Ge later turned himself into a professional video-maker of advertisements for large companies. Mainstream media, ironically, also tapped this sub- and counter-cultural form of entertainment. For instance, in 2006 a *hesuipian* (new year film), *Da dianying* (Big movie), was churned out in the format of *egao*, spoofing twenty other mainstream films. Obviously, the producer was quick at exploiting *egao* as a fashion, and tried to make the most out of it by grafting it onto the already profitable genre of the new year film. *Big Movie* was widely shown in main theater chains in China, although it only achieved a moderate reception.

These new developments of *egao* remind us not only of the "decrowning" of authorities in the way of carnivalesque subversion in the Bakhtinian sense (Bakhtin 1984a), but also of the neoliberal spirit embedded in the Internet on the one hand, and in the postsocialist transformation on the other. The largely deregulated capital, along with the state power that still controls the society and protects the deregulation of capital at once, works to bring the counterculture under control and incorporate it into the mainstream.

Conclusion

Egao emerged as a technology-enabled cultural intervention at a particular sociohistorical juncture in contemporary China. As an individualized comic parody performed among like-minded netizens, it plays with authority, deconstructs orthodox seriousness, and offers comic criticism as well as comic relief. It provides imagined empowerment for the digital generation, exploring an alternative space for individual expression and communal reformation. As embodied in "A Bloody Case," the technology-enabled pastiches, linguistic exuberance, and media carnival create laughter and humor, playfully transgress both social and cultural boundaries, satirize the establishment, and provide a means for emotional catharsis. Audiences'/netizens' active participation further enriches the *egao* discourse and extends the playful subversiveness to a new level. Meanwhile, the self-reflexivity of *egao* further reconfigures the paradoxical role of the author/ authority in cultural production.

As such, *egao* as a cultural phenomenon offers a window into the cultural transformation and alternative empowerment in virtual/social reality in postsocialist China. Its controversial cultural status further betrays a social stratification and class consolidation, a new social reality at the age of transformation when China is actively involved in developmentalism on the one hand, and confronts the ideological ambiguity on the other.

Notes

1 This chapter is a revised version of our article, "Digitized Parody: The Politics of *Egao* in Contemporary China," published in *China Information* in 2010. Since then, we received a large amount of feedback and many new studies of the *egao* phenomenon also came out. This new version was revised to fit into the larger framework of the book and incorporated latest findings in it.

2 Hongmei Li (2011) echoes this point and examines Hu Ge's spoof video within the larger parodic culture on the Chinese Internet. Li views this parodic culture as a form of resistance.

3 Christopher Rea (2013: 170–2, italics in the original) also finds the power of egao in the parodic humor it produces, and explains this power within the paradigm of what he calls "a theory of relativity," exemplified in the following aspects: "a relativistic attitude towards the appropriation and transmission of texts"; "the temporal dimension of *e'gao*'s seeming 'gay relativity'"; and "the discourse of moral relativism surrounding *e'gao*," "amateurism," and "shared sentiment." In Rea's opinion, this theory of relativity helps illuminate what is "Chinese" in this type of humor.

4 Needless to say, similar forms of video parody are also seen in other parts of the world. For instance, a video clip titled "Brokeback to the Future," a parody of both *Brokeback Mountain* (2005) and *Back to the Future* (1985), was wildly popular on the Internet in 2006. *Egao* was new to Chinese people then, due to a large extent to their inadequate exposure to technology-enabled parodic tradition. This is closely tied to the specific socio-political context of contemporary China.

5 We follow Gérard Genette's (1997) terms of "hypotext," which means the original text that parody is based on, and "hypertext," the text of parody.

6 Michele Hannoosh (1989) also reiterates parody as a metatext.

7 Beside these studies, a great many scholars, including Dan Harris (2000), Ella Shohat (1991), Joseph A. Dane (1988), Luiz João Vieira and Robert Stam (1985), Robert Phiddian (1995), Robert Stam (1989), and Wes D. Gehring (1999), also contribute to the understanding of parody in different ways.

8 For example, the employment of parody is manifested in Lu Xun's writing, especially in his collection of short stories, *Gushi xinbian* (Old stories retold), and his *zawen* (essays). There is also a lesser known story: in 1924, Lu Xun wrote the poem "Wo de shilian" (Lovelorn) as a parody of Zhang Heng's (78–139) "Si chou shi" (Poetry of four melancholies) to satirize the overly sentimental lovelorn poem of his own contemporaries. In this poem, Lu Xun comically replaces the classical poetic images of green jade, pearls, embroidered silk, and gold-inlayed swords with trivial, vulgar items such as owls, sugar-covered hawthorns, knockout drops, and red snakes. With the deliberate

discrepancy between the original literati narration and its modern earthy revision, Lu Xun mocks the unchecked lovelorn mood in poetry writing.

Other examples of parody in modern China include Qian Zhongshu's novel *Weicheng* (Fortress besieged) and Zhang Ailing's (Eileen Chang) novellas of the 1940s, which satirize the lifestyles of modern intellectuals, traditional aristocrats, the petty bourgeois, and so on. Although the literary productions of the 1950s and '60s in the People's Republic of China were mainly governed by the revolutionary mandates set up by Mao Zedong, practices of parody can still be noticed in film comedies and new historical plays in this socialist period. Because of strict ideological control, these parodies were so moderate that they could readily be co-opted as a means of strengthening state ideology.

With the end of the Maoist period in the late 1970s, parodies became less restricted and more frequently seen. Among all parodists, two names need to be emphasized: Wang Xiaobo and Wang Shuo. Wang Xiaobo is a freelance writer whose works were mostly written in the 1980s and '90s. Besides his best-known parodic works of the "Age Trilogy" (*Huangjin shidai* [The golden age], *Baiyin shidai* [The silver age], and *Qingtong shidai* [The bronze age]), Wang Xiaobo also comically revised classic Chinese stories such as *Hongfu yeben* (Running away at night) and *Hongxian daohe* (The story of Red Thread). In these stories, Wang twists the original plot and interweaves it with comic language and psychological analysis. In this way, he reconstructs history from a contemporary perspective, while deconstructing it by playing with its absurdity. Wang's goal is to make his writings "fun." Wang has a large number of followers among college students, who have established an online community called "Wang's running dogs."

Wang Shuo is a Beijing-based writer known for his parodic works from the 1990s. Because of his extremely cynical mockery of all orthodoxies, which are for him inevitably hypocritical, he is called a *pizi zuojia* (hooligan writer). However, his huge success in the literary field as well as in the commercial market exemplifies the role that parody plays in dealing with the new reality in postsocialist China. The protagonists in Wang Shuo's novels are mainly glib-tongued urban youngsters. They are "playing for thrills" and claiming "please do not call me human" (both of these phrases are titles of Wang's novellas). In the story *Wan zhu* (Troubleshooters), three young people organize a "Three T Company" and provide a substitute service to help solve people's problems. A series of hilarious stories unfold as each case is performed and deconstructed by the three protagonists. Various humorous episodes show the absurdity of life, and thereby demystify the solemnities of life.

In her study of *egao*, Haiqing Yu (2015: 59) also points out the relationship between *egao* and the use of parody in the forms of cartoon, folk song, popular rhythmical saying (*shunkouliu* 顺口溜), comic books, popular performing arts such as cross-talk (*xiangsheng* 相声), folk dance (*yangge* 秧歌), posters, and comic theatrical skits (*xiaopin* 小品) throughout twentieth century.

9 *China Information* devoted a couple of special issues (issue 19, no. 2 in 2005 and issue 28, no. 2 in 2014) to a discussion of the Internet in China. For recent studies of the topic in English, see Introduction.

10 Berg (2008) is quite optimistic about the liberalizing effect of the Internet on the *egao* phenomenon; Zhou (2008) sees this effect, but is at the same time cautious about the other side. For him, Internet control and censorship in China is a cause of the lack of political activism within the *egao* subculture.

11 This idea of Anderson's is closely related to Stanley Fish's (1980) "interpretive community" in our study, and it will be explored in detail later. Here, we use the term more in the sense that, because of the communicative nature of the Internet, spoofsters are widely scattered but also linked by cyberspace at an unprecedented speed and in a form never seen before. For further discussion of the hyper-connectivity brought about by the Internet, see Chapter 5.

12 The latest statistics show that, as of June 2016, the population of Chinese netizens has reached 701 million (CNNIC 2016: 11). China surpassed the United States as the biggest Internet user in June 2008 (Jacobs 2009).

13 Jameson distinguishes pastiche from parody by the former's absence of depth and critical distance from the hypotext. Hutcheon (1989) argues against this point. However, as Dentith (2000: 156) argues, "it is argument by definition, which affects the terms in which the discussion about postmodernism should be conducted, but not the substance." In a way, *egao* is sometimes more akin to "pastiche" in a Jamesonian sense, because, as it will be expounded in the following part, *egao* does not always engage in the spoofed text critically.

14 For discussions of "postmodernism" in China, see, for instance, Arif Dirlik and Xudong Zhang (2000), Frederic Jameson (1986), Sheldon Lu (2001), and Xiaobing Tang (1993). For discussions of "post-New Era," see Xudong Zhang (1997). For discussions of "postsocialism" in China, see Arif Dirlik (1989), Chris Berry (2004), Haomin Gong (2012), Jason McGrath (2008), Paul G. Pickowicz (1994), Sheldon Lu (2007), and Xudong Zhang (2008).

15 After navigating through the theories of postmodernism of Jameson, Hutcheon, and John Docker with respect to parody, Dentith (2000: 162) later claims that the bond between postmodernism and parody in general seems to be valid and persuasive. However, this grand narrative is

> too epochal, insufficiently alert to the more "micro" and properly historical forces acting in society at any period. What is rather needed is a description of the multiple and varying sources of cultural authority in society, and the capacity of any social order to invent and to reinvent its sacred words as beliefs change, different social classes take the social lead, differing cultural forms come into and move out of prominence.

16 Many studies have been done on this issue. For instance, Chinese sociologist Sun Liping (2003, 2004, 2006) has written extensively on this social transformation. He explicitly uses such concepts as "cleavage" and "imbalance" in describing contemporary Chinese society as an uneven society. Jason McGrath (2008) also points out that "fragmentation" is a significant feature of postsocialist China.

17 For instance, Manfred Pfister (2002b: vi–vii) notes that

> [l]aughter is always caught up in the kinds of distinctions between centre and margins every society employs to establish and stabilize its identity: in one society, the predominant form of laughter can be that which aims from the site of the ideological or power centre at what is to be marginalized or excluded altogether; in another, the most significant form of laughter can arise from the margins, challenging and subverting the established orthodoxies, authorities and hierarchies.

18 *Furong jiejie* (Hibiscus sister), *Houshe nanhai* (Back-dorm boys), and *Wangluo xiaopang* (Net chubby) are such examples. Spoofsters, out of the mindset of sheer entertainment and practical jokes, created a series of anti-idols, vaunting their playful sentiment.

19 In some cases, spoofsters' behaviors border on those of the *qun meng* (mob), a group of people gathering together and exhibiting a homogeneous and uniformed psychological consciousness. They refuse rational and complex thinking. For different kinds of advice, thoughts, and beliefs offered to them, they only give two choices on either extremes: either take them or refuse them entirely, regarding them as either categorical truths or absolute fallacies. Zhu Dake (2006a, 2006b) characterizes such spoofsters as *hongke*, the mob which kicks up a fuss. (See Chapter 5 for further discussion of *hongke* and populism on the Chinese Internet.) For him, this group of people easily falls into *liumang-ism*, or hooliganism. Interestingly, in Zhu's vocabulary *liumang* is

a paradox-charted word that, on the one hand, indicates the conventional meaning of hooligans who disrespect laws and moralities and cause social problems, and, on the other, also implies the ideas of unrootedness, diaspora, mobility, marginality, unshack-ledness, unconstrainedness, and so on. To a certain extent, Zhu's definition best speaks of the double-sidedness of the *egao* culture. It is a product of this multicultural, plural-istic society, in which social values become heterogeneous and social tolerance high. However, it also testifies to the serious challenges to social norms and values and their consequent degradation, which are exemplified in such phenomena as loss of a certain fundamental humanity and lack of social responsibility. Sometimes, the *egao* culture perplexes us as to whether it is to be viewed as "deconstructive" or as being simply "destructive" (Liu 2008). Ethical problems that *egao* aroused will be discussed in detail in Chapter 5.

20 We may also add to these the Hong Kong-based comedian Stephen Chow's films (especially his works *Dahua xiyou* [A Chinese odyssey 大话西游, Part I and Part II, 1995]), which have exerted huge influences on the young urban generation in mainland China, as well as the videos of self-parody, the *Da shiji* (Big histories) series, made by well-known reporters and staff of the China Central TV (CCTV).

21 This statement can be partially justified by popular "folk jokes," which are passed mouth to mouth among people on the Internet, and as short text messages on mobile phones. These jokes sometimes even make fun of political figures and are spiced up with sexual implications.

22 Harris (2000: 7) sees parody in the filmic field as more constructive and argues film parody has become a new canon.

23 For comments on *The Promise*, see, for example, http://ent.sina.com.cn/f/thepromise/index.shtml; http://ent.sina.com.cn/m/c/2005–12–21/1050936192.html; and http://www.360doc.com/showWeb/0/0/48332.aspx. Last accessed August 31, 2016.

24 For instance, celebrities such as Lu Yan (Lisa Lu), Pu Cunxin, Chen Guoxing, Hu Xuehua, and Song Jia openly praised Chen's film (Sina Entertainment 2005).

25 The particular discussion page can be found on a discussion forum at http://www7.tianya.cn/New/PublicForum/Content.asp?flag=1&idWriter=0&Key=0&idArticle=133954&strItem=filmtv, accessed January 19, 2009. The website is no longer available as of August 31, 2016.

26 An ironic footnote to this case is that, at the beginning of each of his works, Hu Ge puts up a warning asking viewers not to disseminate his work for uses other than their own personal entertainment; and at the end, he lists all the works he "cites."

27 Homosexuality in China today largely remains a taboo and the mention of it can be negatively satirical.

28 This is also true for many other spoofs: for example, the spoof of the "Red Clas-sic," *Shanshan de hongxing* (Sparkling red star; http://www.56.com/u54/v_MTMzM TI1MDc.html, last accessed January 19, 2006, no longer available as of August 31, 2016), addresses the problem of rocketing house prices; Hu Ge's "Chunyun diguo" (The empire of the spring festival transportation; http://www.youtube.com/watch?v=JZL_F85AhSg, last accessed August 31, 2016) parodies this stressful annual experience unique to China; the spoof of Ang Lee's film, *Se, jie* (*Lust, caution*; http://you.joy.cn/video/200583.htm, last accessed January 19, 2006, no longer available as of August 31, 2016), mocks the rigid English tests imposed by the state. All these are "petty" problems that common people are most concerned with, and these are also the problems that the government fails to handle satisfactorily.

29 The clips of *The Promise* used in "A Bloody Case" were originally taken from a pirated DVD that Hu Ge bought at a market. This is part of the charge that Chen inflicted on Hu.

30 http://www.tudou.com/programs/view/-itsBrmpbCw/, last accessed August 31, 2016.

31 http://www.tudou.com/programs/view/9AoIu72TgSA/, last accessed August 31, 2016.

Bibliography

Anderson, Benedict. (1991). *Imagined Communities: Reflections on the Origin and Spread of Nationalism*. Rev. and extended ed. London and New York: Verso.

Bakhtin, Mikhail. (1984a). *Problems of Dostoevsky's Poetics*. Trans. Caryl Emerson. Minneapolis, MN: University of Minnesota Press.

——. (1984b). *Rabelais and His World*. Trans. Helene Iswolsky. Bloomington, IN: Indiana University Press.

Berg, Daria. (2008). "Spoofing Subculture, the Beijing Olympics and Web 2.0 in China." Paper presented at International Forum for Contemporary Chinese Studies Inaugural Conference, "Post-Olympic China: Globalization and Sustainable Development after Three Decades of Reform," Nottingham, UK.

Berry, Chris. (2004). *Postsocialist Cinema in Post-Mao China: The Cultural Revolution after the Cultural Revolution*. New York: Routledge.

Boskin, Joseph. (1997). *Rebellious Laughter: People's Humor in American Culture*. Syracuse, NY: Syracuse University Press.

Box Office Mojo. (2006). "*The Promise*." http://www.boxofficemojo.com/movies/?id=promise05.htm. Last accessed August 31, 2016.

Chen, Jiu, Zhang Sheng, and He Shuqing. (2007). "*Egao*: hulianwang shidai de dazhong yule" (Egao: mass entertainment in the Internet age). *Shuzhai* 4: 24–6.

Cheng Qingsong. (2006). "Zhichi Chen Kaige! Zuowei dianyingren he yi ge gongmin" (Supporting Chen Kaige: as a filmmaker and a citizen). http://blog.sina.com.cn/s/blog_476fb4b3010001yb.html. Last accessed August 31, 2016.

Cixous, Hélène. (1981). "The Laugh of the Medusa." Trans. Keith and Paul Cohen. In *New French Feminisms*, edited by Elaine Marks and Isabelle de Courtivron, 245–64. New York: Schocken.

CNNIC (China Internet Network Information Center). (2007). *The Twentieth Statistical Report on Internet Development in China*. Beijing: CNNIC.

——. (2016). *The Thirty-Eighth Statistical Report on Internet Development in China*. Beijing: CNNIC.

Dane, Joseph A. (1988). *Parody: Critical Concepts versus Literary Practices: Aristophanes to Sterne*. Norman: University of Oklahoma Press.

Dentith, Simon. (2000). *Parody*. London: Routledge.

Dirlik, Arif. (1989). "Postsocialism? Reflections on 'Socialism with Chinese Characteristics.'" In *Marxism and the Chinese Experience*, edited by Arif Dirlik and Maurice Meisner, 362–84. Armonk, NY: M. E. Sharpe.

Dirlik, Arif, and Xudong Zhang, eds. (2000). *Postmodernism and China*. Durham, NC: Duke University Press.

Finney, Gail. (1994). "Unity in Difference? An Introduction." In *Look Who's Laughing: Gender and Comedy*, edited by Gail Finney, 1–13. Langhorne, PA: Gordon and Breach.

Fish, Stanley. (1980). *Is There a Text in This Class? The Authority of Interpretive Communities*. Cambridge, MA: Harvard University Press.

Gehring, Wes D. (1999). *Parody as Film Genre: "Never Give a Saga an Even Break"*. Westport, CT: Greenwood.

Genette, Gérard. (1997). *Palimpsests: Literature in the Second Degree*. Lincoln: University of Nebraska Press.

Gong, Haomin. (2012). *Uneven Modernity: Literature, Film, and Intellectual Discourse in Postsocialist China*. Honolulu: University of Hawai'i Press.

Guangming wang. (2006). "Fangzhi wangshang 'egao' chengfeng zhuanjia zuotanhui" (Roundtable on preventing *egao* from becoming a fashion). http://www.gmw.cn/content/wseg.htm. Last accessed August 31, 2016.

Guo Shuang. (2006). "Guowan wangyou qianming zhichi Hu Ge hanwei Mantou" (More than 10,000 netizens sign up in support of Hu Ge's defense of A Steamed Bun). http://www.ycwb.com/gb/content/2006–02/14/content_1068937.htm. Last accessed August 31, 2016.

Hannoosh, Michele. (1989). "Reflexive Function of Parody." *Comparative Literature* 41, no. 2: 113–27.

Harris, Dan. (2000). *Film Parody*. London: British Film Institute.

Huang Qing. (2006). "Parody Can Help People Ease Work Pressure." *China Daily*. http://www.chinadaily.com.cn/cndy/2006–07/22/content_646887.htm. Last accessed August 31, 2016.

Hutcheon, Linda. (1985). *A Theory of Parody: The Teachings of Twentieth-Century Art Forms*. London: Methuen.

——. (1989). *The Politics of Postmodernism*. New York: Routledge.

Jacobs, Andrew. (2009). "Internet Usage Rises in China." *New York Times*, January 15. http://www.nytimes.com/2009/01/15/world/asia/15beijing.html. Last accessed August 31, 2016.

Jameson, Fredric. (1986). *Houxiandai zhuyi yu wenhua lilun* (*Postmodernism and cultural theories*). Trans. Xiaobing Tang. Xi'an: Shaanxi shifan daxue chubanshe.

——. (1991). *Postmodernism, or, the Cultural Logic of Late Capitalism*. Durham, NC: Duke University Press.

Kiremidjian, Garabed D. (1969). "The Aesthetics of Parody." *Journal of Aesthetics and Art Criticism* 28: 231–42.

Li, Hongmei. (2011). "Parody and Resistance on the Chinese Internet." In *Online Society in China: Creating, Celebrating, and Instrumentalising the Online Carnival*, edited by David Kurt Herold and Peter Marolt, 71–88. Abingdon, Oxon and New York: Routledge.

Liang Xiaosheng. (1998). *Zhongguo shehui ge jieceng fenxi* (*An analysis of social classes in China*). Beijing: Jingji ribao chubanshe.

Liu, Xiaobo. (2006). "Cong Wang Shuo shi tiaokan dao Hu Ge shi egao – jian lun houjiquan ducai xia de minjian xiaohua zhengzhi" (From Wang Shuo-style ridicule to Hu Ge-style spoofs – also on the politics of folk jokes under postauthoritarian rule). http://intermargins.net/intermargins/TCulturalWorkshop/culturestudy/mainland/03.htm. Last accessed August 31, 2016.

Liu, Zuoyuan. (2008). "E meiti zhiyi Zhongguo wangmin 'daode baoli'" (Russian media question Chinese netizens' "moral violence"). *Zhongguo qingnian bao*. http://qnck.cyol.com/content/2008–01/22/content_2043200.htm. Last accessed August 31, 2016.

Lu, Sheldon. (2001). *China, Transnational Visuality, Global Postmodernity*. Stanford, CA: Stanford University Press.

——. (2007). *Chinese Modernity and Global Biopolitics: Studies in Literature and Visual Culture*. Honolulu: University of Hawaii Press.

Lu, Xueyi. (2002). *Dangdai Zhongguo shehui jieceng yanjiu baogao* (*A research report on social classes in contemporary China*). Beijing: Shehui kexue wenxian chubanshe.

——. (2004). *Dangdai Zhongguo shehui liudong* (*Social mobility in contemporary China*). Beijing: Shehui kexue wenxian chubanshe.

Mao, Tse-tung (Mao Zedong). (1977). "In Memory of Norman Bethune." In *Selected Works of Mao Tse-tung*, vol. II, 337–8. Beijing: Foreign Languages Press.

McGrath, Jason. (2008). *Postsocialist Modernity: Chinese Cinema, Literature, and Criticism in the Market Age.* Stanford, CA: Stanford University Press.

Meng, Bingchuan. (2009). "Regulating Online Spoofs: Futile Efforts of Recentralization?" In *China's Information and Communications Technology Revolution: Social Changes and State Responses*, edited by Zheng Yongnian and Zhang Xiaoling, 52–67. London: Routledge.

Mulkay, Michael. (1988). *On Humor: Its Nature and Its Place in Modern Society.* Cambridge, MA: Basil Blackwell.

Parkin, John. (1997). *Humor Theorists of the Twentieth Century.* Lewiston, NY: Edwin Mellen.

Pfister, Manfred, ed. (2002a). *A History of English Laughter: Laughter from Beowulf to Beckett and Beyond.* Amsterdam: Rodopi.

——. (2002b). "Introduction: A History of English Laughter?" In *A History of English Laughter: Laughter from Beowulf to Beckett and Beyond*, edited by Manfred Pfister, v–x. Amsterdam: Rodopi.

Phiddian, Robert. (1995). *Swift's Parody.* Cambridge: Cambridge University Press.

Pickowicz, Paul G. (1994). "Huang Jianxin and the Notion of Postsocialism." In *New Chinese Cinemas: Forms, Identities, Politics*, edited by Nick Browne, Paul G. Pickowicz, Vivian Sobchack, and Esther Yau, 57–87. Cambridge: Cambridge University Press.

Rea, Christopher G. (2013). "Spoofing (*e'gao*) Culture on the Chinese Internet." In *Humour in Chinese Life and Culture: Resistance and Control in Modern Times*, edited by Jocelyn Chey and Jessica Milner Davis, 149–72. Hong Kong: Hong Kong University Press.

——. (2015). *The Age of Irreverence a New History of Laughter in China.* Oakland, CA: University of California Press.

Reichl, Susanne, and Mark Stein, eds. (2005). *Cheeky Fictions: Laughter and the Postcolonial.* Amsterdam: Rodopi.

Rose, Margaret A. (1979). *Parody/Meta-Fiction: An Analysis of Parody as a Critical Mirror to the Writing and Reception of Fiction.* London: Croom Helm.

——. (1993). *Parody: Ancient, Modern and Post-Modern.* Cambridge: Cambridge University Press.

Shohat, Ella. (1991). "Ethnicities-in-Relation: Toward a Multicultural Reading of American Cinema." In *Unspeakable Images: Ethnicity and the American Cinema*, edited by Lester D. Friedman, 215–50. Urbana: University of Illinois Press.

Sina Entertainment. (2005). "Pu Cunxin deng mingxing ping Wuji: jinnian lai zuihao de Zhongguo dianying" (Celebrities' reviews of *The Promise*: The Best Chinese Film in Recent Years). http://ent.sina.com.cn/m/c/2005–12–21/1050936192.html. Last accessed August 31, 2016.

Stam, Robert. (1989). *Subversive Pleasures: Bakhtin, Cultural Criticism and Film.* Baltimore, MD: Johns Hopkins University Press.

Sun, Liping. (2003). *Duanlie: ershi shiji jiushi niandai yilai de Zhongguo shehui* (*Cleavage: Chinese society since the 1990s*). Beijing: Shehui kexue wenxian chubanshe.

——. (2004). *Shiheng: duanlie shehui de yunzuo luoji* (*Imbalance: the implementation logic of a cleaved society*). Beijing: Shehui kexue wenxian chubanshe.

——. (2006). *Boyi: duanlie shehui de liyi chongtu yu hexie* (*Gaming: confrontation and harmony in a cleaved society*). Beijing: Shehui kexue wenxian chubanshe.

Tang, Xiaobing. (1993). "The Function of New Theory: What Does It Mean to Talk about Postmodernism in China?" In *Politics, Ideology and Literary Discourse in Modern China*, edited by Liu Kang and Xiaobing Tang, 278–300. Durham, NC: Duke University Press.

Vieira, Luiz João, and Robert Stam. (1985). "Parody and Marginality: The Case of Brazilian Cinema." *Framework* 28: 20–49.

Voci, Paola. (2010). *China on Video: Smaller-Screen Realities*. London and New York: Routledge.

Wang Qian. (2006). "Hu Ge zhuanfang: wo zhizao le 'mantouxue' an'" (An interview with Hu Ge: I created "A Bloody Case Caused by a Steamed Bun"). http://ent.sina.com.cn/m/c/2006–01–18/1952964868.html. Last accessed August 31, 2016.

Yang Tao. (2006). "Falü xuezhe yanzhong de Mantou PK Wuji" (In the eyes of law scholars: the tension between A Steamed Bun and *The Promise*). *Jiancha ribao*, February 17.

Yu, Haiqing. (2015). "After the 'Steamed Bun': E'gao and Its Postsocialist Politics." *Chinese Literature Today* 5, no. 1: 55–64.

Zhang, Xudong. (1997). *Chinese Modernism in the Era of Reforms: Cultural Fever, Avant-Garde Fiction, and the New Chinese Cinema*. Durham, NC: Duke University Press.

——. (2008). *Postsocialism and Cultural Politics: China in the Last Decade of the Twentieth Century*. Durham, NC: Duke University Press.

Zhou, Yongming. (2008). "Egao: Visual Carnival and Iconoclasm in Chinese Cyberspace." Paper presented at the Association for Asian Studies Annual Meeting, Atlanta, USA, 2008.

Zhu, Dake. (2006a). *Liumang de shengyan: dangdai Zhongguo de liumang xushi* (*The festival of liumang: liumang narratives in contemporary China*). Beijing: Xinxing chubanshen.

——. (2006b). "Yi ge songruan de huayu mantou" (A soft discourse on a steamed bun). *Zhongguo xinwen zhoukan* 8: 28–9.

2   Circulating smallness

The dialectics of micro-narratives

As social media is becoming an integral part of everyday life, micro-narratives have become increasingly prominent and attracted our attention in recent years. First, with the sudden surge of really short stories on Weibo (microblog 微博), the Chinese equivalent of Twitter, in the late 2000s, a new genre of microfiction (*wei xiaoshuo* 微小说) has attracted the attention of many readers, both critics and ordinary netizens.[1] Microfiction, defined as online stories of 140 characters or fewer, written, posted, reposted, circulated, read, and commented upon via personal computers or mobile devices, has indeed created a stir. This sensation arises from the promotion of the genre by many websites, such as Sina.com and Rednet. com, and the participation of millions of amateur and professional writers. Sina, one of the largest portal websites in China, for example, launched its Weibo service in 2009 and has hosted a microfiction contest every year since 2010, receiving 232,751, 1,461,420, and 880,733 micro-stories in their 2010, 2011, and 2012 contests, respectively.[2]

Second, with the increasing availability and affordability of personal and mobile digital video-making devices in the 2010s, micro-film (*wei dianying* 微电影) became popular among netizens. Although there is no consensus on what micro-film precisely is, yet as its name suggests, it generally refers to short films online, available on video-sharing sites and social media and accessible through computers, tablets, and smartphones. Micro-film is usually short in length and small in investment. The "Netease Micro Film Festival 2011," hosted by Netease, another large portal website, asked participants to upload their films of less than 10 minutes. The "Sina Micro Video Competition" in 2012 defined the length of micro-film as "30 seconds to 5 minutes."[3] "The First International Mobile Micro Film Competition," jointly organized by *China Daily* and Macworld Asia in 2011, required participants to make 3-minute films with their cell phones (China Daily 2011b). On the website "Chinese Micro Films," micro-films are categorized in accordance with both the genre (romance, action movie, comedy, etc.), and the length (5 minutes, 5–10 minutes, 10–30 minutes, and beyond 30 minutes).[4]

Third, in response to the increasingly short attention span as the result of the overwhelming amount of information at the digital age, Han Han, a well-known writer, racecar driver, and film director, launched a literary app named "ONE·*yige*" (一个) in 2012. "ONE" publishes one picture, one text (a short story), and one answer to one question each day. Within 24 hours when it was available in the Apple Store, it became the most popular free app in China (Ye 2012). Its catchphrase reads: "In the complicated world, one is all." This is a symbolic attempt to simplify the complicated world in the age of information explosion. In an essay titled "Fragment" (*suipian* 碎片), published in the inaugural issue of ONE, Han Han (2012) explains his intention this way: "Everything is too complicated. Everything is too transient. . . . Let's do something simple. . . . This is the ONE you see." Han Han assumes that users' attention spans on ONE is half an hour (Ye 2012). Therefore, all the stories and answers published on ONE are short pieces.

In this chapter, we examine microfiction, micro-films, and literary app-enabled stories from the perspective of their most prominent feature – micro-ness, which exposes and critiques the social barriers that compartmentalize people. Micro-narratives are characterized by their smallness, shortness, simplicity, and lightness. Events organized by Internet companies, such as the Web Culture Festival hosted by Sina in 2012, further extended micro-narratives to a variety of forms, including web literature, screenplays, calligraphy, paintings, photography, and so on. Since then, micro-narratives seem to have gone viral with an explosion of a great many forms, including micro-interviews (*wei fangtan* 微访谈), micro-music (*wei yinyue* 微音乐), micro-events (*wei huodong* 微活动), micro-shows (*wei xiu* 微秀), micro-drives (*wei pan* 微盘), micro-groups (*wei qun* 微群), micro-bars (*wei ba* 微吧), and even micro-philanthropy (*wei gongyi* 微公益) and micro-girls (*wei nülang* 微女郎). Some of them are still popular today, while other have been replaced by newer micro-forms. For many young netizens, it has become fashionable and cool to have a micro- of everything in this age of expansive connectedness via the Internet. It is beyond our scope to examine even a fraction of these micro-narratives, but their inherent micro-ness and adherence to the Internet are instrumental to our conceptualization of new forms of writing and image-making.

We are particularly interested in the dialectical relationship between micro-ness and largeness embodied in the new forms of cultural products, the context of their emergence, and the condition of their existence, the issues reflected in their content, as well as their political implications, particularly those in terms of class restructuring. This dialectical relationship is perhaps best exemplified in the catchphrase that Sina brought up for the first microfiction contest it hosted: "micro fiction @ macro world" (*wei xiaoshuo @ da shijie* 微小说@大世界), which implies the tension that micro-narratives, under the specific sociocultural conditions in contemporary China, are already cast into with the larger world. How should we understand the rise of micro-narratives in light of China's growing national ambitions as well as people's frustration over social division in the process of achieving such a status?

To answer the question, we believe that an investigation of the dialectics between micro-ness and largeness and the political and cultural ramifications of these dialectics will lead to insights not only into micro-narratives themselves, but, more importantly, into the overall sociocultural conditions, of which micro-narratives are a product and to which they respond. Reading micro-narratives as both literary and sociocultural texts, we argue that the smallness is an intrusion upon the largeness and hegemony of grand narratives on the one hand, and a reflection of a broadly changing reality on the other. The narratives at micro-level destabilize the boundaries of the subculture and the mainstream, the mass and the elite, the modern and the traditional, the individual and the community, and the hyper-connectedness and the compartmentalization. They reflect the increasingly stratified society and meanwhile critique the commercial, economic, and technological barriers that stratify people. Our specific focus will be the cultural status of micro-narratives as a reflection of the combination of literary writing, image-making, and online activities, as well as their aesthetic, literary, and cultural characteristics.

The dialectics in a sociocultural context

The dialectics of smallness and largeness manifested in microfiction, micro-film, and literary apps may be explored within the larger sociocultural context. In the introduction to their edited anthology of short-short stories, an offline form of microfiction, in Greater China, Aili Mu and Julie Chiu (2006: xiii–xiv) claim that the short-short genre arises "as Hong Kong, Taiwan, and mainland China join the global drift into the postmodern era." The rise of the short-short genre, they write, is also "closely associated with a passion for speed – easy consumption and instant gratification – and a desire for greater diversity," as well as, in the view of the Taiwanese writer Yin Di, a need to restrain excesses. In another study, Aili Mu (2012: 159–82) further identifies the conditions under which the short-short genre grows and to which it responds as the commercialization that has been taking place over the past thirty years in mainland China, along with the swing of state socialism. As such, the short-short genre on their radar is "a literature both of commitment and entertainment" (Mu and Chiu 2006: xvii). While all these still hold true for the rise of micro-narratives, new sociocultural conditions that have appeared in the last decade have come to shape the particularities of the forms.

Micro-narratives are a product of the age of prevailing yet tarnished "grandeur." It is not coincidental that *micro*-narratives, truly mini-sized forms, arise at the time when extremely *grand* national narratives dominate the theme of the age – just to name a few: the 2008 Olympic Games in Beijing and the 2010 Expo in Shanghai, both involving huge human and financial resources, heralding a spectacular image of China to the world; constructions of massive magnitude, such as the Grand National Theatre in Tiananmen Square, the Birds' Nest Stadium, and the numerous skyscrapers mushrooming all across China, emulating each other and striving to be the largest and the tallest; China's ambitious space project, represented by Shenzhou spacecraft and the Tiangong module, demonstrating China's rising power in outer space; and symbolically, the airing and re-airing of the documentary, *The Rise of Great Nations* (*Daguo jueqi* 大国崛起), on CCTV in 2006 and 2007, signifying China's national ambitions and confidence. However, these grand narratives, unlike those seen, for example, in the revolutionary and socialist periods, when the high collectivism subjugated individual subjectivity, are increasingly losing their ground to a surging awareness of individuality among modern citizens which results from the prevalence of the market economy and globalization. The effectiveness and legitimacy of these grand narratives have constantly been challenged by another reality: the ever-increasing gap between the rich and the poor, worsening environmental conditions, food and drug insecurity, the rampant corruption of officials, and the mass disturbances (*qunti shijian* 群体事件) provoked by the forced demolitions of houses and compulsory acquisition of land.

As narratives of grandness are becoming increasingly unreliable and unsustainable, the search for smallness, or a local reality, becomes increasingly desirable among the common people. Micro-narratives, then, offer a focus on smaller realities, whose localism renders them accessible to common people and provide, in Mu and Chui's (2006: xiv) words, "an antidote to super-sizing and overdose." Against the alienating and disorientating grand reality propagated by official narratives, these small realities imagined in micro-narratives provide a foothold for at-home-ness and the comfort of intimacy. Particularly, for micro-narratives, the "grand" narrative of postsocialist China presents itself in an almost bullying fashion despite (or, perhaps, precisely *because* of) its diminished effectiveness. As a reaction to this condition, micro-narratives offer a tactical adherence, sometimes even to the degree of vulgarity, to small virtues in a small reality, or, in the words of Ibrahim Taha (2000: 64), "one moment of reality." No longer a marginal form and now a quite popular one, micro-narratives sometimes tell "unofficial histories, undocumented memories, unspoken human predicaments, and intimate lifeworlds" (Mu and Chiu 2006: xvii), often dealing with love, affection, and social problems in everyday life. Their small size, along with the small reality they look into, make micro-narratives not only products for convenient consumption and easy gratification, but also something that the common people can, thanks to the Weibo and other Internet platforms, really engage with.

Weibo plays a very important role in the production, circulation, and consumption of micro-narratives. Microfiction is defined on Baidu Baike (undated), a Chinese equivalent of Wikipedia, as "a mini-story published in the form of a Weibo posting," which, in their words, is "a vivid demonstration of the extension of the value of the Weibo." Though micro-films are not directly aired on Weibo, the major film-sharing sites all have their official Weibo accounts to publicize and circulate the short products. ONE registers a Weibo account named "yige App gongzuoshi" (studio of *yige* App). Admittedly, Weibo, as well as the Internet in general, is not innocent from grand narratives, nor is it friendly exclusively to small realities. Studies of the Internet show that the much-anticipated democratization of Chinese society effected by the Internet has always been countered by the growing effectiveness and efficiency of state regulations. Likewise, with the increasing presence of state apparatuses in and tightening monitoring over Weibo, Weibo has become another battlefield on which different forces struggle for control and class reconsolidation and social stratification are manifested.[5]

The dialectics in a technological context: writing on Weibo

Sina loosely describes microfiction as fiction of 140 or fewer characters.[6] Although the simple definition does not specify many unique features of microfiction, particularly in the specific condition of postsocialist China, it nonetheless highlights the importance of Weibo as an inseparable ecological condition under which microfiction exists, and micro-ness as one of microfiction's trademark features.

Situated within the larger context of generic development, microfiction is indebted to many sources in its forming, among which two stand out: the short-short story as a sub-genre, and Weibo as a new digital space. Though there is rich scholarship on short-shorts, discussions of microfiction are scanty.[7] When critics talk about short-shorts, the variety of nomenclature – including the English-language flash fiction, sudden fiction, and the short-short story, and the Chinese-language one-minute story (*yifenzhong xiaoshuo* 一分钟小说), palm-size story (*zhangpian xiaoshuo* 掌篇小说), pocket-size story (*xiuzhen xiaoshuo* 袖珍小说), smoke-long story (*yidaiyan xiaoshuo* 一袋烟小说), and ant story (*mayi xiaoshuo* 蚂蚁小说) – bespeaks the lack of agreement in defining such writings on the part of writers and scholars alike (Qi 2008). Moreover, while shortness is a central concern in these writings, critics have various ideas about *how short* a short story should be so as to qualify as such. This translates into a sheer word count, below which a shorter story might present a qualitatively different reading experience. This, in our view, is rather a moot question because a literary genre is never defined singly in terms of word count. Although microfiction does have a 140-character limit set by Weibo, this limit presents less a generic feature in a literary sense than a technological determinant, which is still experiencing ongoing evolution, and is not directly associated with literary quality.[8] The designated short length in the case of microfiction, with the limited writing space that this form allows, constrains rather than stimulates a creative process in some cases, and urges writers to be more rigorous and experimental in their writing than in others. In any case, given its unique ecological condition of existence and development, microfiction should be more constructively conceptualized under a broader sociocultural context than solely within a literary paradigm. In other words, Weibo, or in a broader view, the Internet, provides a much more complex, and indeed *larger*, space in which the dialectics of *micro*fiction are fashioned.

First and foremost a social networking platform, Weibo provides a unique space for microfiction unseen in other forms of online writing.[9] First, Weibo, with its massive number of users and its multilateral mode, makes itself a ready platform for mass participation in writing, making, circulating, and consuming words and images. The numbers of microfiction works in contests mentioned above have already demonstrated the scale of participation. Weibo largely lowers the bar of literary creation and publication, because virtually anyone with a Weibo account can post his or her "work" on the platform.[10] This extremely easy access to "publication" naturally attracts massive participation. Admittedly, this can result in the production of mediocre material, as well as habits of writing that value immediate gratification over lasting appreciation. But some hidden talents, who would otherwise have no opportunities to publicize their writings, find here a convenient channel to express themselves. In fact, many excellent pieces are widely dispersed.

Second, traditional literary and cultural hierarchies are undone in this space, which leads to a blurring of the borders between the literary and the non-literary. To be sure, many are simply messages intended be shared and spread, while at the same time exhibiting some literary qualities. In the words of communication studies scholar, Meng Wei (2011: 117–21), this mixing of "information and the art of fiction," strengthens the status of microfiction as a form of mass writing. Microfiction can be conceived of, she remarks, as a type of "fiction that has lowered its own [elite] status and thus becomes a part of the common people's everyday lives. When writers of microfiction are more often called 'users,' what they write then becomes more the common people's regular experiences in their understanding of reality and of their self-identification."[11]

Indeed, Weibo as a social networking platform inevitably increases the level of the common people's engagement with everyday reality in microfiction, because information concerning social issues, in the Chinese context, constitutes a significant part of the information spread on Weibo, and thus becomes an important subject in microfiction. With its short length yet high speed in spreading, microfiction on Weibo actively and productively engages with a wide range of contemporary incidents and events, reflecting social changes, ridiculing absurdities, satirizing inequalities, and promoting human intimacy.[12] Moreover, the immediacy and expansiveness that posts enjoy when transmitted on Weibo, arguably a guerrilla tactic that is partly made possible by their brevity, help netizens get their messages across before are censored, at least temporarily.[13] Microfiction is thus usually able to embody broad social concerns, and to do so interestingly, within its small compass.

This extensive literary space, in which human relationships are re-consolidated, creates a new sense of connectedness.[14] In his studies of Internet literature in China, Michel Hockx (2004: 113) has found connections between online literary communities with those based on literary journals in the Republican Period (1911–1949), because of the deeply engrained notion of literature as a "means of social communication." For the same reason, the interaction between readers and authors seen in web literature may also find antecedents in the past. In the case of microfiction, new Weibo technologies render the scale of community forming and author–reader interaction much higher. While netizens of similar literary tastes may find it easy to get connected via the platform of literature websites, entirely disregarding geographical distance, Weibo users may feel even closer to others with instant sharing and diffusional connections. In addition, micro-groups, such as "Literary and Art Youth" (*wenyi xiao qingnian* 文艺小青年) and "Microfiction," perform a similar function as conventional communities, but provide easier and faster multi-directional connections. Not only do authors and readers actively engage with each other, but the line between their roles is also sometimes blurred, or their roles are exchanged. In a way, readers' comments can be regarded as an integral part of the authors' original posts, as the dialogues formed between them extend the meanings and values of the latter. Some readers repost others' works, adding their own words; some writers respond to comments in their new posts, and some incorporate selected comments into their later projects.[15]

Because of the special platform of Weibo, microfiction, small as it is, features mass participation, easy accessibility, extensive connectedness, fast-speed circulation, and vast popularity. This technologically enabled dialectic enriches fiction writing, adding aesthetic uniqueness, which in turn reflects the larger social and political contexts that shape its existence.

Online microfiction is quite inexhaustible. Therefore, in the direct analysis of the genre which follows we will narrow the field by a focus on the pieces selected from contests hosted by Sina, from Chen Peng's (陈鹏) serialized Weibo posts, *The Life of Eiliko Chen in Beijing* (*Eilikochen de jingdu shenghuo ji Eilikochen 的京都生活记*), a highly individual and personal non-fiction, and from Wen Huanjian's (闻华舰) novel, *Love in the Age of Microblogging* (*Weibo shiqi de aiqing 围脖时期的爱情*), arguably the first microblog novel in China.

The dialectics in a literary context

In microfiction, the dialectic of smallness and largeness is manifested in multiple ways, such as those of long and short, macro and micro, individual and communal, talkativeness and expansiveness in vision (as everybody can type a few lines about anything, anywhere and anytime) and the conciseness in expression (140-character limit), and so on. In addition to being a resistance, antidote, and counterbalance to the grand narrative, the smallness, conciseness, and micro-ness also conjure up a rather large picture of social reality in transformation. In what follows, we focus on, with specific case studies, three main features of microfiction, namely the tensions between (1) speedy production and consumption and comparatively timeless topics, themes, and subjects; (2) social alienation and communal intimacy; and (3) the short form online and the long pieces in print.

Micro-tactics against prevalent social disorientation: speedy production and consumption versus timeless subjects

Writing and reading microfiction are closely related to speed, as the 140-character fiction is generally characterized by speed of production and ease of consumption.[16] However, the topics, themes, and subjects of microfiction usually turn out to be relatively "timeless" ones, ranging from love, family relations, and friendship to the humanistic concerns with social issues. This paradox exemplifies a prevalent mindset: that is, when rapid social transformations characterized by rampant commercialization are rapidly disrupting traditional human ties and vulgarizing past beliefs, be they Confucian or socialist, people feel an urge for a (re)turn to basic human feelings that endure as ballast in this age of ruptures and splits. Micro-ness, intriguingly, is at the same time both a product of this restless, impatient society, and its undoing.

The main theme for the 2012 Microfiction Contest, as designated by its host Sina, was love: the love of siblings, friends, lovers, and families.[17] In fact, the

majority of prize-winning stories are stories of everlasting love and speedy satisfaction. In particular, the love between aged couples, which is believed to carry a
transcendent force, is a much-favored subject. For instance, "Wind-Chime Bomb"
(*Fengling zhadan* 风铃炸弹), a first-prize winner, tells a story of the recently
widowed mother, who has to listen to her MP3 player so as to get to sleep every
night. It turns out that what she listens to is the recording of snoring sounds of
her late husband. The stories of Xia Zhengzheng (夏正正) and Zhai Yeqian (宅
夜千), both third-prize winners, describe old couples who, though wrinkled and
losing their hearing, appreciate their mates in ways so romantic that they are even
envied by young couples.[18] The contrast between their age and their "fresh" love,
which remains despite their age, or perhaps because of their age, only foregrounds
the eternity of love. Although this slow and enduring love is desirable precisely
because it is thought to be increasingly rare in a fast-paced consumer society, it
stands in direct tension with the speed at which these stories are produced and
consumed.

In addition, some time-honored, traditional values find their ways back in
microfiction. Filial piety, for instance, is one of the dominant subjects and the
focus of many award-winning pieces. To cite one of many examples:

> Voice in the phone: [in English] "This is a wrong number. Please check up
> and take the telephone number again." [*sic*] Mom speaks on the phone: "Son,
> why do you speak English every day? Mom does not understand. But mom
> misses you . . ."[19]

Short as it is, this second-prize-winning piece of the 2010 contest by Yanis8827
captures a particular moment in modern life: a neglected mother calling her
son, mistaking an automated message as her son talking back in English. This
loaded moment, encompassing geographical separation, technological alienation, linguistic barriers, and generational miscommunication, speaks volumes of
the loneliness and loss that older generations have experienced in the process of
restructuring modern society. As a result, traditional values, such as filial piety,
have been portrayed as a remedy for alienated human relations, if not as an antidote to social disorientation.

Even the "time-travel" genre (*chuanyue* 穿越), a tremendously popular subject in Chinese online writing (as well as in cinema, TV drama, and literature),
is largely related to human affections disoriented in a commercialized society.
In contrast to the stories prevalent in Chinese Internet literature that, to differ-
ing degrees, promote pragmatic and cynical ideologies, as scholar Shao Yanjun
(2012: 16–25) claims, time-travel stories in microfiction tend to return to basic
human emotions that have been disrupted by rapid social "advance" and grand
projects, providing a unique angle to investigate these emotions.[20] The first-prize
piece of the 2011 contest, authored by Jin Yining (金一宁), is a telling example:

> Her mother was critically sick. Her cousin, whom she had never met before,
> came from her hometown and volunteered to look after her mother. It was
> the busiest time in her life, so she agreed. Her cousin stayed in the hospital

everyday and took very good care of her mom. A month later her mother passed away. After the memorial service ended, she wanted to thank her cousin, but she had already gone. Her cousin only left a letter, which said: I am actually you in ten years. I traveled here to assuage my own regret and guilt.

(Sina 2011)

The unnamed protagonist splits into two figures, and her future self travels in time to help her present self in order to compensate for the presently unfulfilled filial duties. In this case, traveling through time provides a means by which the protagonist can act out her devotion, though belatedly, to her mother. More importantly, the bifurcation of the self also epitomizes the schizophrenic society of contemporary China.

Some stories quite directly, yet in a microscopic way, address social problems generated by China's breakneck pursuit of grand development. A large proportion of these little stories devote their attention to environmental crises, social injustice, official corruption, moral degeneration, uncontrolled materialism, and other problems that plague the society. Here is an interesting example written by "biglong Dalong" (biglong 大龙):

His girlfriend asked: "You poor scholar, why didn't you buy a house years ago?!" He bitterly laughed: "Even years ago I still could not afford a house. Maybe I would have been better off being a scholar in the old society." When he awoke he found his arms numb from taking a nap on the table. Wait, where was he? Puzzled, he turned around, and saw a man with grizzled beard. He was the only customer wearing a long gown and drinking wine while standing. He murmured: Do you know how many ways there are to write the character "to rise" (*zhang*), as in "the real estate prices are rising"?

(Sina 2011)

Targeting the skyrocketing real estate prices that so frustrate the majority of ordinary Chinese, this piece pays an obvious tribute to Lu Xun's famous short story, "Kong Yiji," which depicts a destitute, old-fashioned scholar, who falls victim to traditional education and becomes an object of ridicule since he knows nothing but outdated, useless knowledge, such as the obsolete ways of writing a character. Facing the pressure of increasingly unaffordable housing, contemporary scholars seem to be no less helpless and powerless than their impoverished counterparts in the past.

Alienated individual and communal intimacy

Microfiction, as a product of the latest social networking, creates a new sense of imagined intimacy through a reconsolidation of the author–reader relationship in its (re)production, circulation, and consumption. Admittedly, an imagined intimacy is not new in literature, but it figures strongly in microfiction because the

writers, constantly aware of the social network of Weibo, write with his/her audience in mind. The audience, imagined as well as real, variously participates in
the process of producing and reproducing a work. As Wen Huajian (2011: 226,
emphasis added) writes in regard to *Love in the Age of Microblogging*:

> There was no pre-set storyline when I started to write the novel, because
> I didn't know how *you* wanted the plot to develop. My novel may look messy,
> just like our messy Weibo life. I am more of a collector than a writer; I put
> together the wonderful fragments that *you* provide and organize them into a
> novel. It is different from other fiction because of its fragmentary, spontane-
> ous, and interactive Weibo style.

"You" here obviously refers to the followers and fans of Wen's Weibo, who,
instead of being passive consumers, actively engage in commenting, reposting,
and therefore (re)producing stories. This highly interactive process renders microfiction writing more a *collective* and *communal* activity than an *individual* one,
and this generated sense of intimacy thereby counters the human alienation usually seen in grand narratives.

When writing *Love in the Age of Microblogging*, Wen Huajian created a special
account with the name of the "novel" at Sina Weibo and solicited feedback. He
announced, in his very first posting, that he was going to write "the first microblogging fiction tonight," which was reposted ninety-five times and received fifty-
eight comments. His followers expressed their support, interest, and excitement
in the comments. Some said they would stay tuned, and some wished to be part
of his story. One follower shared her own story of falling in love with a person
she knew on Weibo. As Wen serialized his writings, his fans constantly gave him
feedback, with some saying, for example, the style of writing was "subversive"
and "exciting," while others simply liked the "unpredictable" plot. The interaction
between the followers and the author sometimes also transcends the plot of the
story and becomes quite personal. One anxious reader, for instance, even asked
what time he would write online. Wen responded and said he just came back and
would start right away.[21] Through the communication, Wen and his fans share
their thoughts, play jokes, give each other advice, and create relationships.

The personal communication can be best seen in stories that straddle fiction and
non-fiction writing. This type of writing constitutes a significant portion of the
world of microfiction and contributes in a special way to the intimacy of Weibo.
Although these stories often depict mundane details of the writers' lives, for some
reason they nevertheless become popular among a group of fans. In this case the
double privateness, that is the privateness of Weibo and the privateness of personal life experience, almost renders the reader-follower-fans as voyeurs. This
gaze quite certainly affects the ways in which writers present and express themselves, and therefore enhances a sense of *shared intimacy.*

Chen Peng's serial Weibo posts, entitled *The Life of Eiliko Chen in Beijing*,
form an illuminating example of this shared intimacy. Installed on Tencent Weibo
since May 2012, another major Weibo portal, this work chronicles the life of

Eiliko Chen, supposedly the author Chen Peng himself, from his graduation to his first job-hunt and subsequent experience as a professional:

> No. 26: A busy week has started. Today is the second day of the week. "Intense and busy" have become synonyms for my life. A sea of tension has washed away my hunger, and extended my nerves to an extreme. I have tried to write about my situation after work these past few days, but good ideas escaped me. I looked out into the city and relaxed a little bit. Beijing does not believe in tears, but it will never abandon you. . . .
>
> No. 110: On his way home, Eiliko Chen heard people talking about their dreams. This made him a little emotional. There is something about dreams. . . . He realized that he still had dreams. His childhood dreams of fairy-tales . . . could he still remember them? Lying in bed after showering, he closed his eyes and said to himself: #Good night#, #Dream#! [The post was then followed by many emoticons.]. . . .
>
> No. 112: All of a sudden, I seem to have returned to my long-gone college years. After midnight, I write about today with mixed feelings. To be frank, Eiliko Chen is not an exhibitionist who likes to expose his inner feelings to the public – he just feels that it is better to speak out than to hide. Moreover, you never know, maybe a response from you will enlighten this brain-dead Eiliko Chen. The night is quiet, and my heart is bright! Such essential features . . . [The post was then followed by a picture of a bunny.]. . . .
>
> No. 147: I turned off my TV full of boring programs, sat beside my window, and gazed at the full moon in the night sky for a long time. . . . A half moon cake, with its remaining warmth, was in my hand. . . . The clock struck twelve. I realized it was already the day of the Moon Festival. Li Bai's poem "In the Quiet Night" surged into my mind: "So bright a gleam on the foot of my bed. Could there have been a frost already? Lifting my head to look, I found that it was moonlight. Sinking back again, I thought suddenly of home." Until now I had not realized that I haven't been with my family for years. [The post was then followed by a picture of the full moon.][22]

Obviously, there is no storyline in these "stories" – all of them are simply records of personal feelings and thoughts. The shifting relations between the writer, the narrator, and the main character (Eiliko Chen) complicate these writings and blur the line between fiction and non-fiction. Moreover, these fragmentary pieces, together, make a colorful picture of the life of a Beijing vagrant (*beipiao* 北漂) whose emotions, ambition, confusion, and disorientation touch a responsive chord in the lives of so many of those who are also adrift in the metropolis, seeking opportunities, and trying to bear up under manifold frustrations. Further, the author and his followers establish a special bond, as the writer is well aware of his audience and is addressing them directly (No. 112). Responding to Chen's sentimental longing for home expressed in No. 147, his audience shared their own emotional loss. One reader wrote, "I didn't spend the Moon Festival with my family. I don't feel very good." Another posting went, "Poor us! We are the same, being lonely for years!" Chen Peng responded: "Brothers! The same feeling!" (Chen Peng, September 12, 2011). The avid comments and repostings not only impact his writing, but also constitute an indispensable part of the work as a whole, which is, essentially, an organic interactive process.

"Microblog novel": paradox of the short and the long in the ecology of Weibo writing

As mentioned above, the character limit of Chinese Weibo has changed in the course of its evolution. Sina's long Weibo function and Sohu's limit-free Weibo, for example, have largely expanded the writing space. If brevity is one of the most recognizable trademarks of Weibo, then what is the impact of its growing size and capacity on the basic ecology of Weibo writing? Will it change the writing style of the author and the reading, commenting, and reposting habits of the reader, and therefore fundamentally alter their relationship? Will Weibo lose its edge as a form as a result? In terms of media interpenetration, will this change, then, render Weibo more inviting to other media, and in what ways will cross-media maneuvers reshape the aesthetic and cultural features of microfiction in particular and Weibo writing in general? These questions have, of course, yet to be answered, but a study of Wen Huajian's *Love in the Age of Microblogging* may nonetheless yield some insights: Wen Huajian, a professional writer, is regarded as one of the most active promoters of microfiction – he has prolifically produced micro-stories, organized a "microfiction group" (*wei xiaoshuo qun* 微小说群) online, and has written several critical essays on the subject. Yet he is still best known as the author of China's first microblog novel, *Love in the Age of Microblogging*. This work loosely tells the ill-fated love story of "I," a middle-aged "Uncle" (*Dashu* 大叔), and a mysterious young actress, Dai Man. Putting the serialized format aside, this work exemplifies almost all of the features of microfiction discussed above, and complies with what Wen (2010) summarizes as the keys to writing a microblog novel:

> First, there should be cliffhangers and a complete plot in each installment; within 140 characters, one should be able to write a solid and dramatic story. Second, the plot should be concerned with issues related to Weibo itself. For instance, stories should address hot topics on Weibo. Third, the majority of characters should be real Weibo users. Fourth, writers should take advantage of Weibo technologies to realize an inclusion of pictures, video clips, and music.
>
> (qtd. in Men 2011: 162)

Indeed, one of the most prominent features of this work is the intensity with which it engages with Weibo, not only in thematic concerns but also in narrative strategies. Besides touching on many hot topics on Weibo, such as online dating, domestic violence, charity shows, movie-star scandals, business conspiracies, and so on, this story is itself about a relationship developed almost entirely on Weibo, with a way of communication, language, and sensitivity that are characteristic of the virtual reality on Weibo. More intriguingly, the narrative of the story, which mingles a variety of speeches – fictional, real, poetic – is also unique to Weibo, made possible by the nature of Weibo as a tool of social networking. In fact, as Wen admits, some characters in the novel are real Weibo users, his Weibo friends, whose suggestions for plot development, Weibo entries, comments, and responses he has incorporated into his narrative proper (Jiang 2011). To make the work more Weibo-distinctive, he includes hyperlinks to other people's Weibo in the narrative. In addition, each chapter begins with a non-fictional entry similar to prose-poetry, which Wen calls the "Uncle's Monologue" (*Dashu nian* 大叔念). These entries are not directly related to the plot, but they set a poetic ambiance for the following entries, exemplifying Wen's ambition to create a "purely literary work" (Wen 2011: 228).

In all, this intense level of engagement with Weibo itself gives it a self-referential quality, which renders the attachment of microfiction to the Weibo platform even stronger. Yet, with the publication of the work in hard copy in 2011, this so-called "microblog novel" poses new questions to the form of microfiction. Above all, the term "microblog novel" is itself paradoxical. The size that the term "novel" implies is obviously at odds with the scale of microfiction. When it first began to be serialized on Wen's designated Weibo in early 2010, the work granted each post a sense of semi-independence, with a certain degree of conclusion and totality, while at the same time being a part of a larger project, continuing previous entries and anticipating following ones.[23] Overall, however, except for those entries that are loosely related to the plot development, such as the prose-poetry and witty punch lines, most of the entries are still tied closely to the overall structure of the novel. Yet, the process of forming the work involves dynamic interactions between the writer and other participants on the platform of Weibo and, as a result, this process shapes the work as a communal product designed to address common concerns in micro-narratives. The work as a whole, therefore, still figures as an effective expression of the imagined community of Weibo users within the tension of large and small.

However, when printed as a novel in the traditional book form, the work seems to have lost much of its uniqueness as a work of microfiction. Most obviously, the interactive creative process seen on Weibo is no longer possible in the printed form; no hyperlink will work, although its signature @ remains on the page; audio-visual media, though minimal in original posts, cannot be included in the book. These losses, incurred by the change of media, inevitably impact on the nature of the work itself. The original microfiction, to a large degree, is an *open* work on at least three levels: First, it is open to all who would like to participate in the creation of the work as an inclusive discourse of disparate speeches. The book form, however, forecloses this opportunity for potential participation. Second, microfiction generally does not have a conclusion, whereas the book form must end at its last page. As Wen (2011: 227) writes in the "Afterword" of the book, almost none of the plotlines arrive at a conclusion when the book comes to an end, and he will continue the story in his Weibo. Third, microfiction goes viral on the Internet through inexhaustible comments and reposting, which the book form does not allow. As such, the traditional print medium, in the form of a full-scale, orthodox novel, presents itself as a closure, a trophy marking an accomplished work, and a museum displaying bygone glories. Microfiction, in the form of a book, loses its edge, which, in return, demonstrates that this genre of writing is utterly inseparable from the ecology of its production.[24]

The publication of *Love in the Age of Microblogging* in print form, needless to say, involved commercial considerations. The success of many Internet writers in the book market in China is perhaps what Wen strives to emulate. However, the book's lukewarm reception seems to suggest that the experience of Internet literature might not be entirely duplicable for microfiction, which may only survive and thrive in its specific online ecology.[25]

Dialectics in visual images: technological connectedness and compartmentalization

Talking about the smaller screens, Paola Voci (2010: xx) argues that "DV camera, the computer monitor – and, within it, the Internet window – and the cell phone display screen have created new public spaces where many long-standing divisions between high-brow and low-brow, mainstream and counterculture, conventional and experimental are dissolving and being reinvented." Voci sees "lightness" as the marker of the smaller-screen movies because of the "small production costs, distribution ambitions, economic impact, limited audience, quick and volatile circulation, and resistance to being framed into and validated by the market, art or political discourses." Voci discusses the dialectic relation between lightness and deepness: lightness in terms of cost, size, and profit gains, but deep in meaning as it defines ways of understanding the world.

Indeed, just like border-crossing microfiction, micro-film also blurs multiple boundaries. In addition to what Voci has discussed, the borders between the professionals and the amateurs, films and commercials are also mixed (Zhang and Sun 2012: 103–7). Both well-known movie stars and ordinary individuals play roles in the short films. The homepage of "Netease Micro Film Festival," for instance, lists stars to attract participants, fans, and viewers. Meanwhile, non-professionals display uncanny energy in image production. With the widely available video-making apps and software, image-making and sharing are also at everyone's fingertips. The business establishment has also extended its influence to the very micro-form of communication. *Go at a Touch* (*Yichu jifa* 一触即发, 2010), the legendary first micro-film with stunning special effects, gripping plot, and big star crew, is actually a commercial for Cadillac. In addition, as the above-mentioned three micro-film competitions show, the topics of the mini films cover a wide range: youth, love, public service, migrant labor, family, and more. "The First International Mobile Micro Film Competition" (China Daily 2011a) claims "I play the leading role in my world," and encourages individual expression.

Voci's discussion covers a wide range of "smaller-screen realities" that include documentary, animation, *egao*, and videos made by the subaltern. None of these are viable without the pervasive technological device. The reliance on smart gadgets has caused increasing concern and therefore becomes the topic of quite a few micro-films. *Life of Lowering Head* (*Ditou rensheng* 低头人生, 2014), a 3-minute animation directed by Xie Chenglin (谢承霖), satirizes the disastrous consequence of mass infatuation with the cell phone.[26] The film shows that passers-by, clerks, doctors, firefighters – almost everybody – are lowering their heads over their smartphones. They are busy typing and sending messages, taking selfies in front of a dead body of a car accident. As people are addicted to the smaller screens and neglecting their duties, the house is on fire, patients are dying, and the world is literally diminishing. The virtual reality ruins the real world. In a critical tone, the short animation critiques the pathological connectedness enabled by smartphones and exacerbated by human beings.

iPhone Age (*Aifeng shidai* 爱疯时代 2011, dir. Mai Tian [麦田]) tells a story about a girl and an iPhone. Xiao Min, a salesperson at an Apple store, cannot afford an iPhone though. Like many young stylish urbanites, she longs for one. She feels left out as everybody is getting an iPhone. She decides to try every means to save each penny she can to join the "iPhone tribe." When she finally saves up enough money to buy one, she learns from her friend that the iPhone 4 is already out of date, and everybody is buying new phones.

In less than 13 minutes, the film investigates critically many layers of social significance attached to an iPhone. First, the phone symbolizes social classes and status. Three types of people want to buy iPhones in the Apple Store where Xiao Min works. Rich couples do not quite know how to use it but are determined to get one so that they will not lose face in front of their rich friends. A middle-aged father, who looks obviously financially deprived, gathers all the cash he can find in his pockets and buys an iPhone for his son, hoping the well-off students would not look down upon his kid anymore. Stylish young couples negotiate a deal and hope to buy an iPhone to improve the quality of their lives. As a commodity, the iPhone becomes the object of desire for people from all walks of life. It goes beyond a communication tool and is associated with fashion, trends, and social status.

Second, the iPhone symbolizes dialectic connectedness and compartmentalization. iPhone means a "circle" (*quanzi* 圈子). Those with an iPhone feel stylish, successful, and empowered. They belong to a "circle" that is hard for Xiao Min to join as she does not have one. People who are not financially well off feel obliged to have one, for the iPhone is the only luxurious item they could have in common with rich people. The iPhone thus becomes a marker that defines and differentiates people. Xiao Min feels out of place at friends' gatherings, as everybody is busy playing with their gadgets. Without an iPhone, she is about to lose her social connection.

Third, the iPhone also means fashion. It comes and goes at a fast pace. New generations of smartphones keep coming out. To catch up with the style, the young stylish couples want to get iPhones though they just got their new phones a month ago. The new iPhone 4 is quickly outdated while Xiao Min spends a long time to save up enough money. All the efforts she has made – dieting, buying cheap goods, walking instead of taking a bus, and avoiding buying gifts for friends – are meaningless.

Last but not least, the iPhone is also a metaphor of globalization and technological advancement. It disorients and alienates people. For Xiao Min, the possession of it comes at the cost of health and friendship. Finally, it is family value that "wakes up" Xiao Min. She realizes what is most important for her. Towards the end of the film, Xiao Min realizes that the cell phone, no matter what brand it is, is just a tool for communication. She decides to send the money she has saved to her mom instead and calls her family on her old phone.

Both films satirize the very gadgets and technology through which mini films themselves are produced, circulated, and consumed, providing much-needed reflection on the very means of connection and creation. The smartphone is part of the reality, and it also intervenes into real life in a disturbing way. In the short rendition of such problems, the micro-film gives another layer of intervention with a critical tone.

Dialectics of the real and the unreal: the literary app ONE

Literary apps are undoubtedly a new form of hosting literary works. ONE produced by Han Han, Douban Yuedu (豆瓣阅读) developed by the literary social networking website Douban, and Xingke (wakening people 醒客), which belongs to the mainstream literary journal *People's Literature*, are well-known apps. Michel Hockx (2015: 107) reads ONE as a new format to circumvent "any existing controls on literary production," as a format that is outside of both traditional publication (books) and web literature. It is different from conventional websites in that it does not enable interactive functions. Like a virtual magazine, ONE includes several sections. "Homepage" introduces one image of the day, accompanied by one quote from a certain work. "Essay" publishes one short story, and "Question" section provides an answer to one question. "Thing" lists commodities, such as candles, lamps and stationery, for people to buy. "Individual" invites readers to register and become members of ONE. Different from conventional literary journals, ONE has promoted its brand in many other ways. ONE exhibition, ONE bookstore and "ONE life" all exist on Taobao, the Chinese equivalent of Amazon. With its multiple dimensions of literary readings, problem solving, brand making, and commodity promotion, ONE, as Wang Rui and Bi Wenjun (2015: 108–12) argue, constructs a urban-oriented lifestyle.

In the inaugural essay on ONE, "Fragment," Han Han (2012) relates the launch of the app to his experience without cell phones on a highway under the starry night sky, which makes him reflect on his mixed feelings on the smartphone and the virtual reality related to it:

> We have more and more fragments. The news is more and more diversified. Discussion topics are hotter and hotter. Everything comes and goes so fast. We feel disintegrated with the world if we sleep a few hours longer. We feel abandoned by the world if we turn off our cell phones.

While Han Han expresses a sentimental tone on the fast-paced technology and the disappearing quiet time with the starry night, he also realizes: "We cannot go back. We cannot be that simple. . . . We have to move forward."

The more or less nostalgic tone is obvious in the "About Us" page of ONE: "[We are] not into hot spot, current affairs, confusion, and contention. Turn off your Weibo. Leave your WeChat. Go back to the age of Web 0.1 with a smile. ONE is simple enough" (ONE). Ironically, ONE has also registered an official Weibo account which had 1,488,273 followers as of June 2, 2016. The Weibo account updates on a daily basis, sharing stories published on the app and opening space for discussion.

The mixed feelings on smartphones and social media are echoed in three stories published on ONE in 2014: "Suicide Account on Weibo" (*Weibo zisha ji* 微博自杀记 published on March 9, 2014); "Miss S's Friend Groups" (*S xiaojie de pengyou quan S* 小姐的朋友圈 published on September 16, 2014); and "My Boyfriend in the Cell Phone" (*Shouji li de nanpengyou* 手机里的男朋友 published on August 15, 2014).[27] They all become the "hot topics" (*remen huati*) on Weibo. The three stories, written by Fang Hui (方慧) and shared on her Weibo account, raise the ethical question of "reality" in the age of pervasive Weibo and WeChat.

Fang Hui, born in the 1990s, started her writing experience after winning the first place in an essay competition, as many other post-80s or post-90s generation writers did. She has been publishing on ONE since 2014. In "Suicide Account on Weibo," the I-protagonist breaks up with her boyfriend. But she firmly believes he still cares about her and reads her Weibo posts often. With this in mind, she carefully posts photos of the food she eats, the flowers she pretends to receive, and her beautiful pictures to demonstrate that her life is still full of fun. She also frenetically refreshes his Weibo page to see what is going on. However, her boyfriend seems to ignore anything she posts, and she becomes paranoid. In a very bad mood, she posts: "I want to die." Immediately, her boyfriend leaves a comment: "What happened?" Just as she is thrilled by his concern and calculating on a perfect response, this particular post has been reposted by her friends frenetically. Anxious messages flood her page, asking questions, checking on her and comforting her. Seeing how much people care about her, she feels quite good until the discussion goes ferocious. People message her roommate and constantly ask how she is doing and what step she is at as if she *is* in the process of committing suicide. She dares not explain that she had posted the message out of her bad mood and now she is quite content.

Seeing many VIP members repost her message and express their concern, the protagonist feels ecstatic. In order not to disappoint the public concern, she paints her arm red and pretends she is actually committing suicide. The Weibo discussion of her then turns into an online funeral. Some people write about their beautiful memory of her. Her old classmates open blog accounts to commemorate her. Other people choose to gather at her apartment and knock at her door in an attempt to save her. All of these are broadcast live on Weibo. She is horrified that things go out of her control, and she is more worried that people will see her intact. Though the story stops at her sight of a knife nearby, giving an ambiguous ending, it does hint that she does not want to discontinue her performance.

The story reveals several interesting aspects of the intertwined realities of online and offline. First, online sharing is an integral part of life for the I-protagonist, and it blurs the border of private and public. Her personal mood, published on the public site, is magnified and fermented into a collective sensation in the public. Second, the protagonist designs her online image carefully. She performs herself first for her imagined gaze from her boyfriend and then for the expectation of a wider audience. The very attention she draws online, as she had both expected and not expected, gives her a sense of fulfillment and joy, until the online carnival overwhelms the reality and leads to a dead end. Third, her online sharing would not have become a wide-scale sensation without her audience, the onlookers who participate in turning an absent-minded post into an online spectacle. Their curious and anxious anticipation turns a joke into a possible tragedy. In this way, the online and offline realities are closely intertwined and affect each other, leading the way toward the protagonist making a decision on her own life.

The fictional representation is a reflection of reality. In 2014, a nineteen-year-old youngster in Sichuan did exactly the same thing. He broadcasted his suicide process live on Weibo. Neither friends nor police were able to save him. As it becomes a new pattern of life to share everything in social media, there also comes a challenging ethical and moral question on what should be shared.

"Miss S's Friend Groups" and "My Boyfriend in the Cell Phone" address different aspects of technology and people: the escapist fantasy the social media provide and the alienating impact they have on people. In "Miss S's Friend Groups," Miss S, a vagrant in Beijing, does low-pay jobs, lives in a cheap apartment on the borderline of a city, and complains about work on WeChat like many others. Overnight, she transforms her image on WeChat to be a glamorous girl who rubs shoulders with celebrities and consumes luxurious goods. In her WeChat group, she posts photos of expensive restaurants, luxurious cars, concerts, gallery trips, and vacations in foreign countries. Her friends soon find out she has several different groups on WeChat. In one she appears to be industrious and hard working in a group of professionals; in another she is a sexy, seductive girl in a group of young rich guys; in a third, she is a rich girl who enjoys showing off her expensive accessories. Intrigued by the discrepancy, her friends launch a search to look for the real identity of Miss S. It turns out Miss S is actually from a very poor family from the countryside. She rents her car and she has two different boyfriends in two different groups. Just as Miss S's parents appear and pay back all the debt she owes, and her friends think she has already returned to her hometown, they find, from WeChat, that Miss S has kicked all of them out of her groups and has posted a new picture of her enjoying the summer breeze in Sri Lanka in a new group she joins.

"Miss S's Friend Groups" is told from the points of view of her friends, which adds a touch of elusiveness of a real her, or to a large extend, of any person in the city. She has split into different personas and projected each of her ideal selves in different groups. In the urban space where success for a woman is measured by materials and her connections to the rich and powerful, it is not surprising that

Miss S chooses to construct her images in such dimensions. She easily builds her own middle-class lifestyle online, while juxtaposing her hard-working image along with it. In this way, the urban loss is redeemed online. The virtual glamour compensates for her inability and powerlessness in real life. It is where her desire is addressed in an imaginative form.

In "My Boyfriend in the Cell Phone," the I-protagonist is so infatuated with her cell phone romance that the offline reality becomes less important and eventually alienating to her. There are two parallel worlds for the I-protagonist: the boring, listless daily life, and the exciting communication with her boyfriend via WeChat, which is full of anticipation, imagination, and energy. In their virtual dating, she appears to be an energetic girl who loves sports, reads international news, and speaks foreign languages, though she is none of these offline. To prepare for a real meeting with her boyfriend, she collects gym cards and buys used foreign language journals to fulfill her online image. Her fantasy goes perfect until they physically meet each other. He appears to be such a familiar stranger that he is less real than his WeChat avatar. Unable to communicate, she escapes and calls him from her cell phone. Things get back to normal until his voice comes back to her ears and his familiar avatar jumps into her eyes. The virtual image, in this case, is more endearing than the real person. The reality built by the cell phone is more real in the life of the protagonist. The online rendezvous, the only event that enlivens the protagonist's listless life, eventually alienates her from the real world.

Attempting to "simplify" the contradictions, paradox, and uncertainty, ONE nevertheless exposes the complicated nature of reality. The app calls people to leave Weibo and WeChat behind, yet it also heavily relies on both to prosper. In the three stories, the social media space is the fantasy, the imagination, and the daydream. It is also real and pervasive, as it has a significant impact on the offline reality, shaping the way an individual relates to his/her image and his/her realities.

Coda

Against the backdrop of fast-paced modern life and China's grand aspiration to become a great nation, micro-narratives function as a window through which people can see not only virtual reality but also the sociocultural reality of contemporary China. Though sometimes melodramatic and entertainment-oriented, micro-narratives, as we hope to have shown, are a timely response to larger expanding discourses. As literary, cultural, and social texts, micro-narratives feature much more than their obvious brevity. They function as a counter-force to the alienating and disorienting grand narratives of modern China.

As social media increasingly becomes socially engaged, since its space has been employed by disparate interest groups, the business establishment, and political organizations, as well as individuals who are dying to raise their voices, micro-narratives will continue to interact with social issues on the one hand and become a way of self-expression on the other. They redefine the meaning of brevity and also never stop to reflect on the relation of the global and the local, the high-brow and the low-brow, the subculture and the mainstream, and the individual and the community. The short verbal and visual texts reveal the striking gaps among different social groups, and meanwhile critique and destabilize the very barriers that socially divide people. They capture the disparate brief moments of reality and project a vivid picture of a dynamic society in the process of transformation.

Notes

1 This chapter is a revised version of our article, "Circulating Smallness on Weibo: The Dialectics of Microfiction," published in *Frontier of Literary Studies in China*, in 2014. This new version was revised to fit into the larger framework of the book and incorporated latest findings in it.

2 These statistics were retrieved from the official webpages of these microfiction contests: http://www.weibo.com/zt/2010weixiaoshuo/, http://www.weibo.com/z/weixiaoshuo2011/, http://www.weibo.com/z/2012lovewxs/ (accessed July 8, 2012). According to the statistics provided by Sina, there were almost ten times more discussion posts about these stories than the number of stories themselves. Some websites, such as weixiaoshuo.com and 52wei.net, are especially devoted to publishing and reading microfiction, but the stories on these websites are published and read in ways that are more akin to the ways in which those of conventional online literature are published and read in China. This issue will be addressed in detail in the latter part of this chapter. However, in our current discussion, we focus on those micro-stories existing exclusively on Weibo.

3 "Netease Micro Film Festival 2011" can be accessed on http://ent.163.com/special/2011wdyj/; "Sina Micro Video Competition" (2012) is on http://video.sina.com.cn/z/wspds/. The competition also has an official Weibo account http://weibo.com/weishipin. The website of "The First Mobile Micro Film Competition" is http://www.chinadaily.com.cn/2011immfc/ (all accessed on 2 June 2016).

4 "Chinese Micro Films" can be accessed on http://vfilm.china.com.cn/, accessed on September 20, 2016.

5 Jonathan Sullivan (2013: 2) argues:

> although microblogging represents a new challenge to the state's regime of information control, when there is growing discontent with the negative consequences of rapid economic growth, corruption and income inequalities, the government is also using it in multiple ways to maintain control of society.

6 When Sina hosted its first microfiction contest in 2010, it introduced microfiction this way:

> What is microfiction? [A story written in] 140 characters or less. No matter whether it is a comedy, horror, fantasy, sci-fi, love, suspense, or emotional story, all stories can be crystallized into a microfiction of 140 characters or less. Let's share it in Weibo. Come and write your own microfiction!

> The hosting website, http://topic.weibo.com/style/5355?page=4, however, is no longer available as of August 31, 2016.

7 The short-short story, in terms of formal construction, is much akin to the short story, which, as a genre, began to attract critical attention in the West in the 1960s with the moderate resurgence of such writing. Scholarship on the short story represented by critics, such as Mary Rohrberger, Charles May, Susan Lohafer, and Clare Hanson, has illuminated generic features of this literary form characterized mainly by its shortness. Critics have agreed that a short story is not simply a story that is short, but, given the unique literary experience resulting from its length, deserves the status of an independent genre. Indeed, as these critics demonstrate, the shortness of a story does make the creation, appreciation, or consumption of a story discursively different from those of, say, a novel. Literary scholarship on the short story in China, in our opinion, has also

noted how its formal shortness distinguishes itself from other forms of fictional works. For instance, Gao Erchun's book-length study of this genre, *A Theory of the Structure of Short Stories*, investigates in part the ways in which the short structure of this genre shapes its general features, writing skills, and other elements, including characterization, plotting, time and space, and language. The short form of writings in Chinese, in fact, can be traced back to the classical Chinese culture. Ancient mythologies, records of the extraordinary (*zhiguai*志怪), tales conveying the extraordinary (*chuanqi* 传奇), prompt books (*huaben* 话本), and notes (*biji* 笔记) include a variety of micro-narratives. For instance, "Jingwei Filling the Sea" (*Jingwei tianhai* 精卫填海), a widely known mythic story of a girl turning into a magical bird, is composed with less than eighty characters. *The Masters of Huainan* (*Huainanzi* 淮南子) composed in the second century BCE, *A New Account of World Tales* (*Shishuo xinyu* 世说新语) in the fifth century, and *Notes of the Thatched Hut of Close Observations* (*Yuewei caotang biji* 阅微草堂笔记) in the eighteenth century are some other well-known examples recording legendary tales, witty stories, idle talks, and random thoughts in very short forms. Classical Chinese writings, concise in language and extensive in content, engage closely with social, political, cultural, and imaginative lives of their times. In terms of form and content, microfiction in the twentieth-first century does bear resemblance to its classical predecessors. The cutting-edge technology, which makes the new genre more open and accessible, nevertheless initiates a collective unconscious return to the cultural legacy of the past. We borrowed the idea from comments of our reader. For other references, see Charles E. May (2004), Gao Erchun (1985), Norman Friedman (1989), and Robert Shapard and James Thomas (1989).

8 When discussing the small size of the (short) short story, scholars, by tracing the origin of this genre back to ancient oral traditions and literature, tend to make a case that the marginal status of this genre in the literary field, compared to more "serious" genres such as the novel, may find precedents in literary history. Although specific social-cultural-historical contexts are needed in this consideration, it nevertheless offers an interesting line of thought, and may be especially useful in our examination of microfiction in China, where fiction as whole, let alone short pieces, did not have an "orthodox" status until the turn of the twentieth century. However, from the readers' perspective, short stories, with their grassroots concerns and street-side wit, have always been welcomed and widely circulated among common people. They constitute a *necessary supplement* to "orthodox" writings. While never officially recognized in pre-modern China, they were at the same time taken as an important window through which the elite could get to know the lives of common people. Modern short stories arose in China with the emergence of modern print culture. Literary supplements and columns in newspapers, pictorial magazines, literary journals, and the like became the places where short stories were mostly published and read. One can already detect in this general description of the history from which microfiction emerged a persistent dialectical sense concerning the *size*, both physical and metaphorical, of these narratives.

9 According to the *30th Statistical Report on the Internet Development in China* issued by the China Internet Network Information Center (CNNIC 2012) in July 2012, the heyday of Weibo, Weibo user accounts in China reached 274 million by June 2012, accounting for 50.9 percent of all Internet users. About 170 million users, or 43.8 percent, accessed their Weibo accounts via mobile devices.

10 Compared to some conventional platforms of Internet literature in China, Weibo offers a much easier channel for publicizing. Compare Weibo to services such as Under the Banyan Tree (*Rongshu xia* 榕树下), one of the earliest and largest websites dedicated to the online creative writing, where writings are screened, evaluated, and edited before they get published online. See Michel Hockx (2004: 105–27).

11 Ibrahim Taha (2000: 59–84), in studying the Arabic short story, also argues that, generally, the state of openness, fluidity, and blurring of borders among information, culture, and art appears to have contributed greatly to the interaction among various genres.

12　There are many cases of how people use Weibo to expose social injustice (for example, the Wukan incident), to reveal official corruption ("My Father Is Li Gang"), to seek community support, and to "flesh search" (*renrou sousuo* 人肉搜索, which will be studied in detail in Chapter 5).

13　This close engagement with reality makes some stories subject to the government's censorship. As in other media, the government has issued many "forbidden words" (*jinzi*禁字) with a view to maintaining a "harmonious" (*hexie* 和谐) online environment and presenting an image of social stability. For information about the censorship on Weibo, see Hong Kong University's WeiboScope: http://weiboscope.jmsc.hku.hk/. Xiao Qiang (undated), the Berkeley-based scholar of Chinese Internet, keeps updating the list of censored sensitive words on the website *China Digital Times* (www.chinadigitaltimes.net), which he edits. However, a research team at Harvard University led by Gary King finds that "most censorship is indeed not done automatically by keywords filters but based on decisions by human readers, and that there are no specific bans on any individual words or expressions" (Hockx 2015: 10).

14　For discussion of how Internet literature at large reshapes people's relationships with literature, see Ouyang Youquan (2004). In this book, Ouyang, in a comprehensive manner, examines the ways in which Internet literature in China redefines the meaning of literature vis-à-vis its writers, readers, and critics.

15　One may speculate why such a level of closeness is achieved in this expansive space. Besides the new technologies of Weibo that make it possible, another reason probably lies in the participants of microfiction writings. This generation of Chinese netizens is mainly the relatively younger generation of the "One-Child Policy." The increasing geographical mobility and decreasing physical borders, loosening familial ties and distanced communal connections caused by social changes present pressures that diminish their living space in reality. Yet technology-savvy, they tend to find comfort and relief in the virtual reality generated by the Internet, where programs such as Weibo provide endearing, intimate, and fulfilling company. In his study of Chinese Internet literature, Guobin Yang (2010: 335–6) also talks about the association between generations of technologies and their corresponding cultures. He writes, "In a sense, sociological generations are closely linked to generations of technologies such as television and computers – hence terms such as the 'TV Generation' and the 'Net Generation.'"

16　It is arguable that, because of its small size and condensedness, microfiction may somehow entail longer time to write and read. It may be the case for some people; however, according to our research, most of the writers and readers today spend much less time writing and reading microfiction than they do, for instance, writing and reading novels. See, for example, *Xinhua ribao* (2011).

17　It writes on its front page that, "every character is imbued with emotions and jerks tears" (*zi zi han qing, zhi chuo leixian* 字字含情，直戳泪腺; Sina 2012a). Interestingly, while the host strives to promote a sense of touching warmth in human relations, it has no intention, however, to conceal its rather blatant commercial orientation. The 2011 contest opens a special section for enterprises, and as a result, most of the works turn out to be, at best, soft ads (Sina 2011).

18　All of the prize-winning stories can be read at the prize announcement page (Sina 2012a).

19　The original website for this particular piece, http://www.weibo.com/zt/2010weixiaoshuo/zt_hot.php, is no longer available as of August 25, 2016. However, Douban, the leading literary social network, has retained many pieces of microfiction. For details, see https://www.douban.com/group/topic/16215089 (last accessed August 31, 2016).

20　Shao Yanjun (2012: 16–25) laments this "retrogressive" trend in Chinese Internet literary writing, and attributes it to the contemporary sociocultural context characterized by the "dead end of Enlightenment" (*qimeng de juejing* 启蒙的绝境) and "entertainment to death" (*yule zhi si* 娱乐至死). "Time-travel" writings on the Internet will be further discussed in Chapter 3.

21 http://www.weibo.com/1664117350/k4Cc3pGmI, January 31, 2010. Last accessed August 31, 2016.

22 Chen Peng's *The Life of Eiliko Chen in Beijing* was published as an e-book (Chen 2013). The texts we quote are from his Tencent Weibo account: http://t.qq.com/eilikochen.

23 Wen has been writing in both his own Weibo, http://www.weibo.com/wenhuajian, and the Weibo space for his book, project http://www.weibo.com/wbsqdaq (both accessed August 31, 2016).

24 Michel Hockx (2015: 84–93) also points out similar characteristics of *Love in the Age of Microblogging*, including interactions between the writing and his Weibo followers; forming online communities through Weibo writing; experimenting with new techniques in this new form of writing; blurring lines between author, narrator, and reader; capitalizing on the microblog novel in print form; and so on.

25 Overall, microblog novels do not fare extremely well in the market, nor do they receive high recognition in the literary field. After the publication of *Love in the Age of Microblogging*, a few more microblog novels, though in different forms, came out online, including *The Flight to Chengdu* (*Fei wang Chengdu de hangban* 飞往成都的航班), *Love Thief's Time* (*Qing dao shiguang* 情盗时光), *Journey of Double Happiness* (*Xi you ji* 囍游记), *The Diary of Lei Feng* (*Lei Feng riji* 雷锋日记), and *You Are My Cycles of Lives* (*Ni shi wo de shengshengshishi* 你是我的生生世世). Lu Jinbo, a well-known and influential publisher, remarks,

> Microfiction is more apt to circulate on the Internet, but not to be published [in print form]. This is because it does not attain readers' attention for long. Netizens usually pay attention to a piece for only a couple of minutes – they may read it, laugh at it, or show sympathy, but their attention soon shifts to another thing.
>
> (Jin and Gui 2011)

26 *Life of Lowering Head* can be accessed on the Weibo account of the director Xie Chenglin: http://weibo.com/u/3994234599?is_hot=1. *iPhone Age* is available on the Weibo account of the director Mai Tian http://weibo.com/maidao?is_hot=1. Both last accessed on September 21, 2016.

27 The three stories can also be accessed on Fang Hui's Weibo account: "My Boyfriend in the Cell phone" is on http://weibo.com/1623962032/D3uZe9BqP?type=comment#_rnd1465864461597; "Miss S's Friend Groups" can be accessed on http://weibo.com/1623962032/BnUrLfzNd?type=comment#_rnd1465864883194; "Suicide Account on Weibo" is on http://weibo.com/1623962032/Arm0DrvBM?type=comment#_rnd1465864714684 (all accessed on June 5, 2016). The three stories are all included in Fang Hui's collection of short stories (Fang 2015).

Bibliography

Baidu baike. (undated). "Wei xiaoshuo" (Microfiction). http://baike.baidu.com/view/2922884.htm. Last accessed August 31, 2016.

Chen Peng. (2013). *The Life of Eiliko Chen in Beijing*. Beijing, Zhongwen zaixian.

——. (undated). http://t.qq.com/eilikochen. Last accessed August 25, 2016.

——. (2011). http://t.qq.com/p/t/3655107513925/8?&. September 12. Last accessed August 25, 2016.

China Daily. (2011a). "The First International Mobile Micro Film Competition." http://www.chinadaily.com.cn/2011immfc/. Last accessed August 31, 2016.

——. (2011b). "Shoujie guoji shouji wei dianying dasai kaimu" (The first international mobile micro film competition begins). http://www.chinadaily.com.cn/hqzx/2011–07/25/content_12975404.htm. Last accessed August 31, 2016.

CNNIC. (2012). "Statistical Report on the Internet Development in China." https://www.cnnic.net.cn/hlwfzyj/hlwxzbg/hlwtjbg/201207/P020120723477451202474.pdf. Last accessed August 31, 2016.

Fang Hui. (2014a) "Shouji li de nanpengyou" (My boyfriend in the cell phone). *ONE.yige*. August 15.

——. (2014b). "Weibo zisha ji" (Suicide account on Weibo). *ONE.yige*. March 9.

——.(2014c). "S xiaojie de pengyou quan" (Miss S's friend groups). *ONE.yige*. September 16.

——. (2015). *Shouji li de nanpengyou (My boyfriend in the cell phone)*. Beijing: Lianhe chuban gongsi.

Friedman, Norman. (1989). "Recent Short Story Theories: Problems in Definition," In *Short Story Theory at a Crossroads*, edited by Susan Lohafer and Jo Ellyn Clarey, 13–31. Baton Rouge, LA: Louisiana State University Press.

Gao Erchun. (1985). *Duanpianxiaoshuo jiegou lilun yu jiqiao (A theory of the structure of short stories)*. Xi'an: Xibei daxue chubanshe.

HanHan.(2012)."Suipian"(Fragment).http://blog.sina.com.cn/s/blog_4701280b0102eb8d.html. Last accessed August 31, 2016.

Hanson, Clare, ed. (1989). *Re-Reading the Short Story*. New York: St. Martin's Press.

Hockx, Michel. (2004). "Links with the Past: Mainland China's Online Literary Communities and Their Antecedents." *Journal of Contemporary China* 38, no. 13: 105–27.

——. (2015). *Internet Literature in China*. New York: Columbia University Press.

Jiang Wanjuan. (2011). "China's First Microblog Novel Published." *Global Times*. http://www.globaltimes.cn/content/644298.shtml. Last accessed August 31, 2016.

Jin Ying and Gui Li. (2011). "Weibo xiaoshuo: shi wenxue de chuntian haishi duanming wenxue?" (Weibo fiction: is it the spring of literature or short-lived literature?). *Zhongguo zuojia wang*. http://www.chinawriter.com.cn/wxpl/2011/2011–07–20/100204.html. Last accessed August 31, 2016.

Lu, Sheldon H. (1994). *From Historicity to Fictionality: The Chinese Poetics of Narrative*. Stanford, CA: Stanford University Press.

Marwick, Alice, and Danah Boyd. (2011). "I Tweet Honestly, I Tweet Passionately: Twitter Users, Context Collapse, and the Imagined Audience." *New Media and Society* 13: 96–113.

May, Charles E. (2004). "Why Short Stories Are Essential and Why They Are Seldom Read." In *The Art of Brevity: Excursions in Short Fiction Theory and Analysis*, edited by Per Winther, Jakob Lothe and Hans H. Skei, 14–25. Columbia: University of South Carolina Press.

Men Hongli. (2011). "Dianzi chuanmei shidai wenxue de suipianhua xianxiang jiedu" (Reading the fragmentation of literature at the age of electronic communication). *Xueshu luntan* 8: 161–5.

Meng Wei. (2011). "Weixiaoshuo de chuanboxue fenxi" (Analyzing microfiction in mass communication). *Henan shehui xueke (Henan Social Science)* 19, no. 5: 117–21.

Mu, Aili. (2012). "The Rise of the Short-Short Genre." In *China and New Left Visions: Political and Cultural Interventions*, edited by Ban Wang and Jie Lu, 159–82. Lanham, MD: Lexington Books.

Mu, Aili, and Julie Chiu. (2006). "Introduction." In *Loud Sparrows: Contemporary Chinese Short-Shorts*, edited by Aili Mu, Julie Chiu and Howard Goldblattpp, xiii–xxiii. New York: Columbia University Press.

ONE. (undated). "About." http://wufazhuce.com/acercade. Last accessed August 31, 2016.

Ouyang, Youquan. (2004). *Wangluo wenxue bentilun (An ontological research of network literature)*. Beijing: Zhongguo wenlian chubanshe.

Qi, Shouhua, ed. (2008). *The Pearl Jacket and Other Stories: Flash Fiction from Contemporary China*. Berkeley, CA: Stone Bridge Press.

Shao Yanjun. (2011). "Miandui wangluo: xueyuan pai de taidu he fangfa" (Facing Internet: the attitude and methodology of the academia). *Nanfang wentan* 6: 12–18.

——. (2012). "Zai 'yituobang' li goujian 'geren linglei xuanze' huanxiang kongjian: wangluo wenxue de yishi xingtai gongneng zhi yizhong" (Constructing a fantasy space of 'individual, alternative choice' in a heterotopia: one of the ideological functions of Internet literature). *Wenyi yanjiu* 4: 16–25.

Shapard, Robert. (1986). "Introduction." In *Sudden Fiction: American Short-Short Stories*, edited by Robert Shapard and James Thomas, xiii–xvi. Salt Lake City, UT: Gibbs M. Smith.

Shapard, Robert, and James Thomas, eds. (1989). *Sudden Fiction International: Sixty Short-Short Stories*. New York: Norton.

Simmons, Philip E. (1991). "Minimalist Fiction as 'Low' Postmodernism: Mass Culture and the Search for History." *Genre* 24: 45–62.

Sina. (2011). "Time travel! Microfiction." http://weibo.com/z/weixiaoshuo2011/huojiang.html. Last accessed August 31, 2016.

——. (2012a). "The Third Microfiction Competition." http://weibo.com/z/2012lovewxs/huojiang.html. Last accessed August 31, 2016.

——. (2012b). "2012 hulianwang wenhua ji" (Internet culture festival 2012). http://book.sina.com.cn/z/InternetCulturalSeason2012/. Last accessed August 31, 2016.

Studio of *yige* App. (undated). http://weibo.com/u/1766610575?topnav=1&wvr=6&topsug=1&is_all=1. Last accessed June 1, 2016.

Sullivan, Jonathan. (2013). "China's Weibo: Is Faster Different?" *New Media and Society*, 15: 1–14.

Taha, Ibrahim. (2000). "The Modern Arabic Very Short Story: A Generic Approach." *Journal of Arabic Literature* 30, no. 1: 59–84.

Voci, Paola. (2010). *China on Video: Smaller-Screen Realities*. London and New York: Routledge.

Wang Rui, and Bi Wenjun. (2015). "Xin meiti shiyu xia de wenxue qikan yuedu: yi Han Han zhubian de xinrui wenxue qikan ONE. Yige wei ge'an" (Reading literary journal in the social media: The case study of ONE developed by Han Han). *Kaili xueyuan xuebao* 33, no. 5: 108–12.

Wen Huajian. (2010). *Weibo shiqi de aiqing* (*Love in the Age of Microblogging*). http://www.weibo.com/wbsqdaq?page=23&pre_page=1&end_id=3524183151207743&max_msign=-1#1356145648785. Last accessed August 31, 2016.

——. (2011). *Weibo shiqi de aiqing* (*Love in the age of microblogging*). Shenyang: Shenyang chubanshe.

Xiao Qiang. (undated). "Collecting Sensitive Words: The Mud-Grass Horse List." https://chinadigitaltimes.net/2013/06/grass-mud-horse-list/. Last accessed August 31, 2016.

Xinhua ribao. (2011). "Wei Xiaoshuo, yichang 140 zi de wangluo kuanghuan?" (Microfiction, an online carnival of 140 characters). http://news.xinhuanet.com/xhfk/2011–01/11/c_12966222.htm. Last accessed August 31, 2016.

Yang, Guobin. (2009). *The Power of the Internet in China: Citizen Activism Online*. New York: Columbia University Press.

——. (2010). "Chinese Internet Literature and the Changing Field of Print Culture." In *From Woodblocks to the Internet: Chinese Publishing and Print Culture in Transition, Circa 1800 to 2008*, edited by Cynthia Brokaw and Christopher A. Reed, 333–51. Leiden and Boston, MA: Brill.

Ye Anxia. (2012). "Han Han ONE.yige zenme zuoqilai de" (How Han Han develops ONE). https://www.douban.com/group/topic/34709094/. Last accessed June 2, 2016.

Zhang Bo and Sun Jian. (2012). "Lun wei dianying zai dangxia Zhongguo de shengchan ji xiaofei taishi" (The production and consumption of micro-film in contemporary China). *Xiandai Chuanbo* 3: 103–7.

Zhao Dingxin. (2012). "Weibo, zhengzhi gonggong kongjian he Zhongguo de fazhan" (Weibo, public political space, and the development of China). *Dongfang zaobao.* http://www.dfdaily.com/html/150/2012/4/26/782916.shtml. Last accessed June 20, 2012.

Zheng, Yongnian. (2008). *Technological Empowerment: The Internet, State, and Society in China*. Stanford, CA: Stanford University Press.

Zhu Dake. (2006). "Yi ge songruan de huayu mantou" (A soft discourse on a steamed bun). http://ent.sina.com.cn/r/m/2006–03–02/15281003001.html. Last accessed June 20, 2012.

3 Constructing gendered desire in online fiction and web dramas

Online space is gendered. Since the 2000s, a number of new net phrases have been invented in China to describe women. These terms are blatantly misogynistic, reducing women to objects and blaming them for inappropriate relationships. Just to name a few, there are *shengnü* (leftover women 剩女), which refers to women who remain single after their late twenties; *xiaosan* (little third 小三), the mistress of a married man; and *lücha biao* (green tea whore 绿茶婊), a term used to address a *femme fatale* who appears to be innocent. These labels embody sexism, or cybersexism, as Laurie Penny (2013) puts it. In such cases, the male gaze is clearly projected.

Cyberspace has also brought into light many previously marginalized gender identities and enabled new discourses of gender and sexuality. The "lower body poetry" (*xiabanshen shige* 下半身诗歌) in 2000 and Muzi Mei's sex diary in 2003, for instance, find public space online for circulation and consumption. Both the poetic and diary narratives of the body, sexuality, and identity break away from the conventional cultural restraints and morality. Lower body poets such as Shen Haobo, Yin Lichuan, and Duo Yu claimed that the body has been contaminated by the outside influence of culture, tradition, and politics. To restore the alienated body to its true, pure status, poets would have to return to pure corporeality. To highlight the "corporeal experience," their poems are full of imageries of the previously taboo, or invisible, body parts such as breasts and buttocks, and bodily activities such as intercourse, vomiting, and defecation. Their seemingly apolitical approach to the body is quite a political attitude of their resistance to the dominating ideology and social restraints. Muzi Mei's (Sohu 2003) sex diary demystifies the body as a site of physical gratification. She explains her sexual adventure this way: "for pleasure! Of course, I can also study men. Each man has different contents." Her apolitical approach toward her body, nevertheless, involves the reversed power games between men and women: it is a woman who openly mocks and casually consumes men (Yang 2011).

The online narrative of sexuality and the body intermingles with the feminist, intellectual, popular, and commercial discourses. On the one hand, the Internet releases repressed voices and therefore enables resistance against patriarchal institutions. By bringing into light the previously invisible in the online space, poets and netizens explore the personal, the social, and the political implications of the individual body. It is a place where netizens demystify the established, such as morality, virtue, class and family. On the other hand, the Internet also opens up a space for the voyeuristic celebration and consumption of female sexuality. Along with the cultural and political exploration of the body, the Internet fosters a carnivalesque celebration of personal desires.

Rapidly developing, online popular fiction has generated another interesting aspect of gendered desire. It is both conservative and transgressive, permeating almost all popular online writings. For example, Jinjiang Literature City (*Jinjiang wenxue cheng* 晋江文学城 http://www.jjwxc.net), one of the leading websites for popular online creative writing, has published online writings under different genres such as romance, non-romance, fan fiction, creative writing, urban youth, fantasy, time-travel, science fiction, *danmei* (boys' love 耽美), *baihe* (girls' love 百合), and so on. *Danmei*, usually written by and for women, focuses on boys' love and same-sex bonding. *Baihe* expresses girls' love and emotion for each other. Urban romance mostly tells a story of a man from a rich or powerful background who falls in love with a girl of humbler origin, in the recurring theme of "Cinderella." Palace romances re-enact the drama of one man (the emperor) and many women (imperial consorts). Matriarchal narratives (*nüzun* 女尊) highlight a strong and capable woman and her "conquering" of a handsome man, either in a contemporary professional institute or in the distant past. Tomb-digging (*daomu* 盗墓), fantasy (*xuanhuan* 玄幻) and science fiction usually cater to male-focused depictions of adventure, mystery, and conquering the world (and women as well).

Focusing on women's literary production and consumption online, Jin Feng (2013) has conducted a comprehensive study on web romances such as *danmei*, matriarchal narratives, fanfic, and time-travel fiction. She investigates various desires projected, finding that some deviate from the norm and some conform to the conventional power structure. Feng reads these diversified desires as women's negotiations of identity in the digital age. Shao Yanjun (2012: 6–25) also notes the role gender plays in time-travel fiction. For male time-travelers, they travel back to actualize the grand dream of nation-building and establishing political power. For female time-travelers, they realize their own individual fantasy of love and romance. Feng and Shao have provided insightful perspectives on the imagination of gendered desire in online writings.

What has interested us most in these gender narratives is the way in which the gendered desires constructed in online fiction have been translated into the offline imagination. Since the 2010s, it becomes a common practice that online fiction crosses media boundaries and makes its way to larger screens. Increasing numbers of popular online fiction have been adapted into TV dramas and films. *The Biography of Zhen Huan* (*Zhen Huan zhuan* 甄嬛传, 2011), *Nirvana in Fire* (*Langya bang* 琅琊榜, 2015), *Startling by Each Step* (*Bubu jingxin* 步步惊心, 2011), *Journey of Flowers* (*Hua qiangu* 花千骨, 2015), and *Schemes of a Beauty* (*Meiren xinji* 美人心计, 2010), to name a few, all have enjoyed high viewing rates. These stories were first well-received by netizens and then discovered by TV producers. On the homepages of major websites for creative writings, such as Under the Banyan Tree (http://www.rongshuxia.com) and Jinjiang Literature City, there are special columns or webpages which list the titles of fiction published as books or adapted into films or TV dramas. The cross-media migration of the word and image making has expanded their audiences, drawing attention not only from netizens, but also from conventional mainstream media sources.

This chapter focuses on the online/offline, cross-media *constructed-ness* of gendered imagination through a reading of four web fiction and dramas: *Nirvana in Fire*, *The Biography of Zhen Huan*, *Startling by Each Step*, and *Go Princess Go* (*Taizi fei shengzhi ji* 太子妃升职记, 2015). The constructed-ness of the gendered fantasy and desire is at many levels, first completed by the writer online and then revised by online readers. When the fiction crosses media boundaries, gendered desires continue to be revised and remodeled, reflecting the negotiation and con-testation of different ideologies and mentalities in different spaces: the virtual and the real, the playful and the political, and the market and the official.

These four texts were chosen for a number of reasons. First, they are simply good stories with gripping plots, which in many ways restore the age-old tradition of storytelling. Serialized online, the stories have to attract readers and sustain their interest in order to make a profit. On the webpages of Jinjiang Literature City, the initial chapters of any story are always free. When the following chap-ters become "VIP," readers have to pay to keep reading. To invite more clicks, online writers have to tell attractive stories and create suspense at right moments. For instance, *Startling by Each Step* has generated the following responses from readers:

> Your Honor, . . . you can compete well with traditional storytellers. Every time I reach the end of a chapter, it's as if I'm reading a traditional novel that states, "If you want to know what happens, check out the next chapter." Awe-some! You keep us wondering what comes next.
>
> (qtd. in Guo 2015: 79)

The storytelling mode keeps readers' attention and entices them to read on. When online stories are adapted into TV or web dramas, they are also widely popu-lar because of their riveting storylines and the suspense they have created. The costumes, interior design, and performance further add visual spectacle, turning the production into entertaining objects to consume and convenient channels for viewers to project their feelings, emotion, affection, fetishism, and infatuation.

Second, these stories are all set in the distant past, which is closely tied to the current sense of uncertainty in China. Tong Hua (桐华), the author of *Startling by Each Step*, addresses the past this way: "We feel powerless when we face time." The time-travel is "driven by the desire that people want to explore what hap-pened in the past" (Chen 2011). The "time" and the sense of powerlessness, as Tong Hua puts it, are actually deeply rooted in the reality of a rapidly transform-ing Chinese society. People have to handle the constantly changing reality and the ever increasing pressures of everyday life. When the present appears constantly changing and chaotic, the past is not only a nostalgic return which provides some momentary certainty, but also supplies a fantasized space for people to escape from mundane life and reflect on imagined powers, empowerment, or disempowerment. The past, in this sense, offers much-needed distance for people to either reflect on or forget about their own reality.

Shao Yanjun (2011: 12–14) associates the online configuration of the past with the "post-enlightenment" mentality. To achieve enlightenment, to borrow the well-known metaphor, is to break the "iron house," a term coined by Lu Xun (1881–1936) to characterize the rigid, suffocating institution in China at the turn of the twentieth century. People operating with a post-enlightenment mentality, however, do not bother to break through it anymore. Perceiving the iron house to be unbreakable, they are just happy to dream in the form of time-travel fiction and fantasy narratives. Though we agree with Shao that the fictional past can be a daydream, we also see it being reconstructed and deconstructed with a critical lens. The online configuration of the past is more than an escapist fantasy, as it speaks to the lacking within and impossibilities of present life, and reflects the contemporary problem with some critical distance.[1] In addition, many writings of the past, in a way, pay tribute to literary canons. For instance, it is quite apparent that the author of *The Biography of Zhen Huan* imitates the language of *Dream of the Red Chamber* (*Honglou meng* 红楼梦, by Cao Xueqin). Classical poetry writing, which is losing its edge in a technologically advanced reality, finds a space for practice in this work too.

Third, the four stories, as well as a large number of other online fiction, are all written by female authors. Women's imaginings of masculinity, femininity, and gender relation evoke a sense of female agency. While Laura Mulvey's (1975) well-known analysis of the active male gaze and passive female object in visual media speaks to patriarchal gender relations, the Internet, however, enables a reversed lens of an active female gaze. It is women who identify, define, and consume their perception of men, and to a larger extent, love, relationships, and family. Nevertheless, the female gaze in a variety of genres also contributes significantly to fictional constructions of gender stereotypes such as the "dominant magnate" (*badao zongcai* 霸道总裁), a powerful and rich male boss, the "silly sweet girl" (*sha bai tian* 傻白甜), innocent and cute, or "Mary Sue" (*mali su* 玛丽苏), a term that refers to an idealized and flawless yet shallow girl.

Though Laura Mulvey's (1981) "transvestite theory" – women inscribed with patriarchal ideology actively imagine gender stereotypes – could explain this problematic female gaze in online spaces, we argue that female authorship generates more female fantasies than the female gaze, fantasies that are not always in line with critical views on institutionalized patriarchy. Regarding such a "backward" mentality, Jin Feng (2013: 173) notes that "web romances do not universally advocate feminist, progressive, or democratic values. They sometimes seem backward, reactionary, and even offensive." However, Feng cautions us not to read them as merely a return to traditional and conservative values. She argues that web romances, viewed in context, show women's negotiations with "traditional, modern, western and Chinese cultural influences"

(Feng 2013: 175–6). Therefore, female authors create a heterotopia rather than a utopian female space.

Though not necessarily the female gaze in a feminist sense, female fantasy and agency are nevertheless deeply rooted in reality and generate a series of gendered desire. Cross-media adaptations, as well as the interactivity enabled by online publications and the active role played by "prosumers" who both produce and consume the writings, constantly revise female authorship and consequently turn gendered desires into a process of formation, construction, and reconstruction. Scholars have addressed these special modes of producing online writing from the perspectives of participatory culture (Jenkins 2006), taste culture (Lugg 2011), gratification theory (Li, Chen, and Nakazawa 2013), and affective bonding (Kong 2014, Tian 2015). Different genres of online writings address a variety of tastes and generate gratifications from prosumers who consequently develop emotional attachment. In studying the online success of *Startling by Each Step*, Shaohua Guo (2015: 74–83) has discussed the "making" of an online canon. She demonstrates that readers' own visions shape online genres and contribute to the "word of mouth" publicity of fiction, reconfiguring the nature of writing and the circulation of popular literature. Heather Inwood (2014: 6) addresses the "transmedia storytelling" seen in web-game fiction as an emblem of "Chinese netizens' desire to take control of their own story within a larger contemporary reality, the rules and parameters of which lie beyond any individual control." The writers, prosumers, and the transmedia adaptations make writing a complicated process in which gendered desires are projected, added, and revised. On the one hand, traditional values, aesthetics, and practices are evoked, revived, and aestheticized. On the other hand, new discourses of gendered expression are explored, addressed, and discussed. Gendered desire in this context is therefore full of paradox and dilemma.

Idealized masculinity reimagined: *Nirvana in Fire*

Many scholars have discussed the changing masculinity in contemporary China as well as the larger social and cultural contexts behind this transformation. After examining images of masculinity in popular culture, Kam Louie (2012) argues that the buying power of women in East Asia has contributed to the changing images of masculinity, which has become softer and androgynous. The male images designed by women for women viewers have reshaped the conventional masculine type. Geng Song and Derek Hird (2014: 94–100) also discuss different types of masculinity in the digital age, such as the "white gold man" (*baijin nan* 白金男), who is "highly educated, well paid and highly refined"; the "pink man" (*fense nanren* 粉色男人), who transgresses gender boundaries and works in fields that are typically female-oriented; and the "phoenix man" (*fenghuang nan* 凤凰男), who comes from rural regions and gains entry into the city through hard work. These different types of men, they argue, project not only female fantasies but also male anxieties.

The success of *Nirvana in Fire* brings to light another interesting aspect of manhood, which is idealized and traditional, a counter-narrative of the hybrid masculinities addressed by Louie, Song, and Hird. The idealized male hero is not uncommon in online fiction. Jin Feng (2013: 142–5) notices that a kind of perfect fictionalized man combining both modern and western masculinity appears in online fiction. They are "successful, monogamous and reserved," possessing "intellectual power, practical skills and physical strength." Such an ideal hero serves as a prize awarded to the heroine "who wins her battle of wits and will and who overcomes all the obstacles to the marriage" (147). Feng's argument, as well as those of Louie, Song, and Hird, affirms the role of female agency in imagining masculinity online.

The ideal man in *Nirvana in Fire*, however, is devoid of sexual desire and detached from love fantasies.[2] Yet his TV persona has won the hearts of many fans, female and male alike, among netizens, TV viewers, as well as the mainstream media. Written by Hai Yan (海宴), *Nirvana in Fire* was published on the "Girl's Net," a sub-community of Qidian (起点女生网, www.qidianmm.com), printed as a book in 2007, and adapted into a TV drama in 2015. The story tells of a wronged man's revenge against the officials who plotted against his family and caused their death thirteen years ago. Borrowing elements from *The Count of Monte Cristo* (by Alexandre Dumas) and *Romance of the Three Kingdoms* (*Sanguo yanyi* 三国演义, attributed to Luo Guanzhong), the story evokes the tradition of storytelling in terms of storylines, characterization, and styles.

The leading protagonist Mei Changsu is a perfect Confucian gentleman (*junzi* 君子). He exemplifies a typical *wen* figure, according to Kam Louie's (2002) characterization of Chinese masculinity, possessing cultural attainment and moral uprightness. Not only has he had high cultural and aesthetic achievement, he also embodies such attributes as loyalty, altruism, and righteousness. Independent from officialdom, he nevertheless fulfills his social responsibility by helping remove corrupted officials and ushering in a wise emperor and the morally noble leadership. Meanwhile he succeeds in achieving justice for his family, fulfilling a brotherly promise and restoring the country to the right track. In the end, he sacrifices himself to protect the country against invading states and save his people. Mei Changsu's masculinity is established in relation to his social obligations.

Unlike many pieces of pop fiction, there is little heterosexual romance in the story. After Mei Changshu survived poison and a massacre years ago, he became consumptive, physically weak, and fragile. The absence of romance turns the ideal man into more of a brotherly figure than a lover or an object of desire. If heterosexual association inevitably involves imbalanced gender relations and women's sense of insecurity and subordination, taking away a man's heterosexual possibility makes him a safe object onto which all women can invest their affections. Instead of romance, the story focuses on brotherhood, referring to the age-old tradition of brotherly bonding (*xiongdi qingyi* 兄弟情义), a common theme in traditional masterpieces such as *Romance of the Three Kingdoms* and *Water Margin* (*Shuihu zhuan* 水浒传). The protagonist's journey of revenge is intertwined with the brotherly trust he has developed with his close friend, the prince.

The brotherly bonding, to some extent, could be viewed as a part of the female online infatuation with same-sex attraction between males, or "boys' love," which is commonly seen in *danmei* fiction. Usually written and consumed by women, *danmei* features the objectification of men and male love.[3] Such a genre attracts self-identified *funü* (腐女), or female fans who love to consume stories about boys' love (Xu and Yang 2014). The TV persona of Mei Changsu, in Shao Yan-jun's (2015) words, is the "online reincarnation of a classical Chinese beautiful man (*mei nanzi* 美男子)." He is good-looking, handsome, with a calm and regal demeanor. The screen image of his friend, the prince, is also visually pleasant. On the discussion forum Tianya, netizens have expressed that they begin to understand the mentality of *funü* after they watch the television drama: "The two characters are so good-looking. Their personality and appearance are too perfect. . . . It could never go too far no matter how we want to fantasize about the stories of the two perfect men" (Tianya.cn 2015). The cross-media adaptation thus makes the online subculture of boys' love or *funü* more well-known in mainstream culture.

Fran Martin (2012: 365) studies *danmei* stories in Taiwan and argues that the genre offers "no feminist utopia or zone of unilateral sexual-political progressiveness" but rather provides "a participatory space created with immense imaginative energy and generative of great pleasure . . . as well as affective engagement for its largely female participants." In the case of *Nirvana in Fire*, gender roles, hierarchy, and relation *are* reimagined. While men and their bonding become the object of fantasy, female protagonists play very interesting roles as well, serving as imperial officials in the public space and behaving like any capable male figure. Such an obvious twist of the historical reality is a fantasized reconstruction of the past and gender roles. However, women only play an insignificant role in the story, leaving the primary fictional space to the men and their brotherly loyalty.

Different from the conventional "boys' love" stories, brotherly loyalty is placed in the grand context of nation-building and social engagement, which, in turn, elevates brotherhood beyond the personal level and make the story widely acceptable in the mainstream. Though set in the distant, obscure past, the story contains many contemporary references to the social problems permeating society today: corrupt officials who take advantage of land disputes, deprived victims who travel to the capital to appeal for justice, rich and spoiled young kids who randomly kill innocent people, and political factions plotting against each other for power. Though unsolvable in reality, these issues can be all magically addressed in the fictional world via strategy and manipulation by Mei Changsu, who is determined to help the prince become a future emperor. The two directly and indirectly shape all the positive developments in the story. Mei fits the public imagination of a capable official judge, a wise military adviser, and a noble yet humble hero; while the prince grows from an unfulfilled prince, an impetuous young man, to a virtuous and noble emperor. The two finally correct the injustices, protect innocent lives, and restore the state to the right track.

Caught in both national and personal crises, the protagonist places the national, public, and collective interest above his personal well-being. The selfless, altruistic figure generates effective respect from readers and audiences, who bond with the character and become infatuated not only with a classical "beautiful male," but also with the traditional morality, value, and aesthetics he represents. In the discussion section on Qidian, where the novel was first published, there are thirty-four pages of discussion on the story (forum.qdmm.com). Readers have expressed that they are touched by the brotherhood, patriotism, and moral virtue Mei demonstrates. They established QQ groups, an instant messaging network, to express their emotional attachment to the protagonist. The official Weibo account of the TV drama *Nirvana in Fire* had also garnered 771,054 fans by May 16, 2016.

The TV adaption and narrative of Mei's loyalty, duty, dedication, patriotism, and commitment to his mission certainly fit mainstream values. What the idealized Confucian man strives for is not better institutions and systems to come about, but a morally noble person who can be a wise emperor and make the existing institution better. The drama therefore returns to the "main melody" (*zhu xuanlü* 主旋律) promoted by the state.[4] It comes as no surprise that Mei Changsu also receives an enthusiastic response from official media such as Xinhua Net, which asks the CCP (Chinese Communist Party) members to learn from Mei Changsu (Guancha. cn 2015). Xinhua Net especially associates the day of the last TV episodes with the publication of Xi Jinping's "Talk on Arts and Literature." The article praises the integration of family, nation, and all those under heaven (*jia guo tianxia* 家国天下), the plot of "helping the virtuous emperor and carrying out the reform," and the virtue of "self-sacrificing for the nation."

Such an idealized, Confucian type of hero is a nostalgic imagination of traditional masculinity. The perfect man in the past, both visually pleasing and selflessly committed to social engagement, is a counter-narrative to the varieties of masculinity in the digital age. He fits women's imagining of a perfect man, men's ideal of an established, capable figure, and the state's approval of virtues. The official endorsement of Mei Changsu turns the refined Confucian hero into an anchor in a disorienting society. Set in such context, brotherhood is legitimate, noble, and touching. The cross-media adaptation extends the consumption of such male bonding. Ironically, Mei's final sacrifice and death seems to suggest the impossibility of such a kind of ideal and brotherly loyalty. As one netizen's comment mentions, "several (shiny) stars, after all, cannot light up the whole dark night."[5]

Women's imagined participation in history: palace romance

Palace romance, a popular online genre, centers on the drama of one male figure (the emperor) and many women (imperial consorts) who compete for his favor, and hence power. *Biography of Zhen Huan*, henceforth referred to as *Zhen Huan*, written by Liu Lianzi (流潋紫, pen name for Wu Xuelan [吴雪岚]), was published on Jinjiang Literature City in 2006, printed as a book in 2007, and adapted into a television drama in 2012. Also set in an unknown past, the story centers on Zhen Huan's journey from an innocent low-ranking consort to a callous head empress in the imperial palace. The TV drama moves the story to the Qing dynasty and, accordingly, incorporates many Qing-related ritual practices, architecture, and customs. It was widely popular in mainland China and Taiwan, and eventually adapted into an English version titled *Empresses in the Palace*, a web drama broadcasted on Netflix.

According to scholars of cultural and media studies, there are a number of reasons behind the popularity of the televised *Zhen Huan*, and palace romance to larger extent.[6] First, although it is a historical drama, its focus is actually an ahistorical narrative of office politics. The imperial court is a metaphor for contemporary professional institutes. Readers and viewers, especially women, identify with the problems the female protagonist encounters. They find the strategies Zhen Huan employs to deal with her rivals inspiring in handling their own life situation. Second, the detailed depiction of costume, makeup, porcelain, medicine, ritual performance, and cuisine evokes a sense of nostalgia of the distant past. The exquisite taste and connoisseurship transcend the mundanity of everyday life. The speaking style, which is full of classical references, is termed "Zhen Huan style" (*Zhen Huan ti* 甄嬛体),[7] and has been half-jokingly employed by netizens, citizens, and even Taiwanese politicians to satirize their political rivals.[8]

Shao Yanjun (Sun et al. 2012) addresses the appeal of *Zhen Huan* to the viewers from another perspective. She reads *Zhen Huan* as a counter-narrative of love. Love, which used to symbolize individuality, emancipation, and liberation, is a very important component in the mission of enlightenment and modernity at the beginning of the twentieth century. The ideal of love, nevertheless, disappears in *Zhen Huan*. The female protagonist gives up all her fantasies of love and passion to become invincible, and eventually succeeds in attaining the highest level of power in the palace.

The association of the counter-love rhetoric with the discourse of modernity and enlightenment is an innovative way to unravel the public infatuation with Zhen Huan's story, which grapples with the unresolvable conflicts between sense and sensibility, passion and rationality, and the emotional vulnerability and the tough reality people have to deal with. It is certainly not the first time love is demystified and distrusted. Avant-garde fiction in the 1980s and "private fiction" (*siren xiezuo* 私人写作) in the 1990s, for instance, either question the idea of love or reduce love to no more than carnal desire. Indeed, *Zhen Huan*, as well as many other pieces of online fiction, is a continued engagement of counter-enlightenment in a digital age. Nevertheless, what matters to most online writers is less such a grand narrative than their individualized desire. The palace in the past is a fictionalized space for both writers and readers to express their own perspectives on love, life, and institutions.

We propose to read Zhen Huan's fictional journey to the crown as a woman's fantasized participation in history-making and power games. Placed in an imperial court, Zhen Huan gains limited space, resources, and power to intervene in the male-dominated history and eventually shapes it in the way she plans. The very fantasized participation in history-making reveals nuanced, paradoxical layers of gender relations. If we read the palace story of one man vs. many women as a metaphor of the contemporary professional scenario of one (male) boss and many (female) employees, *Zhen Huan* certainly perpetuates age-old patriarchal structures and ideologies. Film scholar Dai Jinhua strongly rebukes such a mentality in palace romance and calls it a "specter of polygamy" (Hong Fan 2015).

Nevertheless, the male characters only play very minor roles. Compared with the well-developed female protagonists, the males serve more as symbols of power (in the case of the emperor), or love interests (such as other male protagonists). Their limited presence and relatively minimal space at the narrative level are mainly to foreground the stories of the female characters. The leading protagonist, Zhen Huan, employs sophisticated tricks to successfully removes all her enemies, lovers, and friends along her climb to power. In her limited space (palace) and capacity (as a consort), she topples the emperor and chooses his successor.

It is legitimate to argue Zhen Huan only tries to conform to the institutionalized power system and make the most out of it, thus perpetuating the age-old patriarchal framework of gendered structures and maintaining a very conservative position. However, her employment of conspiracy, schemes, and strategies also degrades the power structure to a certain degree. The woman's power destabilizes the conventional gendered expectations. It therefore has generated some public anxiety. *People's Daily*, for instance, criticizes *Zhen Huan* for amplifying the evils of human nature and the greedy desire for absolute power (Wang 2012). Such criticism from the mainstream media could be read as a statement repudiating a character that breaks the rules and topples the ruling head of the country. It is also an official attempt to contain women's transgressive endeavors.

Zhen Huan is just one of many palace romances. A large number of online palace stories project a similar fantasy of being close to the center of power and obtaining access to all the associated privileges thereof. *Startling by Each Step* is another example. A time-travel novel written by Tong Hua, the novel was first published on Jinjiang Literature City in 2005. The novel tells the story of Zhang Xiao, a contemporary white-collar girl who has no luck with relationships. Zhang travels back to the Qing dynasty and become an aristocratic girl Ruo Xi. She then becomes involved in romantic relationships with the imperial princes. The novel's adaptation into a TV drama in 2011 led to a larger-scale fascination with time-travel. If, just as Zhang Xiao in the story demonstrates, the present is uncertain, unreliable, and unpredictable, a contemporary person with advanced knowledge in the past would certainly be empowered, for she knows the future and therefore acquires a sense of security. In Tong Hua's own words, "the most attractive feature of time-travel is probably the sense of victory over time" (Chen 2011).

Startling by Each Step enacts many layers of female fantasies. First, due to time travel, an ordinary contemporary girl magically and conveniently possesses social status, beauty, and talent. Her present frustrations are therefore conveniently addressed in the past. The female protagonist also possesses modern knowledge and insight in history. Therefore she can always skillfully balance her own interests and feelings. Second, the handsome princes in the Qing imperial court, with their high status and power, fulfill different fantasies of "prince charming" and the "Cinderella" complex. Different from the polygamy seen in *Zhen Huan*, it is a reversed polygamy: a woman is admired and loved by all the attractive princes.

Last but not least, the female fantasy is enacted as an imagined participation in history: a woman attempts to intervene in history with her knowledge of the present and her self-perceived freedom, equality, love, and individual agency. For instance, Ruo Xi tries to persuade one prince to give up his plan to become the crown prince, for that would lead to his fatal tragedy as history turns out. Nevertheless, she is unable to revise history. She can only helplessly witness as the tragedy unfolds, literally, right in front of her eyes. Eventually she returns to the most traditional way to survive in the palace: seeking a man's protection and love.

The online story of *Startling by Each Step* ends in the death of the protagonist in the past, thus wrapping up the story with unfulfilled love and a failed attempt to change history. The TV drama has the protagonist traveling back to the contemporary moment, adding a layer of self-reflection. The contemporary Zhang Xiao feels at loss while she gazes at a picture of the palace in the museum. All she has experienced, the unfulfilled love and the firsthand experience with history and power, though dream-like, leave an impact on the contemporary figure in the metropolis.

The recurring episodes of palace romance indicate the public infatuation with the spectacle of the past, as well as the problematic reimagining of gender relations. In both stories of palace romance, the escapist fantasy of imagined (dis)empowerment is limited and contained within the patriarchal framework. A woman's presence in the imperial court is a fantasized intervention in the male-dominated history, a reflection on the impossibility and the unattainable at present.

The constructed-ness of gender: *Go Princess Go*

Go Princess Go is another typical online product. Written by Xian Cheng (鲜橙), it was published in Jinjiang Literature City in 2010 and then adapted into a net drama and aired on LeTV.com in 2015. The net drama revises the fiction into a time-travel experience of a contemporary playboy named Zhang Peng. Trying to escape from the revenge of his former girlfriends at a party, he jumps into a pool, gets injured, and loses consciousness. When he wakes up, he finds himself traveling back to an unknown past and inhabiting the body of a beautiful princess Zhang Pengpeng. The whole drama focuses on Zhang's inner struggle to explore her/his gendered identity and sexual orientation, with all sorts of farce, jokes, plays, and comic moments depicting boys' love and girls' love in masquerade. In the end, Zhang finally makes peace with her/himself, falls in love with the prince, and admits she/he is a woman. The seemingly happy-ever-after life is about to begin.

Crossdressing and gender masquerade are not uncommon in Ming vernacular fiction from the seventeenth century. Feng Menglong's "Two Brothers of Different Sex" (*Liu Xiaoguan cixiong xiongdi* 刘小官雌雄兄弟) and Li Yu's "A Male Mencius Mother Moves Three Times" (*Nan mengmu jiaohe san qian* 男孟母

教合三迁), for instance, tell stories of transgressive women, feminized men or androgynous figures. Such figures are lodged with the literati's exploration of their own social status and a reflection on Confucian ethics.[9] Gender masquerading by ancient figures is also a popular theme in Hong Kong cinemas of the 1990s. Wong Kar-wai's *Ashes of Time* (*Dongxie xidu* 东邪西毒, 1994) and Tsui Hark's *Lovers* (*Liang Shanbo yu Zhu Yingtai* 梁山伯与祝英台, 1994) employ cross-dressed figures to address a complicated and subtle interplay of heterosexual/homosexual emotions and desires. In contemporary online time-travel fiction, women often travel back to the past and inhabit the body of men. According to Jin Feng (2013), this derives from women's disappointment in heterosexual relationships. They wish to become men so as to survive in a male-dominated world. Such women-turned-male figures often embody ideal masculinity, projecting women's fantasy, or *YY* (*yiyin* 意淫), as the popular web term goes, of perfect men. The consequent homosexual love is actually a heterosexual relationship in disguise.

While there are many stories of female-to-male transformations, there are not as many writings about men who acquire the body of women. *Go Princess Go* features a contemporary man directly inhabiting an ancient woman's body. To blur the boundary between both men and women, and the present and the past, the web drama blends all kinds of genres such as melodrama, Korean idol shows, silent films, and even revolutionary ballet. The costumes are also designed to appeal to both the traditional and the contemporary, including Chinese and European styles. The pastiche produces a comic effect that also brings boundaries and norms into question.

A man in a woman's body leads to multiple, and contradictory, ways of interpretation. Such a figure could be a metaphor for an empowered, strong woman. Instead of a fragile girl who passively waits to be protected, she is aggressive, playful, and always takes the active role to pursue what she wants. However, her power comes from the male mentality she retains from her previous identity, implying that to succeed and make the best of the situation, a woman has to think and behave like a man. The willful gender-bending princess identifies with man's logic of jungle rules, which makes her life easier and better compared to other women in the story. Zhang's relationship with the prince is therefore also shrouded in an ambiguous light of boys' love. As she/he gradually transforms herself/himself into a woman, she gradually becomes the typical figure of a chaste and loyal wife, conforming to the stereotypical patriarchal norm on the one hand, while demonstrating the fulfillment of same-sex love in masquerade on the other.

In the original version of the online fiction, the prince eventually becomes an emperor, and the princess the queen. While the princess expresses her concern that they are not on an equal footing and she cannot love him wholeheartedly, he gives up his throne, disappears, and then comes back as an ordinary man to reunite with her, thus fulfilling a typical female fantasy of "true love": between love and power, an ideal man will choose love.

However, when transforming the story for the screen, the director of the online drama, Lühao Jiji, leaves the ending open by presenting two different stories. In the first ending, while both the prince and the princess are enjoying the "happily ever after" life in a conventional sense, a group of unknown assassins emerge out of nowhere and slay both of them. The camera then cuts to a black screen and then a modern hospital: Zhang Peng wakes up from his coma and feels deeply confused. He jumps into the pool again in hope of finding the traces of his past. The camera cuts back and forth between him and the princess and the prince, giving an ambiguous image of who he actually was/is. Sometimes he is a bystander, observing the sweet couple of the prince and the princess. Sometimes he participates in the games with them. His image overlaps with the prince and the princess, presenting multiple unknown puzzles. Is everything a dream? Is he the prince or the princess? Are the prince and the princess actually split personas of him, representing his twisted sub-consciousness and his complicated gender identity and sexual orientation? Does he need to kill his subconscious persona to fulfill a right self? Exacerbating the confusion, Zhang's seeking of the past occurs silently, perhaps due to a technological reason or a purposeful arrangement, leaving a dream-like effect on the viewers.

In the second ending, the ancient story ends with the prince and the princess being happily together, and then the camera also cuts to a black screen, accompanied by the sound of a heartbeat, indicating Zheng Peng has been rescued from his pool accident and is recovering in the hospital. He wakes up from his coma, also confused. He runs out of his ward and shouts out the name of the prince. Then he realizes something and calls the doctor instead. At this moment, his doctor turns back, and it turns out he is the very prince in his dream. The whole drama ends with them looking into each other's eyes, transforming the prince and princess romance into an ambiguous male-love bonding in the present day.

The two open endings completely revise the otherwise conventional love story and turn the story into a reflection on gendered identity and disguised desire. Both endings shift viewers' attention to the constructed-ness of both identity and online drama. The contemporary man's struggle to locate his true self is actualized through the cross-gender exploration in the past. The ancient figure comes a long way toward confirming her/his identity, yet the contemporary protagonist is still unclear of what to expect. In this way, the net drama goes beyond a conventional idol drama and comic show, and becomes an avant-garde exploration of gender and genre.

The constructed-ness of identity and online drama becomes even more intriguing when most of the netizens have expressed strong dissatisfaction with the double endings. Some netizens even developed an alternative third ending of their own by editing all the images into a conventional happy ending. Both the prince and the princess return to the contemporary time period and end up living happily ever after. In this way, the netizens revise the reflection on gender identity back to heterosexual love. The State Administration of Radio, Film and Television (SARFT) eventually banned the online drama, clearly indicating the official limit of transgression. The director was forced to keep revising and editing the show. The compromise and adjustment is another layer of the constructed-ness of web drama.

Coda

Online fiction is full of the paradoxes of modernity and tradition, progressiveness and backwardness, and liberalism and conservatism. The media space is cutting-edge, yet the content and genre of the fiction nevertheless can also restore older storytelling traditions. Gaining a seemingly unlimited space to write, some online authors still choose to re-enact the spectacle of the past. Cyberspace provides an accessible public space for the marginalized gender, gendered desires, and gender identity to resist against the hegemonic narrative of the norms, yet the conventional and institutionalized power structures are equally prevalent. In the aforementioned online fiction and dramas, the ideal man is established in relation to traditional virtues and Confucian ethics, and male bonding is constructed against the larger backdrop of establishing a state and social engagement. Female protagonists fantasize about their intervention in history, yet also obey gender hierarchies and adjust their roles to fit into the power structure so as to achieve their personal goals. Ambiguous same-sex desire is invested in the cross-gender, time-travel imagination.

Initially created by women writers online, gendered fantasy addresses female imaginations of masculinity, femininity, love, and the lack thereof. When such fantasy crosses media boundaries, it is revised and rewritten by multiple cultural and ideological players even as it reaches a wider scale of readership. The cross-media migration moves online reconfiguration of gender from the subcultural to the mainstream, turning the online imagination into offline consumption.

The popularity of these stories both online and offline speaks to the public psyche at particular historical moments. The fictional past reflects the impossibilities and insecurities of the present. The constructed-ness of gendered desire and identity is an imagined escape from or resistance to the ever-changing reality. Such online and offline narratives of gendered desires channel both individual and collective anxieties, and also provide much-needed emotional catharsis for people who are fraught with real-life problems in present-day society.

Notes

1 In fact, Shao (2012: 12–18) views some male Internet writers' time-travel works, such as Mao Ni's *Jianke* (An in-between guest 间客), as a heroic and conscientious intervention in present reality. They have inherited and reshaped the realist tradition in offline literary writing, and migrated this popular tradition to the online space.
2 The TV drama slightly enhances the flavor of heterosexual romance and suggests the unfulfilled love between the main characters.
3 For detailed discussion on "boys' love" stories, see Chunyu Zhang (2014).
4 Main melody films refer to those which represent the mainstream ideology the state promotes. For detailed discussion on "main melody," see Ying Xiao (2011).

5 The quote is from the discussion forum of qdmm.com. "Mei Changsu, the deepest emotion" (*Gulai shenqing wei Changsu*), http://forum.qdmm.com/MMThreadDetail New.aspx?threadId=240900095 (accessed June 4, 2016). The review is no longer available.
6 For instance, Yuan Yuan (2013) has discussed the popularity of *Zhen Huan* in the context of contemporary career women.
7 A search on Weibo will lead to many references to "*Zhen Huan ti.*"
8 Sun Rongguang and Li Xinin (2013) have discussed how Taiwanese politicians appropriate "*Zhen Huan ti*" for political battles.
9 In Ming fiction, there are many stories about cross-dressed men and women. This group of people transgresses the gender boundary and takes identities that are different from their biological sexes. Their behaviors challenge the Confucian orthodox gender norms and become morally controversial. However, to what extent their morality is problematic varies from individual to individual. The gender change itself, whether it is male-to-female or female-to-male, does not necessarily make corrupted individuals. This kind of identity change, like other social activities, is subjugated to the overarching Confucian principles. So long as it conforms to the conventional moral principles such as filial piety or chastity, it is positive, legitimate, and virtuous. Otherwise, it is evil, perverse, and decadent. The transvestite case itself is rather a dramatic vehicle or media employed by writers to convey moral messages or cultural ideals. For more discussion on the androgyny in Ming fiction, see Zuyan Zhou (2003).

Bibliography

Chen Yanni. (2011). "'Qingchuan' xiaoshuo jia Tonghua: milian chuanyue yin zai shijian mianqian wuli" (Time-travel novelist Tong Hua: the infatuation with time is because we feel powerless about time). *Liaoshen wanbao*, February 24. http://www.chinanews.com/cul/2011/02–24/2866660.shtml. Last accessed August 31, 2016.
Feng, Jin. (2013). *Romancing the Internet: Producing and Consuming Chinese Web Romance*. Leiden and Boston, MA: Brill.
Guancha.cn. (2015). "Xinhua wang: dangyuan ganbu yinggai jianshou Mei Changsu yongren zhidao" (Xinhua net: CCP members should firmly follow the way Mei Changsu identifies the talents). http://www.guancha.cn/politics/2015_11_19_341812.shtml. Last accessed August 31, 2016.
Guo, Shaohua. (2015). "Startling by Each Click: 'Word-of-Mouse' Publicity and Critically Manufacturing Time-Travel Romance Online." *Chinese Literature Today* 5, no. 1: 74–83.
Hong Fan. (2015). "Dai Jinhua: dangxia xingbie xiangxiang zhong cunzai zhe 'duo qi zhi' youling" (Dai Jinhua: the 'specter of polygamy' in contemporary imagination of gender). http://cul.sohu.com/20151216/n431468714.shtml. Last accessed September 20, 2016.
Inwood, Heather. (2014). "What's in a Game? Transmedia Storytelling and the Web-Game Genre of Online Chinese Popular Fiction." *Asia Pacific: Perspectives* 12, no. 2: 6–29.
Jenkins, Henry. (2006). *Convergence Culture: Where Old and New Media Collide*. New York: New York University Press.
Kong, Shuyu. (2014). *Popular Media, Social Emotion and Public Discourse in Contemporary China*. London & New York: Routledge.
Li, Li, Yea-Wen Chen, and Masato Nakazawa. (2013). "Voices of Chinese Web-TV Audiences: A Case of Applying Uses and Gratifications Theory to Examine Popularity of Prison Break in China." *China Media Research* 9, no. 1: 63–75.

Lugg, Alexander. (2011). "Chinese Online Fiction: Taste Publics, Entertainment, and Candle in the Tomb." *Chinese Journal of Communication* 4, no. 2: 121–36.

Louie, Kam. (2002). *Theorising Chinese Masculinity: Society and Gender in China*. Cambridge: Cambridge University Press.

Martin, Fran. (2012). "Girls Who Love Boys' Love: Japanese Homoerotic Manga as Transnational Taiwan Culture." *Inter-Asia Cultural Studies* 13, no. 3: 365–83.

——. (2012). "Popular Culture and Masculinity Ideals in East Asia, with Special Reference to China." *The Journal of Asian Studies* 71, no. 4: 929–43.

Mulvey, Laura. (1975). "Visual Pleasure and Narrative Cinema." *Screen* 16, no. 3: 6–18.

——. (1981). "Afterthoughts on 'Visual Pleasure and Narrative Cinema' inspired by King Vidor's *Duel in the sun* (1946)." *Framework* 15–16–17: 12–15.

Penny, Laurie. (2013). *Cybersexism: Sex, Gender and Power on the Internet*. London: Bloomsbury Publishing.

Shao Yanjun. (2011). "Miandui wangluo wenxue: xueyuanpai de taidu he fangfa" (Facing Internet literature: attitudes and methods of academics). *Nanfang wentan* 6: 12–18.

——. (2012). "Zai 'yituobang' li goujian 'geren linglei xuanze'huanxiang kongjian: wangluo wenxue de yishi xingtai gongneng zhi yizhong" (Constructing a fantasy space of 'individual, alternative choice' in a heterotopia: one of the ideological functions of Internet literature). *Wenyi yanjiu* 4: 16–25.

——. (2015)."Zhongguo gudian 'mei nanzi' xingxiang de wangluo chongsheng" (Online reincarnation of a classical Chinese beautiful man). *Zhongguo zuojia wang*. http://www.chinawriter.com.cn/wxpl/2015/2015–11–27/259109.html. Last accessed September 12, 2016.

Sohu. (2003). "Muzi Mei: nanren tuole yifu dou chabuduo" (Muzi Mei: men are similar after they take off their clothes). http://women.sohu.com/52/60/article215436052.shtml. Last accessed August 31, 2016.

Song, Geng, and Derek Hird. (2014). *Men and Masculinities in Contemporary China*. Leiden: Brill.

Sun Jiashan et al. (2012). "Duochong shiye xia de Zhenghuan Zhuan" (*Biography of Zhen Huan* in multiple perspectives). *Wenyi lilun yu piping* 4: 27–35.

Sun Rongguang and Li Xinin. (2013). "From 'jianren" to 'jianren': Taiwan Hougong Zhenhuan Zhuan xianxiang de jiedu" (From "low person" to "healthy person:" reading the phenomenon of *Biography of Zhen Hua*n in Taiwan). http://ccs.nccu.edu.tw/word/HISTORY_PAPER_FILES/1492_1.pdf. Last accessed September 12, 2016.

Tian, Xiaofei. (2015). "Slashing the Three Kingdoms: A Case Study of Fan Production on the Chinese Web." *Modern Chinese Literature and Culture* 27, no. 1: 224–77.

Tianya.cn. (2015). "Kanle langyabang, youdian lijie *funü de xiangfa le*" (After watching *Nirvana in Fire*, I begin to understand *funü*). http://bbs.tianya.cn/post-funinfo-6757406–1.shtml. Last accessed September 12, 2016.

Wang Guangfei. (2012). "Yinping gongdou heshixiu" (When will the online palace drama end). *Renmin ribao*. http://news.xinhuanet.com/society/2012–05/08/c_111903733.htm. Last accessed August 29, 2016.

Xiao, Ying. (2011). "'Leitmotif: State, market, and postsocialist Chinese film industry under neoliberal globalization." In *Neoliberalism and Global Cinema: Capital, Culture and Marxist Critique*. edited by Jyotsna Kapur and Keith B. Wagner, 157–79. London and New York: Routledge.

Xu Yanrui and Yang Ling. (2014). "Funü 'fu' nan: kuaguo wenhua liudong zhong de danmei, fu wenhua yu nanxing qizhi de zaizao" (The rotten girl and the "rotten" boy: boys' love, rotten culture and reconstruction of masculinity in transnational cultural flux). *Wenhua yanjiu* 20: 3–25.

Yang, Xin. (2011). *From Beauty Fear to Beauty Fever: A Critical Study of Contemporary Chinese Female Writers.* New York: Peter Lang.

Yuan Yuan. (2013) "Zhichang, minzu, nüxin: cong Zhuan Huan Zhuan kan xinshiji de yishi xingtai" (Profession, nation and woman: ideological manifestation of the new century in *Biography of Zhen Huan*). *Nanfang wentan* 5: 40–4.

Zhang, Chunyu. (2014). "My Double Love of Boys": Chinese Women's Fascination with "Boys' Love" *Fiction*. MA Thesis. Iowa State University. Web. 27 Jan. 2016.

Zhou, Zuyan. (2003). *Androgyny in Late Ming and Early Qing Literature*. Honolulu: University of Hawaii Press.

4   Performing ethnicity

Media, identity, and nationalism

In 2010 Feng Xiaogang's new year blockbuster film, *If You Are the One 2* (*Feicheng wurao* 非诚勿扰2), unexpectedly brought Tsangyang Gyatso (仓央嘉措, 1683–1706), the sixth Dalai Lama of Tibet, to national popularity in China among filmgoers and young urbanites, predominantly ethnic Han Chinese. The film cites lines of so-called "love poetry" attributed to Tsangyang Gyatso at instances of emotional intensity. With the help of the Internet, these lyrical and – for mainstream audiences – exotic lines became household words overnight. It might not be an overstatement that the Tibetan poet, who was previously not well known among the Chinese public, was "brought to light" overnight by the film, the Internet, and Mandarin-speaking netizens in China.

Admittedly, reimagining of ethnic cultures is not new in China; yet, what strikes us as significant in this case is the role that media, especially the Internet, played in (re)constructing ethnic identity. Together with the film, the Internet has helped create and disseminate an image of a "romantic monk" (*qingseng* 情僧), who was a spiritual leader of the highest religious status in ancient Tibet. This young "lover" wrote beautiful love poems, which, to the interest of Han netizens, seemed at odds with his role as a Buddhist monk; his mysterious and premature death, in addition, helped paint an image of a romantic martyr. His unique identity, not surprisingly, fueled the imagination of Han netizens, who viewed his writings as an exotic and enigmatic code. These netizens not only contrived to dig up more of Tsangyang Gyatso's poems, many of which, ironically, turned out to be faked by someone else in his name, but also concertedly churned out what they called "Tsangyang Gystso-style" (仓央嘉措体) lyrics by imitating his writings and made them go viral on the Internet.

In contrast to the wildly popular but problematic reimagination of ethnic minorities by Han netizens precipitated by the Internet, ethnic groups' own expressions of their own cultures and lives on the Internet – which perhaps should play a more important role in the construction of their images and identities in this age of hyper-connectivity and hyper-mediality – nevertheless seem to be much less vocal and visible. Scholarship on the Internet and ethnic minorities' cultural expression, thus, also remains unsurprisingly scanty. Due to China's differentiating, if not discriminative, political, social, economic, and educational policies on ethnic issues, as well as socialist control of media in combination with neoliberal freedom for its consumption, ethnic groups' cultural self-expression has largely been either directly monitored or suppressed, or else incorporated into the mainstream discourse of (self-)orientalization, a phenomenon also affecting the dominant Han ethnicity. Critics' lack of attention to this highly important issue reflects an unawareness on the part of some scholars, and perhaps lack of resources for intensive study on the part of others who are interested in such topics. As Kwai-Cheung Lo (2016: 360) avers, it is highly important

> to examine how the ethnic groups inside China make use of the cyber communication technology in their daily lives to construct, negotiate and redefine identity for themselves, and to achieve greater social equity as a way to exert agency for shaping their futures despite tight government control.

In this chapter, we focus on the understudied subject of ethnic groups' cultural self-expression on the Internet and investigate the ways in which this expression, simultaneously taking advantage of and shaped by digital and cyber technologies, helps groups construct their images and identities not only alongside but in tension with, and sometimes even in conspiracy with, the authoritative discourse of ethnic identity. In what follows, we examine a variety of Internet cultural events in which ethnic minorities assume the role of *subjects* – subjects perhaps best understood in the Althusserian sense of ideological interpellation. These events include Tibetan woman writer Woeser's (*Wei Se* in Mandarin Chinese 唯色) Internet writings, *kuaishan* (flash mob 快闪) singing at Tibet University, and wedding photos of a young Tibetan couple. Through an examination of these cultural events, we would like to suggest that ethnic groups' cultural self-expressions of their ethnic identities on the Internet reflect their desires and efforts to reconfigure ethnic images and identities in cyberspace under the postsocialist condition. Shaped by the Party-state's ethnic policies, ethnic contention and narration in history, contemporary sociocultural conditions, and Chinese Internet culture in general, these cultural self-expressions exemplify complicated features that inform the performance and construction of ethnic identity in the age of the Internet.

Ethnicity, nationalism, and "sinophone" ethnic culture on the Internet

Performing ethnicity/nationality and Chinese nationalism

Chinese ethnicity is one of the most dynamic fields in China studies. Scholars have debated a variety of complex issues, such as the relationships between ethnicity and nationality, ethnic policies, ethnicity and Chinese modernity, reaching some consensus in certain areas. First, *minzu*, a term that incorporates and intermingles different levels of race, nationality, and ethnicity in different social, historical, and political contexts, does not have an exact equivalent in English. It is precisely due to this volatile and complex nature that some scholars prefer to simply use the term in original Chinese instead of any approximate equivalent in English.

Second, ethnic issues in the Chinese context are inevitably interwoven with China's nation-building and nationalism; some even regard ethnic issues as an integral part of Chinese nationalism, as both, in Allen Carlson's (2009: 29) words, are dominated by discourses of "exclusionary dichotomies" that demarcate insiders and outsiders. From the time when it was first introduced in China in the face of Western imperialist colonization in the late nineteenth century, to the contemporary postsocialist period when China is actively engaged in its participation into the capitalist globality as a modern, multicultural nation-state, *minzu*, as a focal issue in China's national crises and state-building projects, has always been manipulated and appropriated in the performative process of construction of Chinese nationalism.

Third, as a result of its inevitable and complex entanglement with Chinese nationalism, which by itself is a highly dynamic locale open to ideological contentions, ethnicity also becomes a site in which a diverse set of positions, assumptions, and voices constantly negotiate and struggle for a power to define it. Many studies have been carried out on the contingent nature of ethnicity, a contingency that is inevitably in line with the "inchoate and incoherent" nature of Chinese nationalism in China (Pye 1996: 87). For instance, Frank Dikötter's *Discourse of Race in Modern China*, Dru Gladney's *Dislocating China: Muslims, Minorities, and Other Subaltern Subjects*, Stevan Harrell's *Ways of Being Ethnic in Southwest China*, and James Leibold's *Reconfiguring Chinese Nationalism*, among many others, have all shown that ethnicity is, in Leibold's (2010: 542) words, "constructed, performed and institutionalized within the specific cultural framework of ethnic difference in Chinese tradition."

As discourses of "exclusionary dichotomies," both nationalism and ethnicity in China seek to "identify where the lines of the community stop. Yet this boundary-making process is never static, single-layered or uni-dimensional: boundaries can shift (often rapidly) depending on the context" (Leibold 2010: 559). Put in another way, in the spectrum of continuous levels of national/ethnic assertions, nationality and ethnicity with defined identities and political registers are a result of signification maneuvers determined by specific social, political, and cultural conditions, a result, understandably, that is to be re-signified when these conditions change. In this sense, ethnicity can be regarded as being isomorphic with nationality, as they can be deemed as two variables of the same signification process.

Thus, some argue that Chinese nationalism and ethnicity are simultaneously performed and constructed in the same process of the so-called "subaltern nationalism," which, in Michael Hardt and Antonio Negri's (2000: 106) opinion, is "a double-edged sword." Following Hardt and Negri's line of thinking, Kwai-Cheung Lo (2016: 356) claims that

> Its progressive nature is the legitimate defense against the domination of more powerful external forces, the right to self-determination and the demand for autonomy and equality. But it can easily manifest its reactionary and regressive aspects in the way that the multiplicity of community itself is always negated. Perhaps nationalist sentiments for building an imagined community

are only truly productive if they do not continue beyond a certain period of existence. Chinese nationalist revolution itself is one good example: as soon as the nation becomes a sovereign state, its progressive revolutionary qualities rapidly fade away, and it erects its own severe structure of domination.

While it is debatable whether the current Chinese nation-state, which is a result of signification and limit demarcation in China's nation-building project, and thus precludes the legitimacy and visibility of other levels of community as a modern nation-state, has therefore lost its progressiveness and become a repressive force against other consequently "sub-national" or ethnic groups, it may nonetheless prove to be constructive to view ethnicity as an isomorphic register with nationality in the same course of ideological contention. It is also productive to view the construction of ethnic identities entangled with the larger scheme of Chinese nationalism, in the Chinese context, as a fluid and ideology-loaded project that has been constantly defined and redefined in terms of its boundaries and ideological implications.

Perhaps the most relevant of such a nationality–ethnicity demarcation to our current investigation of ethnic cultures on the Internet is the existing ethnic register in China, which has taken shape in the tortuous course of the Communist Party's continuous and proactive maneuvering of the national-ethnic discourse for its construction of an independent and multiethnic nation-state. The Party has indeed played an active role in this course – as Elena Barabantseva (2008: 569, our emphasis) explains, *minzu* as a discursive term is not only descriptive and evaluative, but also *definitive*: "This concept is used to *assign* who ethnic minorities are by application of what the Chinese leadership calls an objective set of criteria, but it also incurs certain normative estimations as to what is characteristic of ethnic minorities." Different from ethnicity in the West, which is mostly derived from the Weberian sense of self-ascription, *minzu* in China is greatly influenced by the Soviet Union's "scientific" approach of definitive classification. Basically following the Soviet Union's (mainly Joseph Stalin's) theory on ethnicity, while taking into consideration China's cultural and historical conditions so as to avoid jeopardizing China's national unity, the Party-state orchestrated the "Ethnic Classification Project" (*minzu shibie* 民族识别) in less than a decade following the founding of the People's Republic, which continued to be carried out until the early 1980s. Tom S. Mullany (2011) has examined this project in great detail in his seminal book, *Coming to Terms with the Nation: Ethnic Classification in Modern China*, in which he investigates the ways in which the "scientific" survey, in addition to Republican-era scholarship, was adopted in identifying *minzu* and would become the basis for Chinese policies for nationalities. Moreover, Barabantseva's (2008) study also shows that the Party-state's shift of its official English translation of *minzu* from "nationality" during the socialist period to "ethnicity" during the period of economic and societal transformations – that is, the postsocialist period – demonstrates a change in its approach to and policies on ethnic issues, another example of the *definitive* and performative nature of *minzu* in China.

This project of ethnic classification and the Party-state's later adjustment in its ethnic policies have not only shaped socialist and postsocialist discourses of Chinese ethnicity, but also set a framework within, or against, which most current self-expressions of ethnicity on the Internet are carried out. As James Leibold (2015: 288) observes,

> While sub-minzu attachments are multiple, unstable and unconditional, the state's classificatory register is assigned, rigid and exclusive. . . . In other words, unlike cyber-identities, state policies mobilize and institutionalize minzu-based loyalties and solidary – whether it's Uyghur-ness, Han-ness, or even Chinese-ness – meaning that netizens in the PRC can play with these categories, even distort them, but like one's shadow, they are impossible to shake.

That is to say, the official, authoritative discourse of nationality-ethnicity is writ so large in the Party-state's definitive efforts, that any discussion of ethnicity in contemporary China, including the apparently more "liberal" ones on the Internet, can hardly avoid it but has to be conducted in reference to it. This is the context in which we approach cultural performances of ethnicity on the Chinese Internet in what follows.

Problematics of "sinophone" ethnic literature and culture

Before we proceed, we believe a disclaimer needs to be made. The cultural phenomena in our following discussions all belong to what some would call the "sinophone" ethnic performance. That means, the incidents we look into are all conducted in Mandarin Chinese by ethnic groups, despite the fact that each ethnic group has their own ethnic language – some ethnic languages were "naturally" developed by ethnic groups themselves in the course of their social development, while others had their written scripts created by the central government on the basis of their oral communication, another example of the Party-state's proactive intervention in the construction of ethnicity. The reason that we entirely focus on sinophone ethnic incidents in this chapter are mainly twofold: First, ethnic languages are varied and they are not in our area of expertise; while cultural incidents conducted in ethnic languages are, without a doubt, of high cultural significance, they deserve another project by more capable scholars trained in that field.

But more importantly, in the specific sociocultural space of the Internet, Mandarin Chinese has been playing a more important role than ethnic languages, for better or worse, in shaping the cultural scene thus far. While a native ethnic language is one of the "scientifically" prescribed definitive characteristics of nationality in the dominant discourse of Chinese ethnicity, compared with Mandarin, however, it has not yet achieved commensurate prominence in its indigenous cultural expression on the Internet. According to a study, as of 2011 there were only 389 websites in ethnic languages in mainland China (Li and Zhong 2012), only a tiny fraction of the 1.83 million in total (CNNIC 2011: 24). Needless to say, this figure is far out of proportion with the percentage of ethnic populations in China, even if we take into consideration those ethnic groups who in practice increasingly use Mandarin in their everyday and working communication, such as Hui (Chinese Muslim) and Man (Manchu) ethnicities. Moreover, those existing ethnic websites are much less professionally managed and less popular than their Mandarin counterparts.

In contrast to ethnic groups' less than lukewarm participation in online communication and interactions in their ethnic languages, however, those conducted in Mandarin, though still not compared to that of the dominant Han ethnicity in scale, are much more active. Many Mandarin-language, ethnic-oriented portal websites such as Tibetan Culture (www.tibetcul.com), Yi People (www.yizuren.com), Islam Online (www.islamcn.net), and so on aim at promoting their ethnic cultures and increasing understanding and communication between ethnic people and Han, and they are very popular among ethnic people. Many mainstream Mandarin websites also have set up BBS (Bulletin Board System) and discussion forums that primarily focus on ethnic topics and attract considerable ethnic participation. Further, many ethnic cultural figures, such as Zahi Ciugene, Jin Zi, Xuehong, and so on, have made their names known to a wider population, both the ethnic minority and Han, through their online activities in Mandarin. Online writings by ethnic people in Mandarin have become such a unique cultural phenomenon that they begin to attract increasing critical attention.

However, our current study of ethnic cultural expressions in Mandarin on the Internet is by no means a celebration of a cultural "prosperity" and "harmony" exhibited in China's multiethnic mosaic, as is the theme of many mainstream reports in this regard; nor is it a denial of the hegemony of Mandarin in China as the result of China's social and economic modernization, natural and planned demographic flows, and uneven educational policies (Hansen 1999, Leibold and Chen 2014). In fact, ethnic groups' writing of their own indigenous experience in Mandarin, the *lingua franca* in China, we have to admit, is by itself an ironic paradox. It speaks loudly to the marginal status of ethnic cultures and harkens back to the famous question that Gayatri Chakravorty Spivak (1988) asks, "Can the subaltern speak?" Yet, still, given the ubiquity of this phenomenon, unfortunately or not, we believe our following investigation may demonstrate its relevance by providing a window through which to understand Chinese ethnicity in the specific social, cultural, and political condition in this age of the Internet.

Ethnic writings, ethnic consciousness, and the Internet in China

Recent scholarship on the relationship between race, ethnicity, and the Internet in the West has greatly complicated our understanding of how the vexing issues of race and ethnicity have been tremendously reshaped by the advent of the new medium and technology of the Internet. Some studies paint a quite utopian picture in which new information and communication technologies are taken advantage of by people of color and thus rupture racial and ethnic stereotypes (Nelson, Tu, and Hines 2001). In this case, race and ethnicity for the non-white are deemed a form of lack or deficiency, and the Internet, with its neoliberal liberating power, functions as a kind of magical prosthesis that covers and compensates for the lack and deficiency. Other studies challenge this over-optimistic presumption and delve into the uncanny politics involved in the landscape of digitally mediated race and ethnicity by exploring controversial issues such as the digital divide along lines of race and ethnicity, construction of cultural conceptions of race and ethnicity mediated by the Internet, and so forth (Everett 2008, Nakamura and Chow-White 2012).

Enlightening as these studies are, race and ethnicity in China, as is explained above, carry very different cultural and ideological implications and are defined by and performed in the specific historical, political, and social context in China. Rather than being deemed as a lack or deficiency to be concealed or compensated by new communication and information technologies, ethnicity in China in the age of the Internet, in many critics' view, is more vigorously expressed in the new virtual space of the Internet with the support of new technologies. For instance, the Chinese ethnic literary critic Yao Xinyong (2008a: 223) observes that, while online writings among the mainstream Han ethnic groups tend to subvert conventional writing – not only in terms of language, style, subject matters, and form, but also in the ways in which their works are composed, published, circulated, read, shared, commented, and evaluated – online (as well as offline) writings by ethnic groups, however, "continue to stay with their conventional ways of writing." At the same time, however, these online writings engage in, rather than evade, or circumvent, discussions of ethnic identities, "demonstrating an extensive participation among a variety of social groups in vigorous discussions of ethnic issues" (Yao 2008a: 224). Yao (2008a: 224) thus explains these features, namely staying with rather conventional writing styles and the surge of ethnic consciousness among ethnic groups on the Internet:

> The reason why ethnic literature since the beginning of the "New Era" appears to be more staid (*chenwen* 沉稳) and serious [than Han literature] does not lie in the ethical quality of ethnic groups (*daode zuxing* 道德族性) [that is, "staid 'ethnic characters' with firm beliefs" (*you xinyang de minzu pinge* 有信仰的沉稳的"民族品格")] as Yao explains earlier]; but, rather, it is because of the cultural position that ethnic groups occupy in relation to the Han people – to be more specific, the peripheral cultural position to which ethnic groups are assigned in the cultural discourse of China.

Yao's (2014: 3) views on Chinese ethnic Internet literature are developed from his theoretical framework of "Three-Stage-Development" of ethnic literature in the PRC, that is, a chronological progression from socialist ethnic literature, to ethnic literature with intense ethnic consciousness, and lastly to postcolonial subaltern literature. The current rise of strong ethnic consciousness in ethnic online writings, in this paradigm, is a result of the growing irrelevance of the socialist mechanism of ethnic literary writings, and the increasing impact of the global postcolonial discourse on Chinese ethnic writings.[1]

And this surge of ethnic consciousness among ethnic groups also coincided with the rapidly growing popularity of the Internet in China and was facilitated by the spread of new digital technologies. As Yao (2008a: 225, emphasis added) explains,

> ethnic literary writings entered into the world of the Internet with such an intense sense of *homogenous* (*tongzhi xing de* 同质性的) "ethnic identification" that *naturally* they did not face the literary disintegration that their Han counterparts had experienced. What the popularization of Internet technologies brought to ethnic literatures and cultures was precisely opportunities for more convenient, freer, and more rapid expressions of ethnic sentiments and demands, instead of chances for a subversion of existing ethnic literary authorities and cultural traditions.

It may be true, to some extent, that many ethnic literary and cultural writings on the Internet, particularly those censored and sanctified by the authorities, are rather conventional in the way in which they pursue their "ethnic characters." Yet, this argument, which is representative of many scholars of ethnic studies in China, demonstrates some inherent contradictions. It seems on the one hand to reaffirm the unique characteristics of ethnic literature and cultures online, granting them some self-sufficiently distinctive values other than their Han counterparts; but on the other hand, it virtually denigrates them into a status of an essentialistic object that possesses some "homogeneous" characters and is "naturally" different (from the subject of gaze). In other words, these ethnic cultures, of which fifty-five are recognized as distinct and unique in the official discourse, are not regarded as differentiable online in terms of their pursuits of ethnic identity. As Leibold (2010: 542) summarizes, "Han is often described as an 'empty,' 'invisible' or 'unmarked' signifier, a seemingly 'residual category' that marks all those who are not one of the feminized, exotic/erotic and oppressed ethnic minorities."

This understanding of online ethnic literatures and cultures only reminds us of Rey Chow's discussion about the irony, or uncanniness, of ethnic minorities' assertion of their ethnic identities. In her book *The Protestant Ethic and the Spirit of Capitalism*, Chow finds that the ethnic subject is often under the pressure from the hegemonic culture to explore and perform its "authentic" ethnic culture, and this process inevitably evokes a stereotyped ethnicity from individuals. The coercive social system in effect interpellates ethnic individuals into subject positions and these individuals thus *become* ethnic. Chow (2002: 115) calls these performances of ethnicity "coercive mimeticism":

> When minority individuals think that, by referring to themselves, they are liberating themselves from the powers that subordinate them, they may actually be allowing such powers to work in the most intimate fashion from within their hearts and souls, in a kind of voluntary surrender that is, in the end, fully

complicit with the guilty verdict that has been declared on them socially long before they speak.

This coercive mimeticism, in the final analysis, only strengthens the hegemony of the dominant culture, while ethnic cultures, as a marked other, are objectified and continue to be urged to perform their ethnic "authenticity."

Further, as ethnic online literature and cultures are deemed as characterized – differently from their Han counterparts – by a surge of ethnic consciousness and a single-minded pursuit of ethnic identities, they are thus in effect conceived as, in Lo's (2016: 355) words, "synonymous with untimeliness, non-synchronicity, or non-contemporaneity," and thus deprived of "an agency of time." In other words, ethnic online literature and cultures are believed to be so overwhelmed by the overriding theme of representing ethnic identities that they continue to be seen as objects demonstrating somewhat *timeless* ethnic characters, rather than being viewed as performative constructions shaped by specific social and historical conjunctions.

In this view, the Internet contributes little to promoting thematic or formal experimentations for ethnic online literary and cultural works, in contrast to its flexibility for ethnic groups' Han counterparts. The Internet, then, unlike what it is to Han online literature and culture, is largely *external* to ethnic ones. For example, *The Journal of Selected Poetry* (*Shi xuankan* 诗选刊), an important poetry journal, published in a special column in its second issue of 2009 poems collected from the literary forums and personal blogs on the well-known Mandarin-language Tibetan Culture website "The Culture of Tibetans" (*Zangren wenhua wang* 藏人文化网). As the Tibetan poet Gangcan Gsomsdong (Gangjie Suomudong 刚杰·索木东 [a.k.a. Lai Xinhua 来鑫华] 2009), also the editor of the literary channel of "The Culture of Tibetans," writes in the introduction to the special column in *The Journal of Selected Poetry*, the selection was made following three criteria: new literary rigor (*xinrui* 新锐), folk tradition (*minjian* 民间), and the Internet. Yet, if we put aside the fact that they were first published on the Internet, these poems, in terms of their subject matters, styles, techniques, and aesthetic effects, are not very different from their print counterparts. The fact that they were put into the conventional print form from their original online form without experiencing any drastic transformation shows the affinity between the two categories.

This is why Yao (2008a: 223) claims that "the so-called Internet literature only exists in the cultural sphere of the Han ethnicity in contemporary China; in the cultural sphere of minority ethnicities, there is only 'literature on the Internet' (*wangshang wenxue* 网上文学) but not 'Internet literature' (*wangluo wenxue* 网络文学)." That is to say, in Yao's view, online writings by ethnic groups are no more than an act of simple migration of writings done in traditional media to the new medium of the Internet, a medium that is, however, essentially the same, for ethnic groups, with the former in terms of mediality.

It is debatable as to what extent this claim is true, but it nevertheless reveals an alleged non-synchronicity between ethnic and Han literature and cultures online. This non-synchronicity, further, translates into an understanding, unwarranted yet quite widely accepted, that ethnic literature and cultures online are also out of sync with the postsocialist condition by which Han online culture is tremendously, if not structurally, shaped. Ethnic literature and cultures online, thus, tend to be singly read within the conventional paradigm of resistance and subversion, whereas many varied cultural expressions, unfortunately, remain less noticed. In fact, as Lo (2016: 355) saliently remarks, "from a different angle, China's ethnicity issue designates a multiplicity of temporalities, of which some are repetitions of the past, while others produce fissures, fractures or wrinkles in the era of homogeneous totality." Indeed, these multiple temporalities are at times presented as synchronic with the dominant Han (post)modern, postsocialist temporalities (though the latter itself is also more a mix of multiple temporalities than a "homogeneous totality"), while at other times remain in tension with and offer alternatives to Han temporalities. They demonstrate a plural and more complex scenario that requires further critical scrutiny.

Woeser, ethnic Internet literature, and mediated ethnicity

Ethnic Internet literature and spectrum of ethnic self-expressions

Woeser is perhaps one of the first ethnic writers to take advantage of the Internet in an exploration of alternative ways of composing and disseminating her writings. Although her migration to the new medium of the Internet may seem forced – she was barred from publishing in traditional media in China after her collection of essays *Notes on Tibet* (*Xizang biji* 西藏笔记) was banned in 2003, on the basis of having allegedly touched upon politically sensitive issues (Wang 2004) – her online writings speak, in an intriguing fashion, more than her previous cultural activities conducted in traditional media, to the complexity of the politics involved in her expressions of her ethnic identity.

An investigation of Woeser's online literary writings, arguably, should involve studies of at least three related areas, namely ethnic literatures in China, Internet literature, and ethnicity on the Internet. For ethnic literatures in China, as we explained above, scholarship has been quite active since the founding of the PRC mainly because of ethnic literatures' political and cultural importance, admittedly, for Han-orchestrated nation-building. "Ethnic literatures" (*minzu wenxue* 民族文学), it is agreed, has been such a loaded term in Chinese literary discourse, particularly in the socialist period, that it has gained the status of a special literary genre and has been constantly paid special attention to, largely for the sake of safeguarding its ideological salience in literary and political institutions. However, with the fading of the socialist literary institution in the postsocialist period, which is further precipitated by the introduction of new digital technologies and the new virtual space of the Internet, ethnic literatures was faced with inevitable changes.

The changes that the Internet has brought to Chinese literature in general have also been a widely discussed subject, as we have examined in the Introduction and Chapter 2.[2] Ethnic literatures on the Internet, as many critics see it, continue to remain marginal, not only in the sense that they do not figure largely in terms of their popularity or sociocultural impact, but also because there seems to be an apparent lack in any "organic" interaction between the Internet and ethnic literatures. As a result, ethnic writings online are deemed to be still plagued by their inveterate obsession with ethnic identity, typifying conventional themes and forms and remaining immunized from the postsocialist condition.

However, a brief survey of ethnic literatures online shows that online writings by ethnic groups present a much more interesting scene than is commonly believed. There is a spectrum of ways in which ethnic groups in China engage in online literary and cultural activities with regard to expressing ethnic identity. At one end, some do not touch on issues regarding ethnicity at all, while at the other end, some grapple head-on with hegemonic repression and ubiquitous ethnification. For those who show a scanty sense of ethnicity in their writings, such as Zahi Ciugene (扎西次仁), Liu Wei (刘炜), and Lan Xixi (兰喜喜), their cases raise a critical question: what constitutes ethnic literature in China?[3] If writers such as Pu Songling (1640–1715), Lao She (1899–1966), or Shen Congwen (1902–1988) are seldom regarded as ethnic writers in spite of their ethnic identities, because their works are deemed more as representations of Chinese literature in general than ethnic literatures (Yao 2014), should those contemporary online writers be considered ethnic writers? Perhaps an apparent answer is no. But when these writers are labeled as "ethnic writers," either by popular media for the sake of promoting and reaping more surplus value guaranteed by their imagined exoticness, or by academics for the purpose of foregrounding their otherness, ethnic identity, once again, falls into the unfortunate relationship of objectification, only this time the objectification is caused primarily by commercialization. This situation reminds us of Stevan Harrell's (1998, 2000: 270–82) observation, in a different context, of the ways in which the power of the postsocialist market economy dislodges, restructures, and reinforces the official definition and classification of ethnicity.

If these online writers represent what we would call a "de-ethnification" stance at one end of the spectrum of ethnic online cultural expressions, at the other end we see writers who have strong ethnic opinions and are firm in vocalizing ethnic consciousness. Among them the Tibetan woman writer Woeser may be one of the most well-known figures; her case presents an interesting case of representing ethnicity on the Chinese Internet.

New ecology of Internet writing

Many critics have noticed Woeser's hybrid ethnic identity and questioned, on this basis, her unyielding assertion of her Tibetan-ness. Indeed, Woeser is technically one-fourth Han and three-fourths Tibetan; yet her mixed blood is no excuse for a reinstatement of bio-determinism in regard to ethnic identification.[4] Intriguingly, perhaps it is precisely because of her mixed blood, along with her mixed education, that she feels more attached to her "roots" in Tibet, a point we will elaborate on below.

Woeser's upbringing is equally interesting. Although she was born in Lhasa in a Tibetan family, her hometown in Kham in Sichuan Province is much closer to

Han culture than to Tibetan culture. Moreover, her parents' careers in the military and local government offered her further exposure to (official-sanctioned) Han culture. Later, she received her college education in Chinese literature in Chengdu, the capital of Sichuan Province, and after graduation assumed the post of an editor of the Chinese-language literary journal, *Tibetan Literature*, the official provincial-level literary journal within the national literary institution established during the socialist period (Shao 2003: 22–6).

Her extensive exposure to Han culture, however, seems to have only intensified her attachment to Tibetan culture. She decided to learn the Tibetan language and converted to Tibetan Buddhism. Woeser became an unremitting promoter of indigenous Tibetan culture and criticized the destruction of Tibetan culture by the Chinese government's colonial policy. Her criticisms led to the banning of her works throughout China, as well as her house arrests.[5] Woeser's efforts to pursue a form of Tibetan "pureness" have led to her becoming a cultural symbol and one of the most vociferous voices of Tibet today. Some even argue that she has become a "kidnapped national/ethnic hero" of Tibet – which is to say, due to her fame, she has felt pressured to act and perform the role of representing genuine Tibetan culture (Yao 2005). Not surprisingly, Woeser has firmly refuted such a claim.[6] However, burdened with this hybrid identity, Woeser's fervent and almost pious pursuit of genuine Tibetan roots, which has ironically always and already been a construction overdetermined, is essentially paradoxical.

Indeed, in this globalizing, postsocialist condition in China, perhaps all ethnic literatures, as Dayton (2006: 33–4) rightly points out, "must be assessed for their ties to the native/local, the national culture, and also the global because by speaking multi-vocally (and inter-vocally) they simultaneously (and reflexively) bridge between all of these levels." This claim, in a way, echoes the observation, as a response to the charge that ethnic literature in Mandarin has been "contaminated" by the Han and Western literatures, that ethnic literature "can only be established in the dynamic interactions among a variety of discourses, such as the so-called Hanification and Europeanization" (Zhang 1998: 37).

Dayton's remark may be particularly true for ethnic literatures in Mandarin, the subject of his study, because ethnic writings conducted in Mandarin Chinese, paradoxical as it may seem, prove to be a dynamic site where ethnic identities are most vigorously refashioned by forces at various levels, be they local, national, or global. In the specific case of Woeser, Dayton (2006: 39–58) finds in her writing a sense of "conflicted hybridity," which struggles to balance the two poles of Han and Tibetan cultures. Her work shakes the linguistic, and thus ideological, stability of Mandarin, negotiating for a new identity of Tibet "intricately tied to China" and "caught in the middle of many forces."

What makes Woeser's case more interesting in the context of our discussion, however, is the way in which her conflicted practices and performances of ethnic hybridity are further complicated by the introduction of the Internet. As the Chinese government imposed a ban on her writing throughout mainland China in 2003, Woeser mostly sought to publish her books in Taiwan and overseas; with the growing popularity of the Internet since the late 1990s in China, she also actively explored the opportunities provided by this new technology. Her exploration of online space proved to be fruitful in the following aspects.

First, cyberspace exposes her works to wider audiences across national borders. Although her blogs, where she published most of her online works, were censored and remain so today in mainland China, netizens with some knowledge of proxy servers or VPNs (virtual private networks) are able to circumvent the Great Firewall, the main instrument initiated by the Chinese government to achieve Internet censorship in mainland China, and access her works.[7] Moreover, Woeser's online works are able to reach out to larger international readership, owing much to the help of supporters in different parts of the world. Back in 2004, when her long and politically charged poem "Secrets of Tibet" (*Xizang de mimi* 西藏的秘密) was published online (Woeser 2008), it was immediately translated into English by the supporters of the Free Tibet movement (Dayton 2006: 40). Today, pieces from her current blog, "Invisible Tibet" (*Kanbujian de Xizang* 看不见的西藏), are constantly being translated into several languages. People can find on "Invisible Tibet" links to translations of her works into English, French, Japanese, and Polish. In addition, Woeser has been very active in promoting her works on her Facebook and Twitter accounts, both of which are popular, with 10,600 and 99,200 followers respectively as of August 2016.[8] Although both Facebook and Twitter, as well as her blogs, are blocked in mainland China, and she, along with her husband Wang Lixiong (himself a well-known and prolific dissident writer), have been monitored over the past decade and are sometimes placed under house arrest in mainland China, she is still able to frequently write and publish on these accounts and keep close connections to supporters both in China and abroad. This speaks to Woeser's skills in taking advantage of new digital technologies and her ready adaptation to new forms of literary and cultural production, publication, promotion, and circulation in the age of the Internet.

Further, the Internet also provides Woeser with an opportunity to publish different types of works on the same site. In addition to conventional publications, Woeser actively (re)publishes a variety of her works, including poetry, prose, memoirs, commentaries, travel logs, old pictures, and miscellaneous writings on her blogs. Apparently, without many constraints, her online publications enjoy comparative freedom in many aspects – they are not censored in the way they are by Party-state-controlled presses; they are mostly not restricted by spatial or temporal factors in publication; and they are not too much confined by stylistic consistency either, although it is easy to tag them and group them into different categories. Such freedom in technical terms, in a way, may have exerted some influence on the subjects and styles of her writings. For instance, caring less about the state censorship and more about contemporary incidents related to Tibetan culture and politics, which are accessible and can spread almost immediately online, in recent years Woeser has written more social and cultural commentaries and critiques, and her style has become more critical and satirical.

In addition, the interactive feature of online writing, as we have discussed before, also provides Woeser with opportunities to connect with her readers. However, unlike the case of, for instance, Wen Huajian's microblog novel, *Love in the Age of Microblogging*, which is specifically characterized by its high degree of author–reader interaction and readers' reactions shaping the author's composition, Woeser's online writings, particularly her more recent works for reasons that are unbeknownst to us, do not present as much a degree of interaction as Wen's writings do. For example, her early poem "Secrets of Tibet," which was written in 2004 and reposted on her former blogsite "Map of Burgundy Red" (*Jianghongse de ditu* 绛红色的地图) in 2008, has thus far drawn thirty-one comments posted below the poem (Woeser 2008). This number, which is rather disappointing given the fame and popularity of the author, is about or slightly above the average number of response posts her works have received from readers. Moreover, besides this by far lower number of responses from readers than that in Wen's case, Woeser's responses to her readers are rare in most cases, according to our observations. As presented in her blog posts, Woeser provides hardly any responses to her readers' posts and makes no obvious efforts to incorporate her readers' comments into her writings or revisions. This is indeed very different from the case of Wen's microblog novel. Posts in Woeser's current blogsite, "Invisible Tibet" (*Kanbujian de Xizang* 看不见的西藏), surprisingly receive almost no comments from her readers, although statistics on the site show that, as of August 2016, the site has received almost 5.5 million views. Perhaps it is fair to say that, although the Internet has provided interactive opportunities for Woeser to explore the further possibilities of online writing, this feature has not yet been taken full advantage of by the author and does not figure largely in her current writings.[9]

Lastly, Woeser's online writings exhibit a certain degree of dexterity in her exploitation of multimediality, particularly the visuality of the Internet. Although she does not do literary experimentation, as some writers do (Hockx 2015), with the very mediality of the Internet in composing her works online, her employment of multimedia still provides an interesting case of ethnic expression on the Internet.[10] Take the poem "Flying" (*Fei ya fei* 飞呀飞), for example. This poem was written in 2006 and posted on her blog "Map of Burgundy Red" in 2007. It compares wisdom and bravery to the two wings of a bird. Achieving the balance of these two qualities, the bird is able to fly above the Triloka, the three realms in Buddhism where humans suffer. This is typical of Woeser's meditative poems, which record her spiritual pursuit in Buddhism. Yet what makes this poem most interesting is that the poet attached below the poem a painting by the America-based exile Tibetan painter Losang Gyatso, and this abstract painting, which depicts a warrior accompanied by six flying birds and standing astride a horse advancing forward, visualizes and metaphorizes the poem (see Figure 4.1). In addition, a reader named Anjun posted in the comment area his (or her) poem titled "Fly, My Songs" (*Feixiang ba, wo de ge* 飞翔吧，我的歌) as a response to Woeser's work. Anjun's poem, which rhapsodizes the enlightening power of poetry, forms an interesting dialogue with Woeser's poem.

In another poem, titled "The White of the Snow Region" (*Xueyu de bai* 雪域的白), written on a flight from Shangri La to Lhasa in 2005 and posted online in 2007, Woeser compares the snowy mountains in Tibet to white flower buds and

Figure 4.1 Losang Gyatso, "The Hornblower 3"
Courtesy of the painter

white fire and laments the disappearance of the sacred whiteness where buddhas used to reside. Another meditative poem, this one is also accompanied by a painting called "Disney Plus," painted by the exile Tibetan painter Gonkar Gyatso, that Woeser had found online. While the poem itself is rather conventional in terms of poetic expression and technique, the painting is quite provocative. In the center is an empty silhouette of a sitting Buddha, which is foregrounded by numerous tiny figures – some identifiable but some not – including Spider-Man, the Little Mermaid, Winnie the Pooh, and so on. Most noticeable among these figures is a much larger head of the Atom Boy at the very bottom of the picture, who seems a little angry. All of these are set against the background that resembles a piece of traditional Chinese draft paper, with most of the square letterboxes filled in with indistinguishable Chinese characters.

This painting intriguingly enriches the poem by intensifying the tension between the meditativeness of the poem and the apparent grotesqueness of the painting. Yet, the loss in spiritual purity, which the poet painfully expresses in the poem but does not specify the causes of her pain, is poignantly concretized in the painting. The painting in this context seems to suggest that the disappearance of much treasured spiritualism is inevitable in the contemporary world as the result of assaults from various forces, including Chinese cultural colonialism and entertainment culture from Japan and the West in this age of post-industrial globalization.

In addition, the quite active interactions in the comment area between Woeser and her readers, a phenomenon less frequently seen in later days, also help construct the meaning of not only the poem and the painting, but also the entire post as a whole. The readers in their communications exchange their knowledge about the painting and the painter, inquire about and offer explanations to the meanings of different elements in the painting and the poem, and provide relevant, or not so relevant, information about Tibetan culture. In a way, each element in this case – the poem, the painting, and the comments – are in a dynamic relationship with one another and form an integral part of the work. This case exemplifies a literary practice that is unique to the Internet ecology.

Granting these new possibilities on the Internet, do Woeser's online writings make her cultural expressions of ethnicity more acute and impactful? Perhaps they do at times, as Yao (2008a) argues. But the tremendously diversified and diversifying medium of the Internet, upon which such cultural expressions are based, renders any claim of essentialist ethnicity problematic. Woeser's exploitation of the mediality of the Internet, although more dynamic in some aspects than others, belies the reductionist dichotomy along the ethnic lines between Han netizens, who are said to have proactively experimented with the Internet as a new medium, and ethnic netizens, who are deemed to have been thus far only conservatively stuck with conventional practices online (Yao 2008a).

If Woeser's identity as a representative of an allegedly quintessential Tibetan culture, or simply as a Tibetan, is in fact constructed by a variety of factors, some even "conflicted," in a series of events, aren't Woeser's online writings, too, no more than cultural performances, performances that are inevitably polyphonic, heteroglossic, metamorphic and sometimes even contradictory in acting out her (ethnic) identity online, as well as offline? These performances by which ethnicity is mediated, we should be aware, are inevitably mediated by the Internet. Perhaps this is a more constructive perspective, we believe, with which to view Woeser's online writings.

Performing ethnicity online: synchronic timelessness, creolization

If we argue that Woeser performs her ethnicity through her writings on the Internet, performing ethnicity in physical terms, the focus of our investigation in this part, figures even larger on the Chinese Internet. In fact, being skilled at performing ethnic songs and dances has been deemed one of the most important features inscribed in the Chinese imagination of ethnic minorities since the founding of the People's Republic. Through institutionalized production and promotion of literary and artistic works, particularly the visually effective medium of film, such as *Five Golden Flowers* (*Wu duo jinhua* 五朵金花, dir. Wang Jiayi, 1959), *The Third Sister Liu* (*Liu sanjie* 刘三姐, dir. Su Li, 1960), and *Ashima* (*Ashima* 阿诗玛, dir. Liu Qiong, 1964), this stereotype has been constantly strengthened and has played a significant role in the construction of a modern, multiethnic socialist nation-state.

This stereotype did not fade away from popular discourse with the end of the socialist period. The postsocialist era that ensued witnessed continued strengthening of this stereotypical imagination, although in different and disparate forms. While the Party-state continues to manipulate the means of production that ideologically showcase the multiethnic cultural mosaic, the increasingly commercialized popular culture also capitalizes on ethnic exoticness for entertainment and consumption, and the trope that ethnic groups "are good at singing and dancing" readily feeds this consumerist desire. Popular entertainment TV programs at national and local levels usually demonstrate their "political awareness and correctness" and commercial ingenuity simultaneously by including performers of various ethnicities and featuring joyous and festive ethnic performances. One good example is the "Glorious Blossoming" (*Guangrong zhanfang* 光荣绽放) Concert of Ten Ethnic Young Singers organized by China Central TV in 2012. As an installment of the "Glorious Blossoming" concert series, this concert featured ten of the most popular contemporary young ethnic singers, and had them sing both their commercially successful songs and mainstream ones that propagated ethnic harmony and prosperity.

With the introduction of the Internet, ethnic performances, while continuing to play to this stereotype, have been further diversified and have presented some new features. Recent studies of ethnicity and the Internet in the West have shown that, rather than decreasing or eliminating racial and ethnic differences in the virtual world as some optimists anticipate, the Internet, on the contrary, has complicated related interactions. Although a user's real racial and ethnic identity, as well as gender, age, and so on, can be hidden in this virtual space, and he or she may "randomly" adopt an identity for display, the ways in which he or she constructs his or her virtual identity, and the expression and manifestation of race and ethnicity in the virtual world are no less ideological than those in the real world. In light of this, Lisa Nakamura (2002: 3) coins the term "cybertype"

> to describe the distinctive ways that the Internet propagates, disseminates, and commodifies images of race and racism. The study of racial cybertypes

brings together the cultural layer and the computer layer; that is to say, cyber-typing is the process by which computer/human interfaces, the dynamics and economics of access, the means by which users are able to express themselves online interacts with the "cultural layer" or ideologies regarding race that they bring with them to cyberspace.

Obviously, Nakamura (2002: 5) has "stereotype" in mind when she theorizes its counterpart "cybertype," as she continues to write that "machines that offer identity prostheses to redress the burden of physical 'handicaps' such as age, gender, and race produce cybertypes that look remarkably like racial and gender stereotypes." In other words, racial and ethnic stereotypes in the real world continue to manifest themselves, albeit in different fashion, in the virtual space of the Internet.

Admittedly, the social and cultural conditions under which critics examine the issues of both race and ethnicity and of the Internet are quite different from those in China. Since race and ethnicity carry rather different referential meanings in China than in the West, and the Internet has quite a different ecology in China due to a variety of factors, the issue of ethnicity on the Internet in China should, therefore, be contextualized and historicized.

Yet, studies of ethnicity and the Internet in the West are still instructive to our understanding of this emerging subject in China because, among other things, offline ethnic stereotypes continue to be refashioned into cybertypes online in both China and the West. Construction of ethnicity on the Internet, for both, is admittedly still tightly intertwined with ethnic conditions in reality, and, as a result, ethnic issues in both of these virtual and real spaces should continue to be rigorously examined on ideological terms. In what follows, we will examine two such performances on the Internet: wedding photos of a Tibetan couple and a flash mob performance at Tibet University.

Wedding photos as a performance: exhibiting a simulacrum ethnicity

When Gerong Phuntsok, a thirty-one-year-old Tibetan groom-to-be, posted his wedding photos on social media on the evening of April 5, 2015, he perhaps never imagined that they would bring to him such immediate and enormous popularity. In under four hours of publication, these photos had attracted over 100,000 hits; they were later more widely disseminated on webpages, messaging apps, and other social media in China; and by the third day, they were being circulated by 80 percent of WeChat users. The young couple, Phuntsok and his fiancée Dawa Drolma, a twenty-seven-year-old Tibetan woman, were pronounced the "most blessed bride and groom in the country" by Xinhua, the official news agency of the Party-state, which further reported and populated their traditional/ethnic wedding ceremony held in their native town in Sichuan Province a week later (Wang 2015a, 2015b).

Phuntsok and Drolma's wedding photos, which are acclaimed by Chinese netizens for their "different" and "alternative" flavor (*linglei* 另类), mainly consist of two contrasting kinds: one showing them as young urbanites wearing trendy

attire (pinstripe suits, skirts, oversize sunglasses, wide-brimmed hats) and leading a "modern" life (drinking Starbucks coffee and Western wine, listening to
rock music, driving a Lamborghini sports car, flying a helicopter); the other presenting them as a traditional Tibetan couple wearing "ethnic"/"national" Tibetan
robes, shearling jackets, prayer beads and braids, performing traditional chores
(spinning wool in a yurt, attending yaks, serving butter tea, fetching water with
old-style utensils), and conducting traditional rituals (paying prolonged devotion in the Potala Palace and prostrating themselves in front of the Jokhang
Temple).

Although what immediately attracted Chinese netizens' attention in those photos and made them so popular among them to begin with, as netizens' online
responses show, was largely the attractiveness (what netizens would call in
a coined term *gao yanzhi* [高颜值], or "of high value in terms of the index of
appearance") of the photogenic couple, it is in fact the intriguing play with ethnicity, as many critics point out, that intersects with the active intervention of the
Internet, we argue, that makes these photos a real cultural incident. This incident
exemplifies the politics not only in the entrenched stereotypes in Chinese views of
ethnic cultures in the age of the Internet, but also in ethnic groups' mediated and
ideologized self-exhibition shaped by the postsocialist condition.

First of all, as a form of self-exhibition, Phuntsok and Drolma's photos signify
an ethnicity that is performative in nature and ritualized by a media-saturated and
consumerism-oriented society. Photography is not so much a reflection of reality
as the capturing of a performance. This is not only because the realism claim of
photography has already been challenged – a challenge that becomes particularly
acute in the age of digital technologies, when numerous, easily accessible technologies, such as Adobe Photoshop, make photo editing not only possible but
also sometimes necessary. It is also because, not unlike other media, photographs
are only "pieces" of the world, "miniatures of reality that anyone can make or
acquire," and interpretations of the world that imply "aggression," as Susan Sontag remarks (1977: 4 and 7).

Wedding photos, in particular, are an even more intriguing form of performance. Almost an indispensable part of the matrimony of a Chinese middle-class
couple, wedding photos, with their use of a "cornucopia of performative props"
and predesigned poses, provide couples with the "last refuge of adult fantasy"
(Fan 2015). For all of their acknowledged and imperative artificiality, wedding
photos are even farther away from a claim of recording reality, but are, instead, a
performance of the imaginary overdetermined by social, cultural, historical, and
political discourses.

In the case of Phuntsok and Drolma's wedding photos, the most important part
of the imaginary that the Tibetan couple perform is, arguably, a "modern ethnicity" that rests in a "seamless" merge of a modern and a traditional (read: ethnic)
way of life, or a temporary escape from the former and "return" to the latter. Echoing netizens' responses, Phuntsok said in an interview about the sudden popularity
of his wedding photos, "Maybe we represented thousands of young people from
ethnic minorities, who left their hometowns to pursue a 'modern life' but chose to

return to tradition after feeling a void in the heart." He continued to say, "I think we found an echo with other web users. As we fight for our dreams, some of us get lost. So we wanted to say with the photos: stick to your beliefs" (Wang 2015b; Wendling, Mallya, and Cavallaro 2015).

What we need to be aware of in this imaginary is a discursive exchange of the traditional and the ethnic. Netizens almost non-differentiatingly take Phuntsok and Drolma's photos as *both* ethnic and traditional. This interpretation, in a way reminiscent of the conventional rendering of ethnicity in the socialist discourse as a supplementary, yet indispensable, Other in the mosaic of a multiethnic nation-state, speaks to an inveterate ideology that imagines ethnic groups as a timeless entity. To be more specific, ethnicity under both socialist and postsocialist conditions is invariably perceived as a timeless, perhaps circular, identity that serves as a foil, against which a modern, that is, linear, development of Han is validated, although its timelessness is conceived of in a very different manner.

Further, Phuntsok and Drolma's *modern* images, intriguingly, further fuel the imagination of an ethnicity as *traditional*, as popular imaginations can be summarized thusly: modern as the couple is, they have a tradition that is *more traditional*, that is ethnic, to return to; these ethnic people can be as modern as us, but they are more "blessed" because they are ethnic! This paradox questions the discourse of Chinese modernity in regard to ethnicity in contemporary China, as it testifies to an ethnicity that is ethnic in imagination.

In fact, both Phuntsok and Drolma's ethnic identities have been questioned. Both of them were born, raised, and educated in environments that are more Han than ethnic. Phuntsok is from Kardze (Ganzi) Tibetan Autonomous Prefecture and Drolma is from Barkham (Ma'erkang) county in Ngaba (Aba) Tibetan and Qiang Autonomous Prefecture, both in Sichuan Province and areas with the highest level of penetration of Han Chinese culture. Phuntsok works in an advertising company in Chengdu, the capital of Sichuan, after graduating from Central Nationalities University in Beijing; Drolma ran an online store of artifacts and jewelry after finishing her study of music at Ngaba Normal College. Both of them are Tibetans but highly Hanified. As Phuntsok acknowledges, their native tongue is Mandarin, and their English is better than their Tibetan (Wang 2015b).[11] This fact not only tells of how assimilated the couple is to the Han Chinese culture, but also signifies a global condition in which the power of more hegemonic cultures are present.

Yet, Phuntsok and Drolma in this case are not only imagined as Tibetans with roots, although somehow distanced, in their "original" cultural area, but they in fact actively participate in supplying this imaginary through a form of self-exhibitionism. Woeser (2015) calls this self-exhibitionism a "self negation," a negation that

> turns them into passive objects in an increasingly mainstream and "civilized" world which has secularism as its focus. There is no true expression to be found here, nor any true self-acceptance or identity. Still less is there any sense of an authentic self or a modern Tibetan identity. It's grotesque, like a painting of a tiger based on a photo of a cat. Such images are of "otherized" Tibetans: a pale reflection of oneself in the eyes of others. They have little

new to offer, other than being the empty productions of the current culture among young Chinese people and among young Tibetans who imitate Han culture and its imitation of what looks like Western culture, but is actually Chinese.

Most importantly, these wedding photos going viral on the Internet is a product of postsocialist consumerism. Although Phuntsok claimed that putting their wedding photos on social media was only a personal act, Woeser (2015) suspected that there was an implicit commercial impetus behind the decision. According to Woeser's observation, the person (Phuntsok's friend) who took the pictures for the couple was a professional photographer working for the "Ms. Jin" Wedding Photo Studio, a chain studio with its branches across China. On the webpage of the studio's Lhasa branch, Woeser found wedding photos that looked very similar to the photos of Phuntsok and Drolma, most of them having the same backdrops and props of traditional/ethnic symbols, such as the Potala Palace, Jokhang Temple, prayer wheels, and yurts, and even similar attires and poses. Obviously, Phuntsok and Drolma's wedding photos are not works of art that are meant to represent their unique lifestyle, but instead are simply commodities that are mass-produced for convenient consumption. In other words, their photos are just an ethnic performance governed by the logic of commercialism, a logic that is discursively manipulative in its production and consumption, in this case, of ethnicity in the postsocialist market of China.

As it is remarked in a *New Yorker* report on this incident, the production and consumption of these photos on the Internet have, in fact, ideologically disguised many contradictions in regard to contemporary Tibetan society, particularly those contradictions rendered especially acute by the breakneck economic development in China, such as cultural attachment to rooted traditions made poignant by migration to big cities in China under the economic pressure, commercialization of spiritual and holy cities in the boom of escapist and Orientalist tourism, and so forth. What is most poignant is that on the same day when Phuntsok put the photos on social media, a forty-seven-year-old Tibetan nun set herself on fire as a protest against the Chinese government, the one hundred thirty-eighth case of self-immolation within the previous five years (Fan 2015). Yet, while the wedding photos became an online sensation, the death of the nun was not even heard by Chinese netizens, who were not allowed to know, and were not interested in knowing about (or understanding), such news of "negative energy." Ethnicity on the Internet in postsocialist China, arguably, is partly politically manipulated and largely commercially shaped. Phuntsok and Drolma's wedding photo incident, as the *New Yorker*'s report goes, "is an affect ritualized into performance, like the performances enacted every day in Chinese TV commercials and Internet promotions, and on highway billboards, where affluence is equated with influence and artifice earns cultural currency," and speaks of a China "where optics supersede sustained scrutiny" (Fan 2015).

Further still, Phuntsok and Drolma's wedding photos not only exemplify a mediated and commercialized ethnicity through what Barthes (1981) calls a "derealizing" effect and separation from self/identity, but also signify a society of simulacra that marks contemporary China. Indeed, these photos are not reflections of real life, yet what makes them even more discursive is, as Woeser (2015) finds, the fact that they are *double imitations*: "Chinese Tibet enthusiasts and supermodels dress up as Tibetans, then young Tibetans imitate the Chinese and the supermodels imitating them." The first imitation is an act of Han people's romanticization, that is othering, of Tibetan, and the second is Tibetan's self-othering presented intriguingly as an apparent "return" to their cultural roots, yet via the mediation, ironically, of Han imagination and imitation of Tibetan culture. "There is only one word for this: pseudery," Woeser (2015) continues to write.

These double imitations exemplify a postmodern condition of simulacra and further remind us of what Jean Baudrillard (2000) wrote about the relationship between photography and the industrial age:

> It is perhaps not a surprise that photography developed as a technological medium in the industrial age, when reality started to disappear. It is even perhaps the disappearance of reality that triggered this technical form. Reality found a way to mutate into an image. This puts into question our simplistic explanations about the birth of technology and the advent of the modern world. It is perhaps not technologies and media which have caused our now famous disappearance of reality. On the contrary, it is probable that all our technologies (fatal offsprings that they are) arise from the gradual extinction of reality.

If the technological advance exemplified in photography corresponds to the disappearance of reality in the industrial age, how does the digital age characterized by informational technologies transform reality today? In Baudrillard's (1994) view, reality does not only disappear, but it also implodes into simulacra. In the specific case of Phuntsok and Drolma's wedding photos, ethnicity as the most important signifier in this world of simulacra is not only performed and re-performed in multiple imitations and simulations, but also seems to be on the brink of losing its cling to a form of physicality, on which a performance of ethnicity, fortunately or unfortunately, used to be grounded. The couple's photos, obviously, were not taken on celluloid negatives to be printed on paper, but were instead digitally captured, stored, and processed in the form of magnetic bytes; when they were later put on the Internet, they were circulated and consumed further in the form of optical pixels. Physically still, the latter forms have nevertheless created a virtual condition in which a performance of ethnicity becomes convenient yet flippant, dynamic yet imaginary, multimedia yet mediated.

Finally, unlike conventional photos, which usually carry with them a "melancholic" (Sontag 1977) character and are generally regarded as objects "immobilized" (Barthes 1978), Phuntsok and Drolma's wedding photos going viral on the Internet, on the other hand, are massively joyous and highly mobilized, so much so that they become a sensational *event* among Chinese netizens. If "picture-taking

is an event in itself" rather than a random encounter between an object and a photographer as Sontag avers, circulation and consumption on the Internet of these
wedding photos, then, is no less an event either, an event that is both a result of
a significant, albeit virtual, encounter between an object and its consumers, and
a product of the specific conjuncture of the political, economic, historical, and
cultural conditions of this age of postsocialism and the Internet. The ethnicity
presented in this event, then, signifies the discursiveness of this age that is its
producer, with all its performances that are virtual, commercially-oriented, and
mediated, yet still stereotypical.

Flash mobbing a creolized ethnic identity

Around noon on March 16, 2015, without any prior notice, a female Tibetan singer
came to the center of a student canteen at the new campus branch of Tibet University, the most prestigious university in the Tibetan Autonomous Region, and
began to sing a melodic love song in Tibetan along with recorded accompaniment
to the students who happened to be having lunch there. After the first few seconds
of surprise and bafflement, diners began to realize what was going on; some then
went to join her and sang along, and many more came to surround her, waving
their hands to the rhythm. The entire canteen soon turned into a stage of excitement and exhilaration. This short, surprise performance ended immediately when
the singer finished the song. As the singer packed her minimal performance props,
people dispersed and went back to their normal schedules. The entire performance
was recorded and put on the Internet. In no time the clip became a sensational hit
on the Chinese Internet, and in a few days' time it had attracted tens of millions
of views (CCTV 2015). Penba Dekyi, the singer, was soon dug up by Chinese
netizens and became an overnight celebrity.

This is another case of Internet-driven cultural (self-)performance by ethnic
groups, and this performance is carried out, most prominently, in the unique form
of the flash mob, which arguably contributes most significantly to its sudden and
sensational popularity.[12] While ethnic performances, for disparate political and
commercial reasons, have been greatly diversified in representational forms in
contemporary China, and the flash mob, as a global fashion, was by then not
entirely new among Chinese urban youth, a combination of the two still turned
out to be somewhat eye-opening for Chinese netizens. What kind of ethnicity is
signified in this performance? And how does an appropriation of the form of flash
mob reshape the signification of ethnicity in this case?

Before tending to these questions, a brief examination of the current literature
on flash mobs will provide some background information and a context in which
we explore the issue of ethnicity performed in this form. Studies of flash mobs are
as new as the subject of the studies is young. Among the handful of existing studies, a few explore the performative aspects of the flash mob, with focuses on the
ways in which the flash mob reshapes time and space, particularly public spaces
(Gore 2010, Shawyer 2008, Wark 2011). Some others investigate the role that
new digital technologies of communication and information have played in flash

mob incidents (Nicholson 2005, Rheingold 2003, Schepers 2008). Informative as these studies are, overall these studies almost exclusively focus on the flash mob, though deemed as a global phenomenon, in the Western condition. How does this "global" form of the flash mob inform the local case of ethnic performance in China? Put in another way, how does a flash mob performance so young and fashionable signify a different representation of an ethnicity that is grounded on a rich tradition? We argue that the form of the flash mob does not alter the nature of ethnic performances, but it presents some new problematics in the reconfiguration of ethnic performances in postsocialist China.

First of all, by employing the form of the flash mob, Penba Dekyi's singing heightens its own performative nature in a refashioning of Tibetan ethnicity. Dekyi's performance, to follow Virág Molnár's (2014) categorization, is a mix of a performative, political, and commercial flash mob, as opposed to an autonomous or an interactive one. To be more specific, rather than an event in which people are called in by a non-authoritative organizer via new communicative technologies, gathering to carry out an activity with a more prankish than political or commercial intent, Dekyi's is evidently a performance orchestrated by a special authoritative organizer/leader (the Tibet TV Station), for the specific purposes of demonstrating a performance of art (singing a Cantonese pop song in Tibetan), making an explicit or implicit political statement (presenting to the world a harmonious ethnic community on par with the modern Han society), and promoting the commercial value of the performance (the Tibetan pop). As a later form of the flash mob, Dekyi's performance presents more a quality of orchestration and performativity than the spirit of spontaneity, democracy, and "anti-expression purism" that marked early flash mobs (Molnár's 2014: 49–50). This sense of spontaneity, democracy, and purity, in a way, is still much treasured by many practitioners and critics of the flash mob, who, seeing more expression-oriented flash mob events today, often bemoan that the "authentic" spirit of the flash mob has become passé, or even claim the demise of the form (Nicholson 2005). Dekyi's singing, like many of contemporary flash mob events, is obviously much removed from the flash mob's original pattern as a form of social interaction, but calls attention to its performative feature. This performative feature is not simply determined by the event's nature as a stage performance, but more importantly hinges on the performative way in which a new ethnicity is presented.

The new Tibetan ethnicity in Dekyi's singing is presented as a modern one, characterized not only by its pursuit, along with its Han counterpart, of a global commercial culture, but also by its effort to maintain its ethnic features. The song performed in this event is a Tibetan version of the well-known Cantopop song "Loving You," originally sung by one of the most successful Hong Kong rock bands, "Beyond," in the 1980s. This song is so popular in Hong Kong, Taiwan, mainland China, and other Chinese-language communities that it has been constantly performed. Yet, it is perhaps because Dekyi's remake of the song in Tibetan and her performance of the remake in the form of the flash mob are so refreshing that this performance became an immediate sensation on the Internet and attracted numerous fans in Lhasa, Beijing, Shanghai, Chengdu, Taipei, and diasporic communities.

Admittedly, this flash mob performance succeeds in creating a new ethnic image that is both traditional and modern as well as local and global. This image conforms to the dominant ideology of constructing a modern multiethnic Chinese nation-state – above all, the performance was part of the special program called "Moments of Youth Flash Mob Dance in Lhasa" designed by the Party-controlled Tibet TV Station (Cui 2015). Dekyi was recommended to the station as one of the performers. The orchestration and manipulation by the authorities guaranteed the unmistakable conveyance of the political message of building a modern ethnicity, which also fed into the popular imagination of a new Tibet in the age of globalization.

Yet, this new modern ethnicity is also problematic. If the flash mob, as Molnár (2014: 48) claims, has "sociability" as the more dominant underlying motivation, what kind of ethnic community, "just-in-the-time" and/or imagined, is formed in this event?[13] During the flash mob event, a special time and space was created in which "a heterogeneous public" was transformed, for that space of the song, into "a community with a shared focus" (Gore 2010: 128–9). However, Dekyi's singing had a much stronger and longer spillover effect when the video circulated on the Internet, contributing, in a way that is not unlike traditional media such as newspaper, radio, TV, and film, to the perception of an imagined community of a modern and global yet rooted Tibet. However, this imagined new ethnicity is ironically grounded on a Tibetan *remake* of a Cantonese song from the 1980s. That means that the new ethnicity is a result more of an act of imitation and repacking of the dominant culture than that of an assertion of its own culture. It also reaffirms, in the significant time lag between the dates of the song's original publication in Cantonese in the 1980s and its popularity in the form of a remake in Tibetan in the late 2010s, the hegemonic status of the Han culture. This hegemonic status of the Han culture may be further strengthened and internalized as Dekyi, seeing the popularity of her performance, produces more such remakes, with many other Tibetan singers following suit (Cui 2015). Further, the "new" ethnicity promoted in this flash mob event is essentially a *creole* identity, one that is "in a state of continuous cultural flux, ambivalence and pressure to make new decisions" (Kehoe 2015: 316). Drawing on Ulf Hannerz's and Thomas Hylland Eriksen's works on creolization, Tricia Kehoe analyzes four kinds of representations of ethnic identities in Tibet on the Internet, namely Pure, Hyphenated, Creole, and Depoliticized identities. Dekyi's flash mob performance, like many of other events,[14] falls into the category of Creole identity, as it incorporates into its representation a variety of other elements – linguistic, cultural, and formal. Yet, in Dekyi's flash mob performance cultural creolization largely aids in reaffirming the dominant ideology. Overall, the ethnicity constructed in Dekyi's singing is conventional, if not conservative, although performed in a fashionable form.

Finally, how does this fashionable form of the flash mob help Dekyi's performance achieve its impact, not only on the audience at the scene, but also on viewers online later? Georgiana Gore (2010: 130) observes that a flash mob event, during its implementation, marks out a special space and time, and by doing so reshapes people's perceptions:

> It territorialises anonymous spaces of public passage (streets, steps, halls and so on), which belong to no one, giving them new form, function and meaning, while deterritorialising staked out spaces, such as parks, gardens, galleries, shopping malls etc. Moreover, through its intrusion into individual and collective routines, it disrupts schedules and programmes, tearing into time frames, slowing down the speedy and speeding up the slow. Flash mobbing forces a cognitive shift, dislocating and intensifying experience.

Gore (2010: 130) compares the way in which a flash mob accomplishes the cognitive shift to a form of "soft terrorism" that uses "guerrilla tactics," and calls a flash mob "a kind of mnemonic system." A flash mob, in Gore's view, displays its "difference with the habitual," "create[s] a visual stir," "intrude[s] into or even disrupt[s] the quotidian," and therefore "creates a shift in focus." A typical flash mob performance, Dekyi's singing, it can be said, achieves its effect through this mechanism of "soft terrorism" – it surprises its audience by intruding into their normal schedule, bracketing their lunch time for the duration of the song, and reterritorializing the public space of the dining hall into a stage. By doing so, the performance succeeded in striking a unique impression on its audience.

Yet, it is the video of the performance going viral on the Internet that brought the performance national popularity and granted it a much bigger impact. The impact of the performance is evidenced, arguably, more by the extremely high viewing rate of its video clip circulating on the Internet than by the sensation that the performance per se aroused in a person. Admittedly, the employment of new media, especially visual and mobile technologies and the Internet, as a means of production and postproduction of a flash mob event increasingly became a norm in later forms of flash mobs, namely performative, political, and commercial flash mobs. While the use of these new media may have lessened the spirit of spontaneity and democracy that early flash mobs prided themselves on, as well as, some critics lament, their authenticity; yet new media have helped to lengthen the life of a flash mob, promoted it to a larger audience, and contributed to its broader and more lasting impact. In the case of Dekyi's singing, it is precisely because of the use of technologies of audio-visual production and the Internet that her flash mob performance is able to break through its temporal and spatial limit, and thus be viewed nationwide and at any time. Therefore, it may only seem reasonable to conclude that it is the special form of the flash mob, together with the help of new media, that renders Dekyi's performance an Internet phenomenon.

While it is true that these formal aspects play an important role, what should not be underestimated or overlooked, however, is that what in the end makes Dekyi's case unique is, arguably, its presentation, though conducted in an extraordinary fashion, of the special subject of ethnicity. For most Chinese netizens, a flash mob is perhaps not unusual in itself, but one that is carried out by an ethnic minority is. Also at play is a defamiliarization effect generated by the novel wedlock of ethnicity, the flash mob, and the Internet. For those who find Dekyi's flash mob performance peculiar, the pairing of ethnicity (which has always been imagined as being local, traditional, timeless, unchanged, rooted, essential, etc.) with the form of the flash mob and the Internet (which have been deemed as being global, modern, fashionable, cool, etc.) may seem odd. Thus, the defamiliarization effect augments the performance's unique impact. What is embedded in this defamiliarization effect, however, is no more than a rearticulation of the inveterate orientalist and auto-orientalist mindsets, which reaffirms the objectified and stereotypical image of ethnic groups in the imagination of Han netizens, and, voluntarily or involuntarily, feeds this image on the part of ethnic groups.

Overall, Dekyi's flash mob performance is another product of the prevailing consumerist capitalism, the postsocialist condition, and the age of the Internet that together shape contemporary China. The Internet provides new opportunities of presenting perhaps different kinds of ethnicities. Dekyi's singing appears to embody a new ethnicity that seemingly challenges traditional ethnic images. Yet, finely orchestrated by the authorities for the purpose of showcasing a new picture of contemporary ethnicity, Dekyi's performance gives a surprising, yet ultimately politically correct and commercially successful, portrait of a new Tibetan that exemplifies and strengthens dominant ideologies. This case reminds us of the way in which Kehoe (2015: 316) conceptualizes Zygmund Bauman's idea of liquid modernity in examining the "commodification of ethnicity," only that this commodification is implemented under the auspices and for the benefit of Chinese postsocialist politics.

Conclusion

Ethnic culture on the Chinese Internet, for all the tension, contention, and paradoxes involved in it, and for its nature as a node of many equally dynamic terrains, is a potent field of study. In this chapter we show, through specific case studies, the way in which the Internet has reshaped (or not so much) ethnic cultural expressions in the cyberspace in contemporary China. As an extremely rapidly developing technology, the Internet is increasingly changing almost every aspect of our world and society in a way that is hardly foreseen *in toto* by any one of us. On the other hand, however, ethnicity in China, for all its political, ideological, historical, social, and cultural undertakings, has constantly been imagined and constructed as something contrasting and complementing the dominant Han developmentalist modernity. The growing presence of the latter in the alternative space provided by the former, therefore, demonstrates a contentious, and sometimes uncanny, scene that cannot be conveniently defined, categorized, or dismissed.

In his studies of ethnicity and the Internet in China, Kwai-Cheung Lo proposes to take the Internet as a vehicle, instead of a technological determinant, through which to understand the society, in which ethnicity is defined. He (Lo 2016: 352) thus writes,

> Technology-determined understandings of how the Internet can change society are usually not very accurate since the Internet's impacts are always filtered through the structures and contexts of a particular society. . . . Perhaps, the Internet should not be simply treated as a transforming agent of society but more importantly as a channel for understanding the functioning of power and struggle in a given society.

The Internet, in Lo's view, is a new medium, literally and perhaps more than literally – literally because on this very medium of the Internet ethnicity finds, employs, and creates new means and forms of cultural expression; and more than literally because through studies of ethnicity on the Internet one may attain a new perspective on politics of the society at stake. In other words, these studies of ethnicity mediate a constructive interrogation of sociality. Following this vein, ethnicity is also a special form of new media, maybe on par with the Internet, through which, in Lo's case, we examine Chineseness in particular, and the postsocialist condition in China at large.

Indeed, ethnicity on the Internet is woven quite closely into the larger fabric of Chinese society, of which it is in turn a unique form of embodiment. The dominant ideology of contemporary China that shapes this embodiment is, argued here, the much contested postsocialism. Under this postsocialist condition, socialist ideology of class, which once effectively restructured traditional ethnic relations rooted in different ethnic cultures into one of multiethnic national unity based predominantly on designated class belongings, no longer works; and with this growing irrelevance of the ideology of class, the promise of economic co-prosperity emerged to replace the former and thus fill in the void in official ideology, in the hope of building a new ethnic harmony based on an auspicious economic prospect. Yet, while the residual socialist ideology continues to function to disparate degrees, radical commercialization in Chinese society, which is decidedly marked by the embedded developmentalist philosophy, has created more economic, and consequently social, inequality between ethnic groups and Han, than a promised co-prosperity and equality. Thus, we see marginalization and victimization narratives, interestingly, vented by both ethnic groups and Han (Leibold 2010: 541, Lo 2016, 361). Under this condition, while commercial desire is prevalent in remodeling ethnic discourses, political and cultural reassertions of ethnic identities on the part of ethnic groups, and incorporation of them into the dominant discourse of flattened identities, processes that are carried out implicitly or explicitly, are constantly under way.

The Internet, as Lo avers, does not determine the process of social restructuring described above, but instead works as a channel, or prism sometimes, through which postsocialist China is intriguingly embodied. Presence of ethnicity on the Internet, it can be seen, constitutes a spectrum of political intervention, in which one may find different degrees of agency in ethnic identity construction. At one end, we find practices informed by authority-enforced assimilationist policy, which is further conspired by officially endorsed consumerist policy. Ethnicity presented under these policies, as a result, show a cyber tourist style of hyper-authenticity, which is determined by an orientalist and auto-orientalist mindset that implies little agency. Wai-Yip Ho's (2010: 67) observation of the Chinese Internet in his study of Islamism on the Chinese cyberspace may reflect this condition. Thus he writes,

> By eschewing any controversial or extreme topics that might hurt national feeling, split ethnic solidarity or upset social stability in the eyes of the PRC government, scholars found that the state's "strike hard" regulation has already helped force China's cyberspace into becoming apolitical and further fragmented, the internet further segmented society and internet users are generally encouraged to become atomized consumers.

At the other end, however, we find affirmative, and sometimes radical, assertions of ethnic identity, or even claims of pursuit, to some extent, of national independence. Woeser's online writing investigated above may serve as a good, though largely suppressed, example of this end. Between these two extremes, ethnic cultures present a colorful and contentious scene, in which disparate degrees of agency are manifested.[15]

This study of ethnic cultural expressions on the Internet does not mean to give a comprehensive examination of the field, but instead focuses on the cultural politics in the dynamic encounter of ethnicity and the Internet, each a culturally rich and politically loaded subject in its own right, at the historical moment of the rise of postsocialism in China. The Internet as an apparently entirely new medium has created a virtual space, which on the one hand seems to have provided ethnic groups with new possibilities and means to refashion their ethnic identities within the larger multiethnic discourse in China. On the other hand, however, their refashioning in this cyberspace, which signals efforts to reconstruct ethnicity under the new condition of postsocialist China, not unlike other such efforts in previous decades, is ultimately determined by and embodies this condition, a condition that the Internet is shaped by and embodies as well. If, as Leibold (2010: 559) shows, the hegemonic Han ethnic label and its institutionalization, which are also under reconstruction on the Internet in cases such as Han supremacist events, may serve as a "latent boundary-spanner" that unsettles dominant ethnic assumptions and discourses, perhaps it is also more constructive to view ethnic cultural expressions on the Internet in this vein, in the hope that their redefinition of ethnic identities may in one way or another destabilize and reorient people's stereotypical imagination of ethnicity in China.

Notes

1   The socialist mechanism of ethnic literary writings, Yao (2008b: 122) argues, strove
    to incorporate ethnic literature into the new Republic's nationalistic project of nation-
    building by asserting a view of "objective" and "natural" ethnic identities based on
    the "scientifically" implemented national "Ethnic Classification Project" on the one
    hand, and painting ethnic cultures as exotically colorful in an exhibitionist manner
    on the other. This strategy of representation played an important role in constructing
    a multiethnic mosaic and, in effect, strengthened the embedded Han-centric perspec-
    tive. Therefore, it is quite understandable that any "alien" characteristic of ethnic
    groups which might possess a potential for separatism was scrutinized and ideologi-
    cally contained, and ethnicity was subsumed into the broader demands of "class, peo-
    ple, and socialism" (Yao 2008b: 122). This argument echoes Wang Lixiong's (2002,
    2007, 2009) view that, during the socialist period, class or class struggle was intro-
    duced and took the place of religion, culture, and so forth, as the primary factor of
    ethnic unity.

      With the death of Mao and the increasing obsolescence of class struggle, however,
    an ideological vacuum formed and was filled with the formerly repressed elements
    within ethnic cultures. Yao (2008b: 122–3) thus expounds on this transformation:

    > In all, "ethnic literature" was formed and activated in the 1950s and the 1960s, in
    > the form of repression and self-effacement during ethnic cultures' confrontations,
    > as a cultural other, with the Han culture. In the 1980s, ethnic writings restored
    > their "ethnic self-consciousness" in their imagination and pursuit of their traditional
    > cultures, and their reconstruction of an "ethnic history of the self." They searched
    > for their particular values, and experienced the so-called "sentimental" nationalism
    > ("*ganshang xing*" *de minzu zhuyi* "感伤性"的民族主义), followed by "movement-
    > based" nationalism ("*yundong xing*" *de minzu zhuyi* "运动性" 的民族主义). By
    > then, ethnic writings were no longer simply literary creations, but to a great degree
    > a signal of "ethnic identification."

      This rise, or re-emergence, of ethnic consciousness was further facilitated by the
    growing popularity of postcolonial discourses since they were introduced to China
    in the early 1990s. In ethnic literature, ethnic consciousness was presented to a more
    intense degree in a variety of forms of "specific and dynamic 'cultural nationalism'"
    as opposed to ethnic groups' search for and representation of their unique ethnic cul-
    tures back in the 1980s (Yao 2008a: 224). In Yao's (2008b: 123) view, this surge
    of cultural nationalism among ethnic groups, facilitated by the global circulation of
    postcolonial theories, within the PRC is somewhat ironic, because the founding of the
    PRC as a modern nation-state itself is a result of the global anti-colonial cause and lib-
    erationist struggles against Western imperialism during and after World War II; yet, in
    postcolonial discourses the PRC was regarded as a new "colonial" power suppressing
    sub-national and subaltern ethnic groups. This irony, in a way, echoes the abovemen-
    tioned understanding of ethnicity as isomorphic with nationality, both being a specific
    signification performatively constructed along the spectrum of national identity.

2   Some critics see varying degrees of structural changes and acclaim or embrace what
    some would call the "literary revolution" of Internet literature (Ouyang 2008, Shao
    2003, 2015), while others are less optimistic and find Internet literature no more than
    a product of rampant commercialization and consumerism since the 1990s (Kong
    2005).

3   Zahi Ciugene, a Tibetan musician and writer, is perhaps better known by his Han name
    Luo Bing (洛兵) and by his net name Xinyouxieluan (心有些乱 "a little distraught" in
    Mandarin Chinese). His most well-known Internet stories include "Twelve Nights in
    Autumn Wind" (*Qiufeng shi'er ye* 秋风十二夜, which was awarded the second prize
    in the Second Internet Literature Contest organized by China's most popular Internet

literature website, *Under the Banyan Tree*) and "Perhaps We Have Love Today" (*Jintian keneng you aiqing* 今天可能有爱情, which was included in the collection *Best Internet Literature in 2000*). They tell stories of estranged (anti)romantic love in contemporary urban China and have nothing to do with ethnic experience. By simply reading his works, readers would not have any inkling that the author is Tibetan; given the author's Mandarin pen name, he may not have any intention in letting readers know about his Tibetan ethnic identity. This perhaps can be explained by Zahi Cuigene's personal background: He was born in Chengdu, Sichuan Province, and educated in Beijing. During his studies at the prestigious Peking University, he actively took part in literary activities, including reading and publishing poetry. After graduation he joined the pop music circle in Beijing and became a professional musician and writer. His creations so far operate entirely in Mandarin cultural spheres and he identifies comfortably with the mainstream Mandarin cultural circle. In a literary sense, his connection with Tibet is at best nominal.

Liu Wei, an ethnic Miao who is known by his net name Xuehong (血红), is one of the top Internet writers in China. He is known for his fantasy stories (*xuanhuan xiaoshuo* 玄幻小说), a highly popular genre among Internet readers, such as *The Clan of Rising Dragon* (*Shenglong dao* 升龙道) and *The Song of Evil Wind* (*Xiefeng qu* 邪风曲). Recent studies of Chinese online fantasy stories have shown that this genre may have multiple sources of inspiration, including Western counterparts and some minor traditions in traditional culture, such mysterious rituals (Yang 2008, Ye 2005, You 2011, Zhao 2008). Liu Wei's stories may owe partly to his Miao background, as during his childhood he read quite extensively about Miao myths, ghost stories, and legends. However, Liu Wei does not explore his Miao ethnicity in his writings, but instead thrives in Mandarin-speaking literary circles.

Lan Xixi, an ethnic Hui, is another example of an "ethnic writer" whose writings could be confused for work by a Han author. His most well-known work, *Zero Degree Youth* (*Lingdu qingchun* 零度青春), depicts a group of urban youths who believe they are acting rebelliously but become frustrated and disillusioned in their coming of age. This novel, as well as many of Lan's short pieces, reminds us of the popular genre of the so-called "Cruel Youth Stories," the most famous of which is arguably *Beijing Doll* (*Beijing wawa* 北京娃娃) by the popular Han writer Chun Sue. For the readers of *Zero Degree Youth*, they may not be able to tell the author's ethnic identity by simply reading the story – this story could happen to any urban youth in contemporary China. But this does not seem to be an issue to the author, as his ethnic identity does not function as an integral element in the production and consumption of the work. However, in both Lan Xixi's and Liu Wei's cases, the authors' ethnic identities are taken advantage of as part of their promotional strategy. Lan is lauded as a rising star of Hui Internet writers (Ma 2010, Chapter 3), and Liu, for his status as the most (financially) successful ethnic writer – he has been ranked as one of the wealthiest Internet writers for consecutive years since the list was launched in 2012 (Chen 2013) – is often regarded as a representative figure for ethnic Internet writers to emulate (Yi 2015).

4 In PRC, ethnic policies and laws stipulate that a Chinese citizen of mixed blood is allowed to and will choose a *minzu* as his or her official ethnic designation. Of course, this singular ethnic designation, mainly for the sake of pragmatic management and control, does not correspond to the complex ethnic identity, which is socially, historically, and culturally based rather than institutionally designated. Yet, this official designation, through everyday practices and institutional implementation of differential policies, in effect also constructs, to varying degrees, an individual's ethnic identification. This practice, again, speaks to the complexity of the construction and performance of ethnicity in China.

5 Her acts may be explained, to borrow a psychoanalytical term, as a result of the compensatory mechanism – her hybrid identity gives her such an intense sense of impurity

of or a lack in Tibetan-ness that this sense has to be canceled out or pacified by an even more passionate turn to a "pure" and "essential" form of Tibetan-ness.

6 Yao Xinyong (2008a: 226, 2014: 8) mentions in his published articles Woeser's open response to his claim and provides a link to her response, as well as his later response to Woeser's (www.frchina.net/data/personArticle.php?id=8154), but the link no longer works as of August 31, 2016.

7 In a blog entry dated August 31, 2010, an alleged "International Web Blogger's Day," Woeser (together with her friend Susan Chen) (Woeser and Chen 2010) records, perhaps as a gesture of commemoration or celebration, her blogging career, a tortuous career that is marked by her unremitting struggles with Chinese Internet censorship organs, who repeatedly censored, blocked, and hacked her blogs. Yet, in spite of their persecutions, Woeser unyieldingly launched new blog websites, migrated her blogs to new sites, and renamed her blogs and kept writing.

8 Woeser's blog "Invisible Tibet" can be accessed at http://woeser.middle-way.net/. English, French, Japanese, and Polish translations of her blog entries can be found respectively at http://highpeakspureearth.com/category/woeser/, https://woeser.word-press.com/, http://www.shukousha.com/category/translation/woeser/, and http://www.hfhrpol.waw.pl/tybet/?tag=oser. Her Facebook and Twitter accounts are https://www.facebook.com/tsering.woeser and https://twitter.com/degewa.

9 It is also possible that a large number of netizens are scared to post on Woeser's sites, or the viewership of Wen's blog is artificially inflated by the so-called *Wumao dang* ("fifty-cent party" 五毛党, a colloquial term for hired Internet commentators) or other monitors or even viewer-inflation software. We cannot tell how much each factor shapes the current scene. We would like to thank a reader for bringing this point to our attention.

10 According to Shao Yanjun (2012), most Internet writers in China do not experiment with the mediality of the Internet in their writings.

11 Their photos come with decorative sentences in both Mandarin and Tibetan, the official languages of Tibet and their (supposedly) mother tongues.

12 It is debatable whether this performance is a flash mob event in the traditional sense in the West where flash mobs originated. But as we explain in what follows, flash mobs have developed into many different forms since its first appearance in 2003 in New York, many of which are already to a large degree different from its original form. Dekyi's singing can be categorized as a mix of a performative, political, and commercial flash mob.

13 The Chinese term for the flash mob, *kuaishan*, literally means "flash gathering and dispersing." It does not have the ideological connotations that "mob" in "flash mob" has in English (Nicholson 2005). Instead, *kuaishan* emphasizes the speed and temporariness of the form.

14 For instance, performances of the Tibetan music bands *Yangfendan* (Sheep Droppings) and *Qinglong* (Green Dragon) are characterized by their hip-hop style and use of a mixture of Mandarin, Tibetan, and English languages. Another notable incident is the circulation online of the "Song Dedicated to Mergen, Hero of the Grasslands." This song was reportedly written, sung, and put online by a Mongolian college student, and dedicated to Mr. Mergen, a Mongolian herder who had been brutally killed by a Chinese coal-hauling truck for defending his grazing land from Chinese miners. The song is also marked by its rap style and use of a mixture of Mandarin and Mongolian languages. For further discussion of *Yangfendan* and *Qinglong*, see Kehoe (2015: 323–26); for more information about the "Song Dedicated to Mergen," see SMHRIC (2011).

15 For example, Tzu-kai Liu (2015), in his study on Wa migrant youths' use of mobile communication, demonstrates the ways in which Wa ethnic youth creatively employ, although forced by the limit imposed on them, Internet technologies to write back to the dominant Mandarin discourse and assert their agency.

Bibliography

Barabantseva, Elena. (2008). "From the Language of Class to the Rhetoric of Development: Discourses of 'Nationality' and 'Ethnicity' in China." *Journal of Contemporary China* 17, no. 56: 565–89.

Barthes, Roland. (1978). *A Lover's Discourse: Fragments*. Trans. Richard Howard. New York: Hill and Wang.

——. (1981). *Camera Lucida: Reflections on Photography*. Trans. Richard Howard. New York: Hill and Wang.

Baudrillard, Jean. (1994). *Simulacra and Simulation*. Ann Arbor: University of Michigan Press.

——. (2000). "Photography, or the Writing of Light." Trans. Francois Debrix. http://www.ctheory.net/articles.aspx?id=126. Last accessed August 31, 2016.

Carlson, Allen. (2009). "A Flawed Perspective: The Limitations Inherent within the Study of Chinese Nationalism." *Nations and Nationalism* 15, no. 1: 20–35.

CCTV. (2015). "Meinu geshou zai daxue shitang chang zangyu ban 'Xihuan ni' zouhong" (A beauty singer become popular by singing the Tibetan version of 'Loving you' in a university canteen). http://lady.gmw.cn/2015–03/24/content_15185775.htm. Last accessed August 31, 2016.

Chen Yuan. (2013). "Zhongguo wangluo zuojia fuhao bang fabu" (Release of the list of the wealthiest Internet writers in China). *Renmin wang*. December 4. http://culture.people.com.cn/n/2013/1204/c87423–23737078.html. Last accessed August 31, 2016.

Chow, Rey. (2002). *The Protestant Ethnic and the Spirit of Capitalism*. New York: Columbia University Press.

CNNIC. (2011). "Statistical Report on Internet Development in China." China Internet Network Information Center (CNNIC), July. http://www1.cnnic.cn/IDR/ReportDown loads/201209/P020120904421102801754.pdf. Last accessed August 31, 2016.

Cui Wei. (2015). "Yanchangzhe Bianba Deji: hui fanchang gengduo Zangyu gequ" (Singer Penba Dekyi: I will remake more Tibetan songs). *Guangming wang*. http://edu.gmw.cn/newspaper/2015–03/30/content_105538794.htm. Last accessed August 31, 2016.

Dayton, D. (2006). "Big Country, Subtle Voices: Three Ethnic Poets from China's Southwest." MA Thesis. Sydney: University of Sydney.

Dikötter, Frank. (1992). *The Discourse of Race in Modern China*. Stanford, CA: Stanford University Press.

Everett, Anna, ed. (2008). *Learning Race and Ethnicity: Youth and Digital Media*. Cambridge, MA: MIT Press.

Fan, Jiayang. (2015). "The Viral Wedding Photos That Conquered China." *New Yorker*. http://www.newyorker.com/culture/cultural-comment/the-viral-wedding-photos-that-conquered-china. Last accessed August 31, 2016.

Gladney, Dru C. (2004). *Dislocating China: Reflections on Muslims, Minorities, and Other Subaltern Subjects*. Chicago: University of Chicago Press.

Gore, Georgiana. (2010). "Flash Mob Dance and the Territorialisation of Urban Movement." *Anthropological Notebooks* 16, no. 3: 125–31.

Gsomsdong, Gangcan (Gangjie Suomudong). (2009). "Laizi Ximalaya de xushu he shizhang: Zangzu qingnian shiren shige zhuaji" (Narratives and poetry from the Himalayas: a special issue of poems by young Tibetan poets). *Shi xuankan* 2: 85.

Hansen, Mette Halskov. (1999). *Lessons in Being Chinese: Minority Education and Ethnic Identity in Southwest China*. Seattle and London: University of Washington Press.

Hardt, Michael, and Antonio Negri (2000). *Empire*. Cambridge, MA: Harvard University Press.

Harrell, Stevan. (1998). "From Ethnic Group to Minzu (and Back Again?): Yi Identity in the People's Republic." Paper presented at the 2nd International Conference on Yi Studies, June 19–23, Trier University, Center of East Asian and Pacific Studies.

——. (2000). *Tianye zhong de zuqun guanxi yu minzu rentong: Zhongguo xinan Yizu shequ kaocha yanjiu (Field studies of ethnic identity: Yi communities of southwest China)*. Trans. Bamo Ayi and Qumo Tiexi. Nanning: Guangxi renmin chubanshe.

——. (2001). *Ways of Being Ethnic in Southwest China*. Seattle: University of Washington Press.

Heberer, Thomas. (1989). *China and Its National Minorities: Autonomy or Assimilation?* Armonk: M.E. Sharpe.

Ho, Wai-Yip. (2010). "Islam, China and the Internet: Negotiating Residual Cyberspace between Hegemonic Patriotism and Connectivity to the Ummah." *Journal of Muslim Minority Affairs* 30, no. 1: 63–79.

Hockx, Michel. (2015). *Internet Literature in China*. New York: Columbia University Press.

Inwood, Heather. (2016). "Internet Literature: From YY to MOOC." In *The Columbia Companion to Modern Chinese Literature*, edited by Kirk A. Denton, 436–40. New York: Columbia University Press.

Kehoe, Tricia. (2015). "I am Tibetan? An Exploration of Online Identity Constructions among Tibetans in China." *Asian Ethnicity* 16, no. 3: 314–33.

Kong, Shuyu. (2005). *Consuming Literature: Best Sellers and the Commercialization of Literary Production in Contemporary China*. Stanford, CA: Stanford University Press.

Leibold, James. (2010). "More Than a Category: Han Supremacism on the Chinese Internet." *The China Quarterly* 203: 539–59.

——. (2015). "Performing Ethnocultural Identity on the Sinophone Internet: Testing the Limits of Minzu." *Asian Ethnicity* 16, no. 3: 274–93.

Leibold, James, and Yangbin Chen, eds. (2014). *Minority Education in China: Balancing Unity and Diversity in an Era of Critical Pluralism*. Hong Kong: Hong Kong University Press.

Li Guang, and Zhong Yaqiong. (2012). "Dalu yan ni Zang Wei wen wangluo yuqing jiance xitong, jiankong fenlie fengxian" (Mainland China plans to develop systems monitoring Internet opinions in Tibetan and Uygur languages, controlling the risk of separation). *Fenghuang Zhoukan*. http://news.ifeng.com/shendu/fhzk/detail_2012_06/25/15540422_0.shtml. Last accessed August 31, 2016.

Liu, Tzu-kai. (2015). "Minority Youth, Mobile Phones and Language Use: Wa Migrant Workers' Engagements with Networked Sociality and Mobile Communication in Urban China." *Asian Ethnicity* 16, no. 3: 334–52.

Lo, Kwai-Cheung. (2016). "The Struggle between Subaltern Nationalisms and the Nation-State in the Digital Age: China and Its Ethnic Minorities." In *The Routledge Handbook of New Media in Asia*, edited by Larissa Hjorth and Olivia Khoo, 352–63. London: Routledge.

Ma Ji. (2010). *Wangluo wenxue toushi yu beiwang (A memo of Internet literature)*. Beijing: Zhongguo shehui kexue chubanshe.

Molnár, Virág. (2014). "Reframing Public Space through Digital Mobilization: Flash Mobs and Contemporary Urban Youth Culture." *Space and Culture* 17, no. 1: 43–58.

Mullaney, Thomas S. (2011). *Coming to Terms with the Nation: Ethnic Classification in Modern China*. Berkeley, CA: University of California Press.

Nakamura, Lisa. (2002). *Cybertypes: Race, Ethnicity, and Identity on the Internet*. New York: Routledge.

Nakamura, Lisa, and Peter Chow-White, eds. (2012). *Race after the Internet*. New York: Routledge.

Nelson, Alondra, Thuy Linh N. Tu, and Alicia Headlam Hines, eds. (2001). *Technicolor: Race, Technology, and Everyday Life*. New York: New York University Press.

Nicholson, Judith A. (2005). "Flash! Mobs in the Age of Mobile Connectivity." *The Fibreculture Journal*, no. 6. http://six.fibreculturejournal.org/fcj-030-flash-mobs-in-the-age-of-mobile-connectivity. Last accessed November 22, 2016.

Ouyang Youquan. (2008). *Wangluo wenxue gailun (On Internet literature)*. Beijing: Beijing daxue chubanshe.

Pye, Lucian. (1996). "How China's nationalism was Shanghaied." In *Chinese Nationalism*, edited by Jonathan Unger, 86–112. Armonk, NY: M.E. Sharpe.

Rheingold, Howard. (2003). *Smart Mobs: The Next Social Revolution*. Cambridge, MA: Basic Books.

Schepers, Selina. (2008). "The Power of Many, in Pursuit of Nothing: Flash Mob Communities on YouTube and Beyond." *Cultures of Arts, Science, and Technology* 1, no. 1: 17–34.

Shao Yanjun. (2003). *Qingxie de wenxuechang: dangdai wenxue shengchan jizhi de shichanghua zhuanxing (The inclined literary field: the commercial transformation of the contemporary literary production mechanism)*. Nanjing: Jiangsu renmin chubanshe.

———. (2012). "Zai 'yituobang' li goujian 'geren linglei xuanze' huanxiang kongjian: wangluo wenxue de yishi xingtai gongneng zhi yizhong" (Constructing a fantasy space of 'individual, alternative choice' in a heterotopia: one of the ideological functions of Internet literature). *Wenyi yanjiu* 4: 16–25.

———. (2015). "Wangluo wenxue de 'wangluo xing' yu 'jingdian xing'" (The Internet and classical qualities of Internet literature). *Beijing daxue xuebao (Zhexue shehui kexue ban)* 52, no. 1: 143–52.

Shawyer, Susanne Elizabeth. (2008). "Radical Street Theatre and Yippie Legacy: A Performance History of the Youth International Party, 1967–1968" (Ph.D. Dissertation). The University of Texas at Austin.

SMHRIC (2011). "Rap Song Dedicated to Mergen Banned." *Southern Mongolian Human Rights Information Center*, June 13. http://www.smhric.org/news_390.htm. Last accessed November 22, 2016.

Spivak, Gayatri Chakravorty. (1988). "Can the Subaltern speak?" In *Marxism and the Interpretation of Culture*, edited by Cary Nelson and Lawrence Grossberg, 271–313. Urbana: University of Illinois Press.

Sontag, Susan. (1977). *On Photography*. New York: Farrar, Straus and Giroux.

———. (1997). *On Photography*. New York: Farrar, Straus and Giroux.

Wang Di. (2015a). "Zangzu xinren jiehun zhao zouhong pengyou quan" (Wedding photos of a Tibetan young couple becoming popular in social media). *Xinhua wang*. http://www.sc.xinhuanet.com/content/2015-04/09/c_1114920633.htm. Last accessed August 31, 2016.

———. (2015b). "Across China: Tibetan Couple's Wedding Photos an Internet Hit." http://news.xinhuanet.com/english/2015-04/15/c_134154267.htm. Last accessed August 31, 2016.

Wang Lixiong. (2002). "Reflections on Tibet." *New Left Review* 14: 78–111.

———. (2004). "Xizang miandui de liangzhong diguo zhuyi: toushi Weise shijian" (Two imperialisms that Tibet is faced with: a perspective on the Woeser incident). *Da jiyuan*. http://www.epochtimes.com/gb/4/11/17/n719820.htm. Last accessed August 31, 2016.

——. (2007). *Wo de xiyu; ni de dongtu (My west China, your east Turkestan)*. Taipei: Locus Publishing.

——. (2009). *Tianzang: Xizang de mingyun (Sky burial: the fate of Tibet)*. 2nd ed. Taipei: Locus Publishing.

Wark, McKenzie. (2011). *The Beach beneath the Street: The Everyday Life and Glorious Times of the Situationist International*. London and New York: Verso.

Wendling, Mike, Aditi Mallya, and Cassandra Cavallaro. (2015). "The Wedding Photos that Captivated China." *BBC*, April 18. http://www.bbc.com/news/blogs-trending-32353687. Last accessed August 31, 2016.

Woeser, Tsering (Ciren Weise). (2003). *Xizang biji* (*Notes on Tibet*). Guangzhou: Huacheng chubanshe.

——. (2007a). "Xueyu de bai" (The white of the snow region). *Map of Burgundy Red Blog*. http://map.woeser.com/?action=show&id=28. Last accessed August 31, 2016.

——. (2007b). "Fei ya fei" (Flying). *Map of Burgundy Red Blog*. http://map.woeser.com/?action=show&id=2. Last accessed August 31, 2016.

——. (2008). "Xizang de mimi" (Secrets of Tibet). *Map of Burgundy Red Blog*, April 23. http://map.woeser.com//?action=show&id=455. Last accessed August 31, 2016.

——. (2015). "Jiangshu 'xiandai Zangren' de xingfu gushi ru jia bao huan" (A hyper-authentic story of the happy life of a 'modern Tibetan' couple). *Radio Free Asia*, May 7. http://www.rfa.org/mandarin/zhuanlan/weiseblog/ws-05072015100559.html. Published in English as "Aren't They the Lucky Ones?" *Radio Free Asia*. Translated by Luisetta Mudie. May 15, 2015. http://www.rfa.org/english/women/lucky-05152015103956.html. Both last accessed August 31, 2016.

Woeser, Tsering (Ciren Weise), and Susan Chen. (2010). "From Map of Burgunday [*sic*] Red to Invisible Tibet: Tsering Woeser's Blogging Career." *Invisible Tibet Blog*, August 31. http://woeser.middle-way.net/2010/08/blog-post_31.html. Last accessed August 31, 2016.

Yang Guihua. (2008). "Xuanhuan xiaoshuo xianxiang jiqi yanjiu" (A study of the phenomenon of the fantasy novel). MA Thesis. Shanghai: Shanghai University.

Yao Xinyong. (2005). "Bei bangjia de 'minzu yingxiong': guanyu Weise shijian de sikao" (Kidnapped 'national hero': thoughts on the Weise incident). *Zuojia (Hong Kong)* 12: 66–75.

——. (2008a). "Wangluo, wenxue, shaoshu minzu ji zhishi: qinggan gongtongti" (The Internet, literature, ethnic minorities, and knowledge: affective communities). *Jiangsu shehui kexue* 2: 223–6.

——. (2008b). "Zhongguo 'shaoshu minzu wenxu' de houzhimin piping" (Postcolonial criticism of 'ethnic literatures' in China). *Ershiyi shiji* 4: 119–29.

——. (2014). "Shaoshu minzu wenxue: shenfen huayu yu zhutixing shengchan" (Literatures of ethnic minorities: discourse of identity and production of subjectivity). *Jinan daxue xuebao* (*Zhexue shehui kexue ban*) 36, no. 2: 2–17.

Ye Yonglie. (2005). "Qihuan re, xuanhuan re yu kehuan wenxue" (The fever of the fantasy fiction and science fiction). *Zhonghua dushu bao*, July 7: 14.

Yi Hua. (2015). "Shaoshu minzu wenxue ruhe yingjie wangluo wenxue de 'huangjin shidai'?" (How should ethnic Internet literature embrace the 'golden age' of Internet literature?). *Zhongguo minzu bao*, October 30: 9.

You Jie. (2011). "Shi lun xuanhuan xiaoshuo jiqi shenmei jiazhi" (On the fantasy novel and its aesthetic values). MA Thesis. Nanjing: Nanjing Normal University.

Zhang Zhixin. (1998). "Hanhua? Ouhua? Shaoshu minzu zuojia hanyu xiezuo de wenti tansuo" (Hanification? Europeanization? An exploration of writing styles of ethnic writers' writing in Mandarin). *Minzu wenxue yanjiu* 4: 35–41.

Zhao Qiuyang. (2008). "Zhongguo dangdai wangluo xuanhuan xiaoshuo yanjiu" (A study of online fantasy novels in contemporary China). MA Thesis. Chengdu: Sichuan Normal University.

5 Caught in the web

Ethics of Chinese cyberspace

On January 10, 2008, an interesting article titled "The Cultural Freak Behind the Case of 'Very Pornographic and Very Violent'" was published in the influential Beijing-based newspaper, *New Beijing Daily* (*Xin Jing bao* 新京报). In this article the following lines appeared particularly outstanding:

> [The Human Flesh Search Engine] relies on unverifiable facts, but it claims to stand on a moral high ground. It gathers together anonymous and irresponsible mobs to expose common people's privacy.
>
> It has the masses fight among themselves, the disadvantaged assault the more disadvantaged, and lies disclose lies.

This article is about the massive assaults on the Internet of a thirteen-year-old girl, who, in an apparently staged "man-in-the-street TV interview," had critiqued the current Internet culture in China for being "very pornographic, very violent" (*hen huang hen baoli* 很黄很暴力). Having seen the interview aired on the seven o'clock Primetime Nightly News on the national China Central TV (CCTV), netizens were enraged and castigated the journalist for coaxing a young girl into acting as a mouthpiece of the government, whose propagandist campaigns on the so-called "vulgar" culture on the Internet signaled further state control of the Internet as a whole.[1] Netizens then started to spoof this event – as well as the girl – in cartoons and edited photo images; they also mimicked the phrase "very pornographic, very violent" on different occasions in satirical ways, and the phrase soon went viral (Benney 2015: 39–40, Li 2011: 77–8, Tang and Bhattacharya 2011).

Similar to other *egao* cases investigated in Chapter 1, this case is also characterized, among other things, by the younger generation's dissatisfaction with and disobedience to the establishment's oppressive moves, which leads to the rise of a cynical subculture facilitated by digital technologies. However, in this case netizens pointed their satirical barbs not only at the "perpetrator" – the journalist and the state TV station – but also at the victim. In fact, the girl interviewed received most of the attacks from netizens, while the journalist and the TV station remained mostly off the netizens' target. To make the matter worse, netizens identified the girl by the means of what they called the "Human Flesh Search Engine" (*renrou sousou* 人肉搜索, abbreviated as RRSS hereafter) – a method of tracking down offline individuals by putting together pieces of information different netizens provide – and then exposed her personal information online.

Those online assaults on the victim rather than the perpetrator and the use of the RRSS on a minor aroused huge controversy. The commentator of the article quoted above, for instance, denounced this case as a "freak" (*guaitai* 怪胎) of the Internet subculture of youth, a subculture that started as an interesting phenomenon for its deconstruction of the orthodox culture, but later became nonsensical, rendered by a growing group of the bored and the aimless, and sometimes became violent as it turned to extremes (Mai 2008). Particularly, the RRSS became a focus of the controversy, because it raised many questions about the moral and legal status of this phenomenon. Moreover, this "Internet violence" – so it was called – had caused real damages. The girl's daily life was hugely disturbed by verbal and physical abuse from strangers as a result of the exposure of her personal information online.

It is not surprising that the RRSS became a focus of current controversies, because since it first appeared in 2006,[2] it has been a topic of continuous debates online and offline. These debates mostly concern the legitimacy of the RRSS and its ethical validity – according to academic researches on the RRSS, both in China and abroad (Benny 2015, Chao 2011, Chen and Sharma 2011, Downey 2010, Herold 2011b, Li 2011, Tang and Bhattacharya 2011, Wang et al. 2010).[3] People have been discussing issues such as whether it is moral or legal to expose someone's personal information online; whether it is proper to pry into the privacy of others in the name of maintaining morality and justice; how to strike a balance between protection of freedom of expression and privacy protection; where the limit of such a search is, and so on.

Indeed, the RRSS has posed challenges to the current legal system and moral standards in China, mainly because the virtual space in which the RRSS mostly takes place is conceived of as a somewhat "outlaw area," an area where current laws are not entirely applicable and moral standards offline are regarded as mostly irrelevant. But the RRSS as a phenomenon involves more critical issues than legal and moral ones – its *cultural* implications, for instance, may tell us more about not only netizens and the virtual space of the Internet, but also the larger socio-cultural conditions in contemporary China. Moreover, the RRSS does not simply cause problems to society either. As David Kurt Herold (2011b) and some others (MacKinnon 2009, Martinsen 2009) have demonstrated, for instance, the RRSS does not singly target "wrongdoers," but netizens also help find grassroots talent, missing relatives, and those in need through the RRSS.

Yet, an examination of current literature on the RRSS seems to show that scholars and intellectuals mainly conceive of the RRSS as problematic, if not entirely illegal or immoral. Popular opinion and imagination have also shown increasing concerns about some (mis)conduct by participants of the RRSS, and legal and moral problems that the RRSS has brought about, although a great many netizens are still actively participating in it with the conviction that they have accomplished some moral deeds or served justice.[4] These growing concerns about the RRSS on the parts of both "elite" and not-so-elite groups (if this division is valid in this case) exhibits a general sense of anxiety in contemporary Chinese society about the ethics in the virtual space of the Internet, which are determined by the characteristics of the online space and the culture that netizens developed, and which are also shaped in one way or another by the ethics and sociocultural conditions of the offline space. Therefore, it may not be too farfetched to argue that this general sense of anxiety about the RRSS signals an overall concern about the cultural order, or the lack thereof, as a result of a larger social transformation of the Chinese Internet in general in the postsocialist condition.

In this chapter, rather than engaging in the discussions on legal and moral issues concerning the RRSS, we examine how the RRSS is represented and imagined in novels and films, and focus on their cultural and symbolic dimension. Literary and cinematic representations of the RRSS, hitherto an understudied subject, are important for our understanding of this phenomenon, or (sub)culture, not only because they provide us with an alternative perspective to perceive it, but more importantly they offer us a (self-)reflectiveness. This (self-)reflectiveness, as the works we examine manifest, is seriously lacking in current online activities, but is crucial for an online culture that is constructive. Also, this quality of (self-)reflectiveness is reminiscent of the humanist and Enlightenment undertakings of the New Era of the 1980s, as well as of the May Fourth period of the 1910s and 1920s, and is taken as an antidote to the "(neo)liberal" forces that are receiving increasing favor in the name of human dignity and freedom in China, the unregulated forces of the market and personal (consumerist) desires unleashed by the "(neo)liberal" forces and their rather predictable consequences. These neoliberal forces find a particularly apropos place on the Internet in China, since the Internet, as we have explained in the Introduction and will show in the study of specific cases of the RRSS in what follows, is overdetermined by the neoliberal cyberculture embedded in the Internet from its place of origin in the US, and by many conflicting forces that became active during China's social turn to postsocialism. The postsocialist turn was characterized by an adoption of, or a mediation by, neoliberalism in the 1980s, which continues to play a part in the Chinese postsocialist condition today. It is precisely this quality of (self-)reflectiveness that those writers and filmmakers intend to bring to online culture in China through their literary and cinematic creations.

The works that we investigate include Sun Haoyuan's (孙浩元) popular mystery novels *The Human Flesh Search Engine* (*Renrou sousuo* 人肉搜索, 2008) and *Fatal Searches* (*Zhiming sousuo* 致命搜索, 2010); Wang Jing's (王竞) film, *Invisible Killer* (*Wuxing sha* 无形杀, 2009); Chen Kaige's (陈凯歌) film, *Caught in the Web* (*Sousuo* 搜索, 2012); and Wen Yu's (文雨) (pen name for Zhang Wenxuan 张雯轩) Internet novel, *Death on the Internet* (*Wang shi* 网逝, 2007; a.k.a. *Please Forgive Me* [*Qing ni yuanliang wo* 请你原谅我], and later published in print as *Search* [*Sousuo*] in 2012 and *Will You Love Me Tomorrow as You First Did* [*Mingtian, ni shifou ai wo ru chu* 明天，你是否爱我如初] in 2015), on which Chen Kaige's film is based. These works touch upon the issue of netizens' invasion of individuals' privacy while playing moral vigilante, which is a central subject of many ongoing debates: people contest whether it is legal or moral to expose someone's private information for public denunciation, if he or she is perceived to have done things against social ethics. And this central contention leads to many related questions, such as: What constitutes social ethics? Do social ethics have identical implications online and offline? Who and what determines whether a deed is ethical or not?

While these questions are closely related to their cultural reflections, these literary and cinematic works, particularly *Invisible Killer*, *Caught in the Web*, and *Death on the Internet*, do not show a strong intention to answer these questions or simply pass any judgment. Rather, through representations of specific cases of RRSS and explorations of human relations in these cases, and by confronting the audience with the confusions and frustrations that people experience in their online and offline activities, these works, to different degrees, demonstrate the ethical, cultural, and political complexities in understanding the phenomenon, and invite us to comprehend the dilemmas and their cultural ramifications.

In examining these works' cultural engagement with the RRSS, we further explore the following issues: the problematics of the Chinese Internet that cause ethical deficiency in netizens' online and offline activities; the politics of *mediality* embedded in the Internet and other media's manipulations of public and individual opinions, and in the literary and cinematic *representations* of these manipulations; literary and cinematic reflectivity and self-reflectivity in their intermedia and meta-media practices, and the importance of this (self-)reflectivity in a construction of online ethical identities;[5] and, finally, the cultural implications of the online construction of ethical identities under the postsocialist condition. We argue that literary and cinematic representations of the RRSS, as a form of cultural intervention into the subject, go beyond passing simple judgments on the legitimacy or moral validity of the phenomenon, but probe into the problematics of ideology, mediality, power relationship, and identity construction. By displaying the complexity of the phenomenon and the importance of a cultural intervention, these writers and filmmakers show that RRSS exemplifies participants' attempts, although or because those attempts are skewed, to imagine and construct an ethical online identity. The problematics in these attempts, which these works strive to capture, reveal not only ethical questions that affect the moral and legal validity of the RRSS, but also the ideology of the Internet as a medium, a product of neoliberalism migrating to the postsocialist condition. In their final analysis, a self-reflectivity based on constructive communications, with a restoration of affective connection counteracting the flattening hyper-connectivity, may serve as a corrective to the problem.

Popular imaginations of the RRSS and representations of moral anxieties

"Internet Violence," a general perception of the RRSS among its detractors, is also how the RRSS is mainly portrayed in Sun Haoyuan's two suspense novels *The Human Flesh Search Engine* and *Fatal Searches*. As popular genre fiction, these two novels in many ways follow their generic conventions and mostly reflect, conform to, and reinforce the dominant perceptions of the RRSS. But do they in some ways also offer alternative understandings of the RRSS? What can we learn from their cultural intervention into the issue?

The Human Flesh Search Engine was published in 2008, the heyday of the RRSS.[6] This mystery fiction is about a series of spine-chilling murder cases associated with dissemination of an online curse message. The detective, He Shao-chuan, who is in charge of these cases is at the same time involved in a love triangle with his friend's newly-wed wife, Yan Sixi. Sixi breaks up with her husband at their wedding ceremony, when a video clip of her husband having sex with a prostitute is accidentally played on a large screen for all the wedding guests to see. As the story develops, more mysterious murders continue to take place, including a journalist killed in a car accident, obviously having been tied up and poisoned before his murder; a manager of an Internet company engaged in the RRSS who is stabbed to death and whose body is hung from the ceiling, signifying the act of "keeping a post at the top of a discussion forum" (*zhiding*) that he had been in charge of; a cartoonist killed by his own pencil, thrust into his throat; and a popular musical star taking her own life after humiliating herself in public by doing a striptease while hallucinating in front of thousands of her fans during a concert. Finally, it turns out that the murderer is none other than Sixi, who, when a minor, was "human flesh searched" after she had been put in a staged interview as a whitewashing strategy for government corruption, an incident reminiscent of the case of the girl in "Very Pornographic and Very Violent," mentioned at the beginning of the chapter. Not able to withstand the bullies and harassment from her family, classmates, and strangers on the Internet, Sixi escapes to a place where she thinks nobody knows her, only to be forced into prostitution. Devastated, she is determined to revenge herself on those who have caused her suffering, in ways that she believes can do justice to the "atrocities" they have committed by participating in the RRSS.

Fatal Searches, published two years after *The Human Flesh Search Engine*, is a sequel to the latter. In a similar narrative style, Sun Haoyuan churns out a similar mystery fiction, taking the RRSS as a central prop. *Fatal Searches* tells another story of a serial murder case: nine victims including five who have on different occasions done things that are disrespectful to elderly people, and four who have been involved in a twist of RRSS plots. All of these murders, it turns out, originate from a TV interview conducted several years earlier, in which a middle school girl has candidly and boldly expressed her support for those who are unwilling to give up their seats to seniors on the bus. The girl, Wan Jing, is soon the subject of an online manhunt and becomes a target of online and offline denunciations. She and her family have to move to another city where they are unknown, but in a rare coincidence she is humiliated in class for her earlier words in the interview while her professor and classmates are entirely unaware of her former identity. Despairing, she commits suicide. It so happens that her boyfriend, Hong Yuezong, is a policeman who is in charge of the murder cases linked to the "human flesh search" of her. It is even more coincidental that Yuezong, after Jing's death, comes across Jing's sister of a different surname, Zhou Xuan, and they fall in love. During the police investigations, Yuezong realizes that Xuan, using a pseudonym, has launched several "human flesh searches" for four people who have caused her sister's death by actively participating in the RRSS of the sister earlier. Those four, now disgraced as a result of the RRSS that Xuan has launched for their other immoral deeds, such as extramarital affairs and corruption, set up an online discussion forum in order to lure out the one who has caused their disgrace. More intriguingly, Xuan launches another RRSS upon herself for a minor defect, and, therefore, passes herself off as a victim of the RRSS similar to those four who are tracking her down. Finally, with the return of the hero in *The Human Flesh Search Engine*, Shaochuan, who has taken a year off to recover from the psychological trauma he has experienced with Sixi's death, it becomes gradually clear that it is the policeman, Yuezong, who has conducted all of those murders. Yuezong, crushed by the death of Jing, comes to seek vengeance on those who have once mistreated the elderly, as a way of compensation, he claims, for his former girlfriend's unfulfilled apologies to them. Later when playing tricks with those who have determined to track her down, he realizes that his current girlfriend Xuan is in danger, so he kills them one after another, when they come closer to the discovery of the truth.

Admittedly, these two novels were written and promoted for popular consumption of the RRSS. Particularly, *The Human Flesh Search Engine* quite obviously is intended to capitalize on the RRSS as a newly emergent and highly controversial phenomenon that was then in a blaze of publicity. Upon its publication, this novel was billed as an "encyclopedic novel about the RRSS" and a "recommended work of the year by Mop.com" (Sun 2008, front cover), arguably the website on which the very first RRSS was conducted and most of the early RRSS cases took place. However, despite its claim of a close association with the RRSS, the novel in fact fails to tap into the complex mechanisms by which the RRSS is conducted or its sociality, let alone entertain any serious reflection or critique. Rather, it simply takes the RRSS as a cause, which can be reasonably replaced by another, of the murder cases that follow. In other words, the RRSS in this novel is mostly taken advantage of as a selling point, and is thus turned into an abstract concept of "Internet violence" without much substantial unraveling.

Fatal Searches was advertised upon its publication as a work of "the top writer of the News-Suspense Novel" (*xinwen xuanyi xiaoshuo* 新闻悬疑小说) (Sun 2010, front cover) – although the "News-Suspense Novel" is more a neologism coined for promotional tactics than a real literary genre. Even though it is not promoted, unlike *The Human Flesh Search Engine*, as a novel of the RRSS, this novel, compared with its predecessor, exemplifies a closer engagement with the RRSS, and, as a result, represents the phenomenon in a more complicated light. One reason that contributes to its more complicated representation of the RRSS is that, as a "News-Suspense Novel" – regardless of what this term really implies – *Fatal Searches* incorporates into its narrative a great many real cases of the RRSS that have taken place in the years preceding its publication, which happens to be the years in which the RRSS gained steam. This is an advantage that its predecessor *The Human Flesh Search Engine* did not have, as the novel was composed in haste, so to speak, at the moment immediately after the phenomenon began to attract attention, so much so that by the time the novel was published, many different forms of RRSS had yet to happen. Therefore, the writer was not provided with enough real-life cases for a more sophisticated understanding, nor was he given an adequate space for much critical reflection. As a result, the RRSS in *The Human Flesh Search Engine* is represented as a rather one-dimensional phenomenon that simply causes online violence, which inevitably leads to offline violence. This is exemplified, most forcefully, in the writer's incorporation of the lines from *New Beijing Daily* cited in the beginning of this chapter into the novel as his unreflective condemnation of the violence incurred on individuals caused by the RRSS.

Fatal Searches, in contrast, brings out some degrees of complication of the RRSS, as it incorporates real cases of the RRSS that include both those that have harmed individuals by being a form of vigilante justice or invading their privacy, and those, participants believe, that have worked as a form of social enforcement to withhold moral justice where perceived wrongdoings were a blind spot, or beyond the scope, of the legal enforcement. But for most of those cases, harm and accomplishment coexisted and did not offset each other, making the RRSS a "double-edged sword," as one character says (Sun 2010: 20). These real-life cases are mostly cited by the characters in their debates on the social effects, legitimacy, and ethical validity of the RRSS, echoing the debates going on simultaneously in reality.

Moreover, the two novels' different degrees of engagement with the RRSS are exhibited in their different views on the Internet as a medium. *The Human Flesh Search Engine*, imputing murder cases of disparate nature to the single cause of the RRSS, seems to denounce not only the RRSS, but also the Internet at large, as a cause of violence. As Sun Haoyuan (2008: 198) writes, the reason why those apparently unrelated cases are conducted by the same murderer is because all of the victims have, in one way or another, been involved in some online activities, and "only the Internet can bring people of different nationalities, ethnicities, occupations, locations, and genders together." Further, in the author's view, the reason why the Internet becomes a cause of violence is because it is susceptible to manipulation by other hegemonic powers, an opinion that Wen Yu and Chen Kaige share in their different versions of the story *Caught in the Web*, which will be discussed below. In *The Human Flesh Search Engine*, the major power that manipulates the Internet is the sweeping commercialization and consumerism that have grown with and been facilitated by the Internet. For instance, one victim, Xue Mubo, the CEO of the "Far Vision Net" (*Zhuiyuan wang*), the most popular website on which the RRSS is conducted in the novel, once promoted in public his so-called "Theory of Agenda Setup," which is a method that a commercial group uses to blatantly manipulate public opinion by setting up certain "agendas" on the Internet through tricks such as "keeping a post at the top of a discussion forum" (*zhiding*). Xue is later killed and hanged from the ceiling, literally showcasing the killer's revengeful act of *zhiding*.

Fatal Searches, on the contrary, shows a more balanced view of the Internet. While acknowledging the problems that the Internet has brought about, it also recognizes the positive effects it has on the society. On the one hand, the writer believes that netizens participating in the RRSS are driven by a "blind sense of righteousness"; when their "curiosity is decorated by the veneer of morality" in the RRSS (Sun 2010: 82), it will bring problems. On the other hand, however, the fact that a great many people are taking part in RRSS events with enthusiasm seems to suggest, the writer remarks, a rising attention to public issues among individual netizens and a growing desire for justice and equality. The RRSS, one character suggests, has a power that equals the supernatural or religious powers of the past, and functions as a weapon of the masses in modern society seeking justice and equality (Sun 2010: 21). It only needs some more regulations in order to avoid those negative effects and to function properly. Of course, the problems with the RRSS entail much more sophisticated considerations, but the writer's efforts to balance disparate views suggests a more complicated engagement with the phenomenon.

Indeed, both *The Human Flesh Search Engine* and *Fatal Searches* are typical genre fiction composed for popular consumption. Both employ formulaic narration, dramatic development, and surprise ending, techniques that are characteristic of such fiction. For instance, the stories in both are moved forward by using the narrative devices usually seen in conventional detective or mystery genres, such as intensely building interlocked suspense and then resolving it with unexpected twists. Moreover, as a popular genre, detective fiction, it is commonly assumed, mostly reflects and conforms to a culture's dominant ideology, and thus its close engagement with infringement and imposition of law and order usually mirrors social uncertainties and anxieties, as well as attempts to restore some reassurance of social organism (Cawelti 1976, Moretti 1997). If this understanding is still relevant today, which we believe it is, both novels speak to a moral crisis in contemporary Chinese society that comes with the RRSS and the Internet at large.

The fact that the RRSS and the Internet have become a subject of detective fiction demonstrates problematics in popular imaginations of them. And the fact that they are oftentimes depicted as something that can be so violent (this is also the case in the other works that we will study in what follows) cannot be simply taken as a result of the commercial drive on the part of the press, but also shows some real problems with Internet ethics within the large sociocultural transformation.

The most poignant of these problems that the author depicts in these novels is, arguably, the absence of social morals as the result of a lack of sufficient ethical (self-)regulation in the online space. The RRSS, it can be argued, is a most telling manifestation of this problem, as it constantly tests and contests existing offline moral conventions online. In both novels, the virtual space in which the RRSS is conducted is represented, to a large extent, as an actual jungle, a space in which the law of the jungle prevails.[7] Those who are in power, whether it is economic, political, technological, or self-assumed moral power, are prone to mindlessly take on those who are not, disregarding – ironically – moral standards in the real world. In this space, people's primitive desires, predisposition for brutality, and many other propensities that are controlled in the process of civility and sociality by laws and moral rules in reality, seem to have found an opportunity to break loose the constraints of the real world. This is because the virtual space on the Internet, to some, is such a "free" space that laws and regulations in the real world are deemed irrelevant, while at the same time its own rules online are not yet established. That is why many participants of the RRSS, as we see in the novels, lead two different lives online and offline – they usually have decent jobs and live an ordinary life in reality, but they can be very insulting, aggressive, and uncontrolled in their online activities. As Daniel J. Solove (2007: 9) reminds us, "cyberspace norm police can be extremely dangerous – with an unprecedented new power and an underdeveloped system of norms to constrain their own behavior."

This sense of "freedom," distorted and ironic as it is, is arguably a product of the sudden deregulation in and by the market during the postsocialist transformation, which has rippled to almost every corner of Chinese society. However, this sense of "freedom" also comes along as a revengeful reaction to the repression and suppression on all fronts in the socialist period, and yet, ironically, also is reminiscent of the "freedom" that most people (ab)used during the Cultural Revolution (Capstone 2013, Downey 2010, Eberlein 2008, MacKinnon 2009).[8] Yet, once this "freedom" was first introduced to China in the 1980s, with its neoliberal vision and mission to free Chinese society in the spirit of an unregulated market, the neoliberal morals that were supposed to secure the freedom of the rule of the market were taken by some as freedom based on sheer power, be it newly unleashed commercial power or the inveterate bureaucratic state power. The postsocialist turn brings an overlapping of these conflicting yet complicit powers, and witnesses an imaginative and yet, to some extent, more realistic manifestation of this problematic in the alternative dimension of the virtual space on the Internet.

The lack of regulation is further facilitated by the fact that participants of the RRSS, as well as those of most other online activities, use pseudonyms or remain anonymous. Despite several efforts of the Chinese government to enforce a real-name registration system for online activities, anonymity still remains the default on the Internet in China. "Anonymity, on its own, is value neutral," as Kenneth Farrall and David Kurt Herold (2011: 166) point out in their study of this issue. "It protects vital outlets of truly creative, democratic discourse," but it "at the same time afford[s] abuses of human body and spirit, such as those from lone, unaccountable bullies engaged in flaming or the nameless, vengeful on- and offline crowds of Human Flesh Search Engines."[9] In the case of the RRSS, unaccountability, more than protection of privacy, is at stake in the practice of anonymous participation. "Anonymity is freedom from being identified, freedom from the personal accountability that identification affords," Farrall and Herold write (2011: 166). As depicted in these novels, it is exactly because netizens are aware of their own anonymous identity when they participate in the RRSS – and therefore they cannot be tracked down and thus held accountable for whatever consequences that may come up as a result of their deeds – that most of the participants tend to behave in a reckless manner. For them, the RRSS is like a safe and costless ambush protected by the new media of the Internet. Some provide information for crowdsourcing without considering any legal or moral consequences, some blatantly speak loud and clear their desire for peeping into others' privacy, and many simply express their "justified" outrages in mindless cursing. It may be an overstatement that the RRSS renders the Internet "a sanctuary for mankind's most transgressive desires and urges, a dark playground where human depravity could go unchecked" (Chen and Sharma 2011: 67), but indeed there is some truth in it when anonymity remains as the default for online activities.

The fact that identities of participants of the RRSS remain anonymous, in contrast to their aim of exposing their targets' identities, as well as the fact that those anonymous participants usually lead two different lives – an offline life in which they are common, law-abiding citizens versus an online life in which they can be vilifying and irresponsible netizens – raises the questions of double ethical standards, which usually leads to moral bankruptcy. This bankruptcy is primarily grounded in an unfortunate divide between self and others, as well as their two different selves. While searchers hold the searched accountable for their "wrong-doings" and thus justify an exposure of the latter's privacy and an attack on them, the very fact that they choose to remain anonymous while exposing others' privacy only exhibits their unwillingness to be held accountable for their own acts yet insisting on others' accountability. This is indeed an application of unequal accountability and double standards regarding ethos on the Internet. In fact, when the self is *self*-complacently deemed beyond any questioning, it is precisely this very self that is in a more urgent need for interrogation. As Sun Haoyuan (2008: 73) reprimands the participants of the RRSS in his novels, their acts exemplify their personal moral hypocrisy, and, by extension, ethical deficiency in the Internet culture because they assume the role of "moral guards" and justify their attacks against "wrongdoers" simply because "their own wrongdoings are not exposed online." They tend to exaggerate others' errors while being less forgiving; some even pretend that they are immune to the same mistakes. But their very exaggeration, unforgiveness, and pretension, as the writer remarks, only indicate their looming sense of anxiety and guilt that they try to conceal. Even more disturbingly, some netizens actively abuse the searched, with an unwarranted feeling of smugness simply because they, unlike their target, are not caught red-handed for the same wrongdoings which they may have also committed. Their moral high ground, ironically, is based only on a matter of luck.

Indeed, in a way, these participants of the RRSS, tainted by their moral ambiguity, seem like more deserving subjects to interrogation than those assumed wrongdoers, the novels' authors seem to suggest. While the crimes of the murderers in the novels are quite clear-cut, the accountability of the participants' deeds is rather controversial. In fact, these participants exert more harm on social morality because their double ethical standards are backed by a *warped* sense of justice and equality, which makes them believe that they are seeking justice and equality, but, in fact, they are simply distorting these values.

In addition, these participants' eager assertions of justice and equality online are driven more by a *compensatory mechanism* than by a real pursuit of justice and equality. In the novels, some become fervent *online* moralists and vigilantes, because they believe they have been unjustly treated and cannot find equality *offline*. Their heightened sense of justice online seems to make up for the lack of it offline. However, instead of seeking real justice, they tend to be more vindictive and abusive, retaliating against "wrongdoers." This distorted "compensation" finds an unlikely yet reasonable echo when one anonymous character claims in a post in an online discussion forum that, if possible, he would be more than happy to switch places with the "wrongdoer" under the human flesh search and "enjoy" whatever the "wrongdoer" has experienced in his bureaucratic corruption. It then becomes clear that this compensatory mindset, if not supported by a genuine pursuit of justice, only aggravates the moral deficiency that ails the RRSS. The unfulfilled sense of justice and equality, the compensatory mechanism, and the imagined replacement bespeak not only a condition marked by severe social imbalance, but also a problematic ethos caused by this social condition and intriguingly expressed in this online space of anonymity.

Moreover, some participants develop a habit of voyeurism. They simply enjoy prying into others' privacy, particularly when the targets under the human flesh search are somewhat well-known personalities who have been involved in scandals. They love to see them exposed in public and disgraced, and even gain pleasure in being unaccountable abusers taking advantage of those people who seem unreachable in the past but now, fallen, seem subject to violation at will. This voyeuristic desire is unleashed in this unregulated, "free" virtual space of the Internet, and further fueled by surging commercial powers, exemplified by the Far Vision Net's blatantly manipulative consumerist pursuits that specifically aim at feeding netizens' desires.

Thus, the hunting down of criminals, a central motif in mystery genres, becomes a process of *double hunting* in both *The Human Flesh Search Engine* and *Fatal Searches*. While the reader follows the gaze of the investigators and tries to find out who the murderers are, the murderers are at the same time hunting down those who have caused their misfortune by participating in the RRSS. In effect, both novels blur the boundaries between perpetrators and victims, as the murderers are at the same time perpetrators and victims of the "Internet violence" caused by the RRSS, and the murdered have caused the murders' traumatic experiences in the RRSS. Arguably, it is the latter hunting, while less depicted but looming large throughout the novels, that is more revealing of the social and ethical complexity in both novels. This double hunting, rather than "resolv[ing] the deep anxiety of an expanding society," as Franco Moretti (1997: 143–5) claims, increases the anxiety and exposes the deep deficiencies in existing ethical codes, as the "criminals" are at the same time victims, and when the "criminals" are punished – juridically and morally they *have to* be "punished" – by the existing laws, huge sympathy is generated for them, leaving people more perplexed than reassured that "society is still a great *organism*: a unitary and knowable body."

All these moral ambiguities and confusions point to the issue of the ethical validity of the RRSS. If the RRSS as a search engine is by itself value neutral, as it can both help find missing ones and infringe on human rights, then the fact that it becomes mostly a tool by which people commit the latter in China only signals an ethical problem on the part of the Chinese Internet and its netizens, as well as the Chinese society in transformation. To be more specific, the moral problems exemplified in the cases analyzed above, arguably, lie largely in a deficiency in the spirit of introspection and self-reflection. Pitting the self against other, a practice that underlies most controversial human flesh searches and causes ethic and legal problems, is a most telling manifestation of this deficiency. Hannah Arendt (1951, 1977: 191) argues in another context that the ability of thinking, or this spirit of introspection and self-reflection, constitutes the humanity of human beings and the essence of human existence; it enables us to exorcise the evil. Moreover, this thinking, in Arendt's (1977: 186) view, first and foremost should be "consistent with self," and should also put "ourselves in the place of any other man," as she cites Immanuel Kant (Arendt 1982: 43). Only by doing so can we possibly avoid falling into a moral bankruptcy that shrouds the RRSS.

Further, the fact that this deficiency in the spirits of introspection and self-reflection comes along with a celebration of the advent of "freedom" brought about by the neoliberal deregulation only reminds us of Rüdiger Safranski's conception of evil as the "drama of freedom," or the price for freedom. In Safranski's (1997) opinion, evilness is just the other side of freedom, because when people are free, they are able to do evil things – of course, they can also choose to do good things. What is at stake here, we believe, is an Arendtian commitment to thinking that resists the evilness that is prone to come along with freedom.[10] In the case of the RRSS in China, this "freedom" produced by the neoliberal deregulation, and further guaranteed by the virtual space of the Internet, is taken by some as a form of categorical freedom, or a carnivalistic kind of freedom, that is exempt from any form of social or moral constraint. When this sense of freedom rejects any human dialogue with self and other, as is the case with many RRSS participants, and thus fails to generate a sense of morality, it becomes seriously problematic. Further, this freedom became a dominant ethos following, and as a result of, the collapse of communist ideals and the ebb of the "New Enlightenment" (He 2010) during the short-lived "high culture fever" (Wang 1996) and found its most fortuitous venue to thrive on the Internet.[11] The spiritual vacuum left by the desertion of the old socialist beliefs and the cynicism about the current revival of traditional values was soon filled by a fervent pursuit of power.[12] In particular, economic power was suddenly unleashed by the deregulated market and buttressed by the bureaucratic state power. Thus, the law of the jungle prevails in many online practices, such as the RRSS.

Concerned about this ethical problem online, many intellectuals called for an immediate reestablishment of a responsible online ethics. For instance, Shao Yan-jun (2012a: 71) saw the dynamics and chaos in Chinese Internet writings, and called for a concerted effort on the part of influential and serious Internet writers to re-enact a law (arguably a law that is different from the law of the jungle that is currently in charge) in the alternative world of the Internet, and "reset an ethical bottom line and a psychological order" among netizens. In fact, the state has never ceased its efforts to extend its rule over this virtual space. Since the beginning of the 2010s, it has carried out the so-called "Campaigns of Cleansing the Internet"

(*Jingwang xingdong* 净网行动) for five consecutive years. These efforts, particularly the 2014 Campaign, are regarded, in terms of cultural production and consumption, as a decisive act by the state to facilitate its plans to incorporate the virtual space of the Internet into its existing cultural mechanism for the construction of a state-orchestrated "mainstream literature and art" (*zhuliu wenyi* 主流文艺) (Shao 2014: 68, Shao et al. 2015). The Internet is decidedly losing its carefree "outlaw" cultural status, and becoming increasingly a significant factor, if not an "independent" one on par with that of the political and economic power, in shaping the cultural field (in a Bourdieuian sense) of contemporary China. Thus, critics such as Shao Yanjun and Zhuang Yong require that Chinese netizens play a more proactive role in the process of revamping the current cultural field in order to gain a leading position in the ongoing production of the "mainstream literature and art" (Shao 2012a, 2012b, 2014, Zhuang 2014).

Yet, the state's imposition of political and cultural laws onto the Internet is, for many, a tactic "meant to appeal to mass morality and to legitimize control over the internet" (Li 2010: 71). Given the questionable nature of the state's rule and discipline, netizens' ability of introspection and (self)-reflection becomes all the more important for the building of a constructive ethos on the Internet and netizens' bid for a leading role for the future cultural sphere. Further, as Internet ethics is a contested site characterized by constantly ongoing negotiations and confrontations among all netizens, without an Arendtian thinking that is inclusive of both self and others, moral bankruptcy as a product of unconstrained freedom will inevitably prevail.

Mediality and society of imbalance: the Internet and other media

In this part, we will focus on the issue of *mediality*, not only the mediality of the Internet but also that of other media, such as cinema, DV (digital video), and TV, and the relationship among these media, which figures large in Wang Jing's, Wen Yu's, and Chen Kaige's works. The questions we ask include: How does mediality serve as a condition for the production of these works? How is the mediating nature of these media manipulated, particularly that of the Internet? What social condition does this manipulation inform and what are its ideological implications?

Mediality as a condition for literary and cinematic productions

While both *The Human Flesh Search Engine* and *Fatal Searches*, with their ingenuity in dramatizing controversial social issues and dexterity with generic narratives, present and, to some degree, explore a popular concern about problems with Internet ethics exemplified in the RRSS, the three works that we investigate in the following sections especially engage, with a much higher degree of vigor, the ways in which the *mediality* of the Internet shape the construction of Internet ethics. The Internet, as a heterotopia, is rapidly reshaping human beings' relationships with media as well as the relationships among human beings themselves. Therefore, this process of reshaping also figures in a process of redefining social ethics online and offline. The three works under investigation – namely Wang Jing's film *Invisible Killer*, Wen Yu's Internet novel *Death on the Internet*, and Chen Kaige's film adaption of Wen Yu's novel, *Caught in the Web* – demonstrate, with disparate approaches, the paradoxical effects on human behavior and psyche that the Internet has generated, the ideological complexity embedded in the manipulation of media, and an urgency for reestablishing an online ethics that may stand for human dignity.

Wang Jing's film *Invisible Killer* is based largely on a well-known and highly controversial real RRSS event, called the "Bronze Whisker Gate" (*tongxu men* 铜须门), which took place in 2006. This was an alleged extramarital scandal between a modestly well-known Internet gameplayer ("World of Warcraft," or WOW) whose net name was Bronze Whisker, and a married female player. A denunciation, declared to be written by the cuckolded husband, was posted in a discussion forum on Mop.com on April 12, 2006, implicating the head of the WOW gameplayer association, Bronze Whisker, for having an extramarital affair with his wife, and immediately caught the attention of thousands of netizens. Queries, rumors, and curses soon swarmed the Internet and Bronze Whisker was put under the human flesh search. Bronze Whisker's personal information was dug up and exposed online in no time. Yet, while netizens denounced or even physically harassed Bronze Whisker, playing the role of moral vigilantes, some netizens found, and the husband later admitted, that some of the information about the affair was fabricated. The event gradually moved out of people's focus, but it left them with more questions than answers, not only in regard to the truth of the event, but also its ethical ramifications on the Internet.

The film mainly follows this event, but gives it a spin of mystery. The film begins with an accidental encounter between the police and Gao Fei, the role of Bronze Whisker, who is caught for using a fake identity card. It turns out that he does so in order to escape from harassment at home. The discovery days later by the police of the body of a girl, later affirmed to be that of Lin Yan, Fei's online game partner, leads to the exposure of her extramarital affair with Fei and the cause of her mysterious death. When Yan's husband finds out about their affair, he makes an open denunciation against Fei online. This denunciation immediately triggers a large-scale human flesh search against the "adulterous couple." Unable to bear the vicious verbal and physical attacks from the RRSS participants, Fei escapes to an isolated island. Yan, after having failed to obtain any understanding from her husband and family, or receive any comfort from Fei, and having been sexually harassed by people both known and unknown to her, commits suicide out of despair.

Wen Yu's novel, *Death on the Internet*, tells another tragic story of death and destruction related to the RRSS and modern media. Ye Lanqiu, a white-collar office girl, finds that she has a terminal cancer. Exhausted and upset, she hesitates to offer her seat to an elderly passenger standing by her, and this causes a squabble between Lanqiu and other impatient passengers on the bus. This incident is, however, recorded on the cell phone of Chen Ruoxi, a young journalist working for the local TV station, who happens to be on the same bus. Ruoxi ingeniously makes it a hot topic for debate by airing the video clip in the Primetime Nightly News, along with street interviews and expert discussions, and, most importantly, promoting discussions on the Internet. These acts soon result in a human flesh search for Lanqiu. Lanqiu's personal information then is exposed by Mo Xiaoyu, the wife of Lanqui's boss Shen Liushu, who, out of jealousy, also vilifies Lanqiu for being her husband's mistress. In a dramatic twist, Ruoxi's boyfriend Yang Shoucheng meets Lanqui and feels sympathy for her. He accompanies her to a remote place to escape from the harassments brought about by the RRSS, and spends the last few days with her before she takes her own life. In the meantime, Liushu, the boss, knows about his wife's betrayal and Ruoxi's treatment of Lanqui's case, and is mad at both of them. So he takes advantage of his social power and makes netizens believe that Ruoxi's public defamation of Lanqiu is out of her personal grudge against Lanqiu, as Lanqiu had taken Ruoxi's boyfriend away from her. Further shocked by Lanqiu's suicide, netizens almost unanimously sympathize with Lanqiu and reprimand Ruoxi for abusing public resources and power for personal gain. The story ends with Ruoxi being under her own human flesh search and, thus, disgraced both in her career and personal life. Chen Kaige's filmic adaptation largely follows the main story of Wen Yu's novel, with only a few changes that were meant to add some dramatic and romantic spins to the film.

In all of these three works, the issue of Internet ethics raised by the RRSS depicted in Sun Haoyuan's mystery novels are further interrogated with more critical intensity. What makes their interrogation more intensive, arguably, is their special critical engagement with the *mediality* of the Internet, particularly the mediality of the Internet in relation to that of other "traditional" media, such as TV. After all, the mediality of the Internet is a central concern of all three works from the very beginning of their creations. *Invisible Killer*, as the director Wang Jing confessed, was first motivated by the well-known "Cat Abuse and Killing" incident which took place in February 2006, and was one of the first major incidents in the development of the RRSS in China.[13] A serious reflection on this incident and the role the Internet played in it led to the director's further explorations of the RRSS and his later decision to take another equally well-known RRSS incident, "Bronze Whisker Gate," as the main story of the film (Sina 2009). The Internet as a new medium, as the director explicitly indicates in the title of his film, is an "invisible killer" that causes the tragedies.

The publications of Wen Yu's novel, on the other hand, signals complicated negotiations among considerations for social intervention, critical investigation of modern media, and popular consumption. The novel was first published on the Jinjiang Literature City with the title *Please Forgive Me*, in 2007. When it was selected by the website to compete for the prestigious state-run "Lu Xun Literature Prizes" in 2010, it was retitled as *Death on the Internet*, aiming explicitly at drawing public attention to its status as an Internet novel, a novel not only published *on* the Internet, but also *about* the Internet. The novel was later shortlisted as a finalist, and was the only Internet novel on the shortlist, although it did not win a prize. But its candidacy marks the first time an Internet novel was ever shortlisted for a mainstream, prestigious national literary award (Anonymous 2010).

Arguably, the novel is more than a work simply about the Internet; as its original title suggests, the author's central concern is more about human relations warped in this age of media oversaturation, and chances of restoration and forgiveness. Yet, when the novel was made further widely known as Chen Kaige adapted it for film, an opportunity presented itself to capitalize in the book market on a printed version of the novel, and it was published in the traditional book form with the same title as the film, *Sousuo* (literally "search"), in 2012. Obviously the publication sought to take advantage of the popularity of the film, which itself was exploiting the then ardently debated issue of the RRSS; however, the publication of the book fell short of the publisher's expectation in the market. The vice chief editor of the publisher, the newly established Shanghai Purui Cultural, Inc., believed that it was the "social subject" of the work, a subject that was less attractive in the tremendously entertainment-oriented, commercialized ecology of Internet literature in China, that negatively affected its popularity (Wu 2012). Yet, it is rather ironic that the very act of the promotion of the book as a work *of* the Internet and capitalizing on the RRSS was precisely the target of the work's social criticism. The mediality of the Internet and traditional media, as we will further explore, is a focus of the work's social intervention, but this very mediality was exploited in real life, ironically, for the promotion of the work that interrogates this exploitation. Most recently, the novel was repackaged as an Internet romance, *Will You Love Me as You First Did Tomorrow*, and published by another publisher, Hunan People's Press, in 2015. The result of this move is yet to be seen.

Chen Kaige's filmic adaptation of Wen Yu novel, presumably, involves a personal entanglement with mass media. As we explained in Chapter 1, in 2005 Chen's much hyped epic fantasy film, *The Promise*, failed to achieve its expected commercial and aesthetic success, and was spoofed and made a target of online satire by the amateur director, Hu Ge, in his short video. It was precisely the Internet and other digital technologies that were becoming increasingly accessible to the young digital generation that made this spoof possible. Viewed in this light, it is widely presumed that Chen took advantage of this film to reiterate his stance against the "Internet violence" (He 2012). Indeed, this film is more than a simple castigation of Internet violence, nor is it a product of a personal grudge, as Chen remarked on many occasions; yet, the role that the Internet and other media play in this urban romance is undeniably a focus of critical reflection, as well as a selling point.

"Invisible" netizens represented: visualizing "*hongke*" (哄客)

In questioning netizens' accountability, if not holding them unequivocally blameworthy, as they usually hold the searched accountable while evading their own answerability in the RRSS, these works, unlike *The Human Flesh Search Engine* and *Fatal Searches*, feature the unique power of the Internet in the hands of *common* Internet users in their *everyday* life. As a result, the netizens in these three works are not involved in any mysteries, and, therefore, may be exempted from an accusation of, wittingly or unwittingly, dramatically abusing their power granted by the new communicative technology of the Internet. Yet, their rather quotidian and *un*dramatic use of this power can be equally destructive and deadly, and, worse still, the users are not aware of their share in the abuse of this destructive power.

Further, those common netizens presume that they may submerge or conceal themselves among the millions of like-minded, indistinguishable netizens and, thus, become unidentifiable or invisible – that is, not accountable – when they conduct the RRSS. Their presumed invisibility is further guaranteed, as discussed above, by the prevalent anonymity of the Chinese Internet, which produces the effects of "deindividuation" and "diffusion of responsibility" that constitute the ethical deficiency of the Internet in China in general, and of the RRSS in particular. As Chian-Hseung Chao (2011: 653) remarks,

> The state [of deindividuation] is characterized by diminished awareness of self and individuality. This in turn reduces an individual's self-constraint and normative regulation of behavior. Deindividuation is an important part of depersonalization when a personal decreased sense of self-identity, self-awareness, and with lower level of self control [*sic*].

Chao continues to explain: "diffusion of responsibility effect" – "When a person is a member of a group, he/she will find the group action is a shared responsibility that can be dispersed or vague." Deindividuation and diffusion of responsibility, both characterizing netizens' psyches when participating in the RRSS, account for the participants' "invisibility" or, translated into a narrative term, unrepresentability.

Thus, the "invisible killer" in Wang Jing's film refers not only to the invisible but ubiquitous Internet, but also to those Internet users who choose to remain invisible and unanswerable. Interestingly, however, in *Invisible Killer* the usually anonymous and nondifferentiated netizens are, by narrative necessity or choice, concretized, or to be more specific, *visualized*, in a specific character, Zhou Qiang. This visualization of a depersonalized netizen not only provides the viewer, via the lens of cinema, with specific visual accounts of "invisible" netizens, but also signifies a complicated relationship between cinema and the Internet, particularly with regard to their mediating nature. The mediating nature, or mediality, of the Internet, cinema, TV, and other media is also a focus of the other two works' thematic concern, sometimes constituting their auto-referential twist and critical edge.

The visualized figure in *Invisible Killer*, Zhou Qiang, whose "net name/ID" is "Sword of Justice," is a netizen "representative" selected by a news/entertainment website for a mission to track down and dig out further information about the already shamed adulterous couple. In many ways, Qiang, a typical nobody, externalizes ethical flaws that many common netizens in China would find familiar. He works as an ordinary salesman in a small company; his overall dissatisfaction with, or resentment for, his own life and society is shared by many other netizens, particularly those who actively participate in the RRSS. That is why he is selected to represent them for this mission. A sideline sequence in the film is a telling example of Qiang's mentality in his rather fanatic devotion to the "search" for the couple. When he is walking across a street, he is almost run over by a Mercedes Benz that fails to yield to him; seeing the luxurious car, he is immediately infuriated and vents his grudges against the entire society, saying, "The rich people in China are the worst. None of their money is got in legal ways. All of them should be executed!"

This sequence quite effectively demonstrates an overall discontent with social injustice and inequality prevalent in contemporary China, which, without constructive engagement and rational reflection, easily translates into a contagious sentiment of cynicism and irrationality both online and offline. This incident showcases a prevailing sense of frustration that common and marginalized Chinese experience in their everyday life, and of which those in power are believed to be the cause. For the author, this sense of frustration and power imbalance account for an online and offline unrest, especially an online irrationality that informs the RRSS. The new medium of the Internet, with its embedded spirit of "freedom" further guaranteed by the practice of anonymity, provides those disgruntled netizens with an ideal space to vent their dissatisfaction. For instance, Qiang turns his real-life frustration into online vituperation, which is, ironically, masked in the form of a cyber-posse, aiming at upholding social and moral norms online and offline. The fact that his self-assumed role as a moral vigilante online is presumed to be empowered by his subaltern and marginalized status offline only testifies to our earlier claim that the sense of moral justice that many RRSS participants believe they represent is based more on an *imagined sense of justice* than a real upholding of social justice, and is thus constructed by virtue of a *compensatory mechanism*. That is to say, many of these participants believe they are morally and legally justified to conduct human flesh searches, because what they are doing is for the sake of social justice and equality.

For example, the T-shirt that Qiang wears during the course of his "mission" speaks of this imagined justice and compensatory mechanism. That T-shirt is a popular kind in contemporary China, with the famous logo of Che Guevara in the front (see Figure 5.1). This explicitly revolutionary logo, however, is a product of not only the lingering history of the socialist period, but also the looming nostalgia in the New Era for the socialist past (Dai 2009). Just as this nostalgia figures an *imagined* return to an irretrievable past, a sentiment shaped by disparate social forces including discontented common people, disillusioned intellectuals, and all-encompassing commercial power, the sense of justice and equality that this nostalgia points to and that RRSS participants presumably defend is also more symptomatic of social ailments that these participants experience and contribute to, rather than to an unproblematic upholding of social ethics. Qiang once forcefully claims that he is on this mission, "representing all netizens in China,"

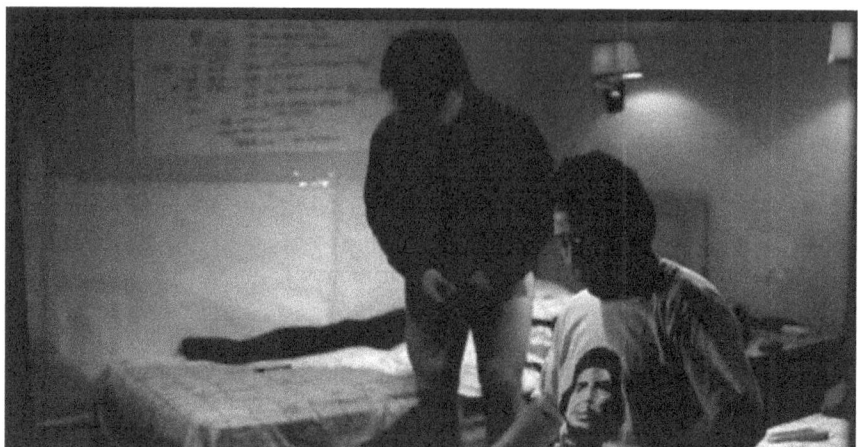

Figure 5.1 The iconic Che Guevara printed on Qiang's t-shirt
In Wang Jing, *Invisible Killer*

to "ask for an explanation" (*jiaodai*) from Fei for the latter's adulterous act; yet Qiang's presumably high moral stance, arguably based greatly on moral kidnapping, immediately turns into physical violence once Fei refuses to respond.

In another instance in Wen Yu's novel *Search* (the print version of *Death on the Internet*), a group of young students in their late teens and early twenties are instigated by media reports of Ye Lanqiu's disregard for social etiquette on the bus and immorality in love affairs, and gather in front of her home to protest. They reprimand Lanqiu especially for her presumed sexual misconduct and call for a severely humiliating punishment. A girl standing out as an opinion leader is particularly active and effective in arousing the crowd: she claims that they are protesting for the sake of "ridding the people of a public enemy" (*weimin chuhai*), and the crowd responds with a concerted shout of affirmation with overwhelming power (*paishan daohai*) (Wen 2012: 141–2). This scene simply harks back to images of public denunciations during the Cultural Revolution. As Tom Downey (2010) records in his essay in the *New York Times*:

> Rebecca MacKinnon, a visiting fellow at Princeton University's Center for Information Technology Policy, argues that China's central government may actually be happy about searches that focus on localized corruption. "The idea that you manage the local bureaucracy by sicking the masses on them is actually not a democratic tradition but a Maoist tradition," she told me. During the Cultural Revolution, Mao encouraged citizens to rise up against local officials who were bourgeois or corrupt, and human-flesh searches have been tagged by some as Red Guard 2.0. It's easy to denounce the tyranny of the online masses when you live in a country that has strong rule of law and institutions that address public corruption, but in China the human-flesh

search engine is one of the only ways that ordinary citizens can try to go after corrupt local officials.

Herold (2011b: 132) echoes MacKinnon, remarking, "if an individual netizen manages to attract large numbers of netizens to his/her cause, then they are free to begin harassing other Chinese individuals." Yet, what is ironic here is that these contemporary "Red Guards" are more individualists than collective soldiers – the leader exhibits her idiosyncrasy by her ripped jeans and affected mannerisms.

Both Qiang and the young students' acts not only expose the problematic nature of their moral stance, but also reminds us of the deeds characteristic of what the cultural critic Zhu Dake calls *hongke*, people who boo and hoot as a mob. Particularly problematic among the *hongke*, in Zhu's view, is the group of what he terms *make* (骂客 verbal-abusers). This is how he describes them:

> Hidden behind the logic of those verbal-abuses is a solid moral pillar, that is, a stand for "justice" which takes as its aim chastising social problems in China. This concern about social values has become an internalized faith of the verbal-abuser. Yet, for the sake of "catching viewers' eyes", "venting off their sentiments regardless whatsoever", and "upholding the so-called justice" they forsake their rational analyses, but take vituperation as their weapon instead. As a result, this only seriously weakens their reflective power and causes prevalent social resentment.
>
> (Zhu 2015: 12)

The characters of most RRSS participants, in many ways, fit quite nicely with Zhu's description of the verbal-abuser. Yet, what is unique about RRSS participants is the fact that their acts are decidedly shaped by the modern medium of the Internet. Indeed, one may find in the RRSS a pursuit for moral righteousness that can be traced back to Confucianism (Chen and Sharma 2011: 52), or a "bandwagon effect" that also characterizes mass movements of the Cultural Revolution (Chao 2011: 653); however, what is unique about the RRSS is arguably the fact that the Internet not only marks the distinctive ways in which the RRSS is conducted, but also informs social problematics of which the RRSS is symptomatic. This is not to overemphasize the role the Internet plays in shaping a social phenomenon; instead, it is to bring to our attention the fact that, as we have explained above, the neoliberalist spirit that the Internet carries with it,[14] which is further conditioned by the postsocialist reality in China, determines the unique features of the new medium of the Internet in China and of activities conducted in this new virtual space, and informs the new problems, particularly ethical problems, that are symptomatic of the postsocialist condition.

In the case of the RRSS, the usually anonymous and invisible netizen participants are concretized by the traditional print and visual media in the three works under investigation and, thus, rendered more palpable for specific inspection and examination. This, then, raises further questions about the mediality of the

Internet and the inter-mediality among the Internet and other media. An exploration of these questions is in order.

Manipulation of mediality and the issue of inter-mediality

In his influential book, *The Future of Reputation: Gossip, Rumor, and Privacy on the Internet*, Daniel J. Solove (2007: 11) convincingly argues that shaming others by circulating gossip and rumors can be traced back to the dawn of time, but "[t]hese social practices are now moving over to the Internet, where they are taking on new dimensions." In other words, the Internet has unprecedentedly, or structurally, changed the nature of the issues of privacy and free speech. A critical engagement with the very mediality of the Internet, a focal issue that these three works are concerned with, may therefore yield further understanding of the ways in which Internet ethics are shaped by manipulation of the Internet as a new medium.

The "compensatory mechanism" that marks the logic of the behaviors of many RRSS participants tells a stringent reality, against whose rules many netizens desire to establish alternative ones in the virtual space of the Internet. This stringent reality is explicitly laid out at the outset of *Search*, where Shoucheng is continually frustrated by a variety of unnecessary inconveniences set up by public services, such as the telecommunication bureau and the police department, when he only asks to cancel services and report to the police after his cell phone has been stolen. Lanqiu even falls into a catch-22-like dilemma, when she calls to claim her medical insurance and is only told to prove she will die in six months. What makes them even more frustrated is that they realize that they are stuck in a structural gridlock in which they are reasonably helpless and hopeless. For instance, Lanqiu is required to prove exactly how soon she will die because it is written specifically in her contract with the insurance company. Yet, Lanqiu, like most other people, has not read and is not able to understand every entry in the contract, which entails professional knowledge. What is worse, the associate from the insurance company makes a clear distinction between her personal opinion and how the contract should be carried out (Wen 2012: 16–17).

These incidents reveal, to borrow Douglas Rushkoff's (2010) seminal ideas, how ordinary people like Shoucheng and Lanqiu are controlled in their daily life by "programmed" institutions, programmed just as is digital technology. In other words, not unlike digital technology, those institutions that ordinary people deal with on daily basis are shaped by those who have written the rules; understandably, those rules favor those who have written them and, as a result, ordinary people are directed by the "programmers." But what is not so obvious – or what people may be aware of but do not think too much about – is that the social restraints they encounter are more than a result of an ordinary maneuver of "ideology." Here, as Shoucheng's and Lanqiu's cases show, institutional rules are programmed in such a "professional" way that their credibility seems to stand on their own right, and their "impartiality" is further guaranteed by a mechanical neutrality. Those rules are not meant to be deciphered by ordinary people, and the more undecipherable they are, the more impartial they seem to be. This is even more so with digital technologies, which are programmed in an even more "professional" fashion. A crucial point here is that ideology in this age of high professionalism is further mediated. In other words, mediality becomes a key issue in our understanding of the Internet. Rushkoff offers in his book what he calls "ten commands" for us to assert our agency in order to program, rather than to be programmed by, digital technologies. Yet, the three literary and cinematic works we have examined seem to alert us, in a more pessimistic manner, of how the Internet is manipulative of people's opinions and behaviors, and is manipulated by powers that master it.

Apparently, the most important power that masters the RRSS and the Chinese Internet at large, these works seem to suggest, is the increasingly prevalent commercial power, a power that has freed Chinese society from its past political controls, but put it into a more intangible constraint, namely the logic of the marketplace. In fact, none of the RRSS cases depicted in these works is driven merely by the innocent sense of correcting wrongs, but is always in one way or another governed by an interest in profiteering. For instance, as we mentioned above, the blatantly profit-oriented "Theory of Agenda Setup" that the Far Vision Net practices in *The Human Flesh Search Engine* may tellingly exemplify the manipulative commercial power behind the RRSS. In *Invisible Killer* and *Caught in Web*, human flesh searches are calculatedly "promoted" (*tui*) – that is, to reach out to most viewers in case the searches submerge into a swarm of information – by the websites, as well as the TV station, which host the searches for the sake of profit making. What these websites usually do to promote their RRSS include feeding voyeuristic desires by highlighting scandalous elements, arousing or even inventing controversies, and so on. In a way, they are concerned less about social justice than about commercial gains that they can receive from mass participation.

Perhaps the most poignant satire of this prevailing logic of commercialism on the Internet is the episode in *Search*, in which netizens who later believe Lanqui is a victim of personal grudges and the abuse of public power then decide to create a website in commemoration of her, only to realize a year later that the website will be revoked by the server which does not offer the service for free, and no one intends to pay the fees. Wen Yu (2012: 230) writes, "Perhaps this is the value of the Internet: it is free to curse someone on the Internet, and it is also free to express regret online; but a space of commemoration on the Internet is not free of charge." This line only reminds us of the physicality or materiality of the Internet, and the logic of capital from which this alternative space is not exempt. The logic of capital, further, is not only exemplified in a pursuit of profit over any other matter, including affection, on the Internet, but also in a replacement of time-honored value with exchange value, as a search for truth and justice is oftentimes taken over by a carnivalistic restlessness. To be more specific, the RRSS has to continuously move on in order for those who manipulate it to extract maximum capital.

Further, the RRSS is a typical product of what we call an economy of Web 2.0, which is characterized by "prosumption," an "implosion of production and consumption" (Ritzer and Jurgenson 2010: 19). As George Ritzer and Nathan Jurgenson (2010: 21–3) argue, prosumption is a new form of capitalism, whose differences from traditional forms of capitalism are determined by the ideological underpinning of cyber-libertarianism that is embedded in the Internet. Therefore, exploitation in prosumption is less clear-cut and control more difficult. Yet, it seems the three works suggest otherwise. Not only are the exploiters and their acts of manipulations in these works explicitly exposed, but the logic of capital in the manipulations seems to exemplify a more primitive rather than a more "advanced" feature. For instance, in *Search* and *Caught in the Web*, although Ruoxi and Yang Jiaqi, Shoucheng's cousin who works as an intern journalist under Ruoxi's supervision, orchestrate the RRSS on Lanqiu, they are doing this, as Ruoxi candidly tells Jiaqi, because as ordinary persons in a highly competitive society they are driven by the "absolute principle of the survival of the fittest." This survivalist ethos, ironically, leads to Ruoxi's own downfall in the end, as Jiaqi takes advantage of Ruoxi's minor negligence and turns against her. Their survivalist acts not only exemplify the prevailing law of the jungle in this age of the Internet, but also reaffirms Manuel Castells' (2000) convincing argument that the logic of the network society is only an extension of that of capital. Only here the logic of capital still has a rather bloody face that characterizes its early ruthless stage.

Perhaps the most intriguing exposure of capital magnates' manipulation of the Internet is the added episode in the film *Caught in the Web*, in which Liushu throws a party in front of his potential collaborator from abroad, celebrating the fifteenth anniversary of his marriage with Xiaoyu. In fact, their fifteenth anniversary should be a month later, but in order to put on an image of a responsible husband in front of his collaborator, and as a strategy to offset the negative impacts that the publicity of Lanqiu's incident has caused to his company, Liushu designs this party and even fakes the date of his marriage. He also manages to have his men take "candid pictures" of them and hype the event as another of his extramarital romances on the Internet, only to attract netizens' attention to him and "discover" the "truth" – he *is* a faithful husband. This episode is indeed an ingenious addition to the original book, as it poignantly exposes how skillfully Liushu manipulates public opinion by mastering new visual and communicative media and by taking advantage of the weaknesses of netizens' psyches. Further, given the heated controversy about the private and the public in this movie, as well as in discussions about the RRSS at large, Liushu's act reveals that the demarcation between what is private and what is public held sacred in modern civil society can be, and usually is, manipulated by those in power. That is to say, protection of privacy, a core issue in people's reflections of the RRSS, can be a moot issue if manipulation of media is so intriguingly carried out. This is indeed a dire picture of the future of the Internet and a timely warning for us. Perhaps Liushu's remark, "Media are like undercovers; they are everywhere," best characterizes the situation that contemporary people are inevitably faced with – the ubiquity of media, which are panoptic and can be violent; and ultimately, media embody power relationships that are as ideological as exploitative.

In addition, the fact that the whole event of celebration is exposed to be no more than a show in front of a camera and on the Internet, a performance of affection mediated by lenses and screens of electronic devices, further foregrounds the nature of *performance* in the manipulation of and through media. This sense of performance is literally exhibited in the episode in which, when the two invited academic discussants, in a more rational and less confrontational manner, exchange views on the Ye Lanqiu incident in the pre-recording of a talk show program, Ruoxi becomes impatient and cuts their conversation short. She knows their bland exchange of views will not arouse any interest among entertainment-thirsty viewers, so she requires the discussants to put on a show of verbal combat in front of the camera. This show of verbal combat not only feeds viewers' desire for irrationality and entertainment, a feature that Ruoxi immediately captures as she envisions the economic potential of the RRSS, and thus turns the Ye Lanqiu incident into a commercial success; but it also reveals that this success is professionally orchestrated by specifically targeting participants' consumerist desires, and by skillfully exploiting the mediality of modern technologies.

Most intriguingly perhaps is how, in *Invisible Killer*, the website journalist who is sent to accompany Qiang along the way records his mission with his DV (digital video), so that website editors can attract viewers by informing them of Qiang's "progress" with frequently published and most recent recordings. The underlying ideal about which this act seems reminiscent is the "New Chinese Documentary Film Movement" started in the early 1990s, and one of whose most vociferous slogans is "My camera doesn't lie" (Berry, Lü, and Rofel 2010, Zhang 2006). Indeed, the journalist seems to make efforts to maintain the "objectivity" of his recording by "faithfully" following every step of Qiang's mission while keeping some distance from him. He even records Qiang's final arrest by the police for his physical attacks on Fei, which infuriates Qiang, as Qiang believes the journalist is his comrade of the same "cause," not an onlooker who laughs at and takes advantage of his downfall. In fact, the journalist has never been, or intended to be, an objective recorder. The moment when he asks Qiang to pose in front of his camera early in the film already reveals an exploitation by his camera. Just as their mission is aimed at raising the popularity of its sponsoring website for the latter's ongoing fundraising project rather than asserting social justice and equality, the camera's claimed objectivity is inevitably belied by its specific commercial intent.

Moreover, the director Wang Jing uses his camera to capture those scenes of media maneuvers, and reveal the very mediality of the new technologies, including the Internet and the digital camera, as well as the manipulative nature of their mediation. These inter-media dynamics brings to mind the critic Nie Wei's comments on Chen Kaige's *Caught in the Web*, which also instantiates interesting inter-media entanglements among the film, TV, smartphones, and the Internet. In Nie's opinion, Chen's film reveals his elitist view of new media in China. Not unlike *Invisible Killer*, *Caught in the Web* also exposes the ways in which mobile devices, the Internet, and TV are intriguingly and intensely exploited in a variety of implicit, or not so implicit, schemes; yet Chen's critique of those media is grounded on his assertion of the validity of the film, the very medium that he as the director employs. Thus, Chen establishes a "hierarchy of media," with the film on the top, overseeing other media (Nie 2012: 30).

Arguably, Nie's remarks resonates with the popular speculation, as mentioned above, that Chen produced *Caught in the Web* as a delayed counterattack against Hu Ge's spoof of his *The Promise*, a speculation the Chen flatly denies. Whether we agree with Nie or not, his argument points to an inter-media, or a meta-media, relationship that features all of these works, in which the mediality of the Internet and other modern technologies is constantly exposed by literary and cinematic representations. Indeed, in line with Nie's argument, we may say authorial assertions are an inevitable dimension in these representations, which, however, by themselves are a form of mediation. Yet rather than viewing these works as elitist attempts to create a hierarchy among representational media, attempts that signify endeavors to reaffirm a conventional literary hierarchy that is under growing challenges from burgeoning digital forms of art, perhaps it is more constructive to perceive them as mediated reflections of mediality at large, and the mediality of the Internet in particular.

After all, Wen Yu's novel was first published online; its critique of the manipulations of the Internet, as well as other media, offers her work a degree of auto-referential quality. That is to say, it does not take the more "orthodox" media of print literature and film to evaluate or rectify, still less in a condescending manner, the newly arisen Internet culture. In fact, Internet writings, in some people's view, is in the process of establishing its own rules of production, evaluation, and consumption in its own alternative space (Shao 2009, 2011, 2012a, 2014, 2015, Shao et al. 2012). Yet, the fact that Wen Yu's online novel was known to the wider readership outside of netizens only after it had been shortlisted as a finalist for the Lu Xun Literary Prizes, which led to its further popularization after Chen Kaige adapted it into a film, and the fact that, after the adapted film became a box-office hit, the author went after publications of her novel in book form twice, both testify to a negotiation among the different media of Internet, film, and print, if not an incorporation of the Internet by the latter two.

Indeed, this negotiation is inevitable in China because, as Shao Yanjun (2009: 12) convincingly argues in her seminal studies of the drastic institutional and structural transformation taking place in the literary field in China, while Internet productions are surging as an increasingly prominent power in the market and the contemporary cultural scene, conventional print literature and film productions, with their existing institutional control and consequently the structured reading and viewing habits they have developed over the years, are still keeping a tight grip on the so-called mainstream cultural production. The two production-evaluation-consumption systems, which are determined more by different "media civilizations" (*meijie wenming*) than institutional differences, generational gaps, or disparate literary principles, will continue to struggle and negotiate for discursive power. What is instructive to our discussion is that mediality, perhaps more than any other factors, plays a decisive role in China's latest cultural transformation. The negotiation among different media in the contentious cultural field informs an inter-media dynamic that is exemplified in the representations of the Internet in the works under discussion, and a meta-media tension that is instantiated by the production of these works.

The ethical aspect of hyper-connectivity and intimacy

Poignant enough in the end of *Search* is when Wen Yu (2012: 190–1) compares media (*meiti*) to matchmakers (*meipo*), a term that carries a rather pejorative connotation in Chinese, as the two terms share the character, *mei* (mediation). Perhaps for the author, media manipulate people's views in a similar way that stereotypically matchmakers exploit people's opinions. The mediality of the Internet is further exemplified, in an ironic fashion, in the paradox of deficient communication in hyper-connection.

In Chapter 2, we have discussed the heterotopic role cyberspace plays in enabling hyper-connectivity and intimacy, and the dialectics of virtual connectedness and physical alienation. How should we view the issue from an ethical perspective? Critics have written abundantly about how communication among people are often disrupted, distorted, and superficialized by the hyper-connectivity of modern means of communication. For instance, Sherry Turtle (2011) questions people's over-reliance on technologies of communication, which ironically results in a deficiency in real and deep communications. In the case of the RRSS, it is precisely this paradox of deficient communication in hyper-connection facilitated by manipulations of the Internet in China, we argue, that accounts for the ethical problems on the Internet at large, and in the RRSS phenomenon in particular.

In these three works, through numerous scenes of ubiquitous cell phones, cameras, landline and mobile connections, screens of a variety of sizes – smartphones, laptops, desktop monitors, program editors' screens, TVs, and large screens in public squares – we are presented with a world that is saturated with all forms of media. This media saturation leads to a hyper-connectivity that undeniably characterizes the world today. Yet, this hyper-connectivity, rather than bringing people closer, seems to alienate them further from each other. For instance, in *Caught in the Web* Liushu and Xiaoyu play tricks on each other by employing new media, such as when Xiaoyu makes an anonymous call to a live TV program slandering Liushu and Lanqiu, or when Liushu tracks Xiaoyu's call history and, as mentioned above, fakes their anniversary in front of a camera. They have numerous means through which to connect with each other, but they exploit these means of connection for various other purposes than communication, only to find, as they unwillingly concede, "we don't share a topic of same interest, and we have nothing to say to each other anymore." Super convenience in human communication made possible by new technologies, ironically, only results in human beings losing a fundamental trust in each other and an ability for true communication.

This sense of alienation within hyper-connectivity is also explicitly suggested in *Invisible Killer*. The easy connection made possible by the Internet and the alternative space created thereby make Yan believe that the relationship she has developed online with Fei is true love, which she takes as a replacement for the emotional vacuum that her husband leaves. Yet, when she turns to Fei for help after their affair is discovered and exposed online, and Fei refuses to stand with her, she then comes to the realization that things taking place online are not real. This disillusionment leads to her despair and suicide. Fei's experience with the

Internet, similarly, begins with a desire to find consolation online for his emotional emptiness, which leads to the final destruction of his real life. He requires Yan, during their loving making, to say she loves him, only to reveal unmistakably a sense of a spiritual void that he strives to fill with coercion. Moreover, he uses a fake ID card he has bought in the black market during his escape, which not only tells of his stranded situation in society, but is also symbolic of a questioning of his own identity. To be more specific, when his alternative identity on the Internet messes up his real-life identity in his affair with Yan, Fei simply loses control of his life and has to adopt another fake identity.

This hyper-connectivity also alienates people from themselves. For example, in *Caught in the Web*, Shoucheng refuses to lie in a wedding ceremony in order to cover the money hoax that the groom's father has played on the bride's father, leading to the abrupt cancellation of the ceremony and the loss of his job. His boss scolds him, "Are you going to die if you lie?" Lying, in this world of high informational fluidity, has become a basic skill for survival, and refusing to lie – that is, to be untrue to others and to himself – makes Shoucheng out of place and, in a way, a loser. Unlike his girlfriend Ruoxi, Shoucheng is depicted as far from "successful," professionally or in his personal life.

This paradox of hyper-connectivity and deficient communication, in fact, contributes to the very formation of the RRSS. In Wen Yu's story, for example, the RRSS on Lanqiu is possible because people do not know the whole story as a result of the lack of communication among netizens. These netizens simply notice the fact that Lanqiu refuses to give her seat to an elderly passenger, and exaggerate it without bothering to know the other parts. What they want from the Internet is more sensational messages than can only be delivered through rational investigations. Moreover, it is also precisely because of the hyper-connectivity of the Internet that the RRSS becomes so "efficiently" and "effectively" conducted. Further, this paradox inevitably leads to an irrationality that renders the online ethos problematic. For instance, after Shoucheng is later tricked into believing, as a result of Liushu's scheme, that Ruoxi first initiates the RRSS on Lanqiu, and later blemishes her on the TV because Lanqiu has attracted Ruoxi's boyfriend, netizens' opinion immediately shifts from condemning Lanqiu as an immoral person to rhapsodizing her as a "saint girl," particularly after she is dead, while blaming Ruoxi for an abuse of public power for a personal interest. This immediate change of opinion, again, reveals a deficiency in rational meditation online as a result of lack of deep and constructive communication, and this deficiency will spread far and wide online because of the hyper-connectivity provided by the Internet.

The sense of alienation brought about by this paradox, in a way, can be traced back to the human alienation that came along with the commercialization in the market economy. After all, the market flattens the world and creates atomized, rather than positioned, individuals, who are to be re-"connected" by modern relations and technologies. This "reconnection" restructures human relations, in which traditional bonds, be they based on blood ties or sociocultural affinities, are disrupted, and modern communications become increasingly fluid and more grounded on exchanges of interests rather than values. This replacement of exchange value for use value, as mentioned earlier, is increasingly visible on the Chinese Internet, and is exemplified in the pursuit of hyper-connectivity over real communication.

Moreover, this process is no less ideological than the fetishism of the commodity. In fact, the Internet, particularly the most commonly used device by which people connect to the Internet – the smartphone – is depicted as something increasingly indispensable to people's daily lives, or even as becoming part of human bodies (Wang 2009). For instance, at the beginning of *Caught in the Web*, Shoucheng is so disconcerted when he loses his smartphone because he has stored some intimate pictures on it. With some other important "part" of his life associated with the phone, such as bank accounts, he indeed has reason to be disconcerted. Later in the film, smartphones continue to perform as eyes/I's of their holders in the episodes, such as when Jiaqi records the incidents of Lanqiu refusing to give her seat to an elderly passenger, onlookers take pictures of the "celebrity" Lanqiu in the housemaid market, and Shoucheng takes pictures of Lanqiu on their way to her resort where she spends her final days. These witnessing, voyeuristic, threatening, and intimate "eyes/I's," connected to the Internet in one way or another, closely merge the devices with personal identities. By so doing, they seem to have naturalized the functionality of new technologies and concealed their mediality, in a comparable way in which the market naturalizes its mediation of modern human relations. After all, it is exposed in all of these three works that the mediality of the Internet is, by and large, manipulated by commercial powers in China (Gong 2016).

Affection, it is suggested in these three works, can be used as an antidote to the moral degeneration on the Internet. The lack of communication within hyper-connectivity on the Internet, not surprisingly, always generates some problems with human relations among characters, as described earlier. Very tellingly, for another example, in *Search* Ruoxi feels extremely alienated and desolate after she is "discovered" to have framed Lanqiu; her sense of alienation and desolation is particularly poignant as she no longer receives calls, text messages, or online messages from her friends, in sharp contrast to the time when she is in charge of the TV program about Lanqiu's incident, while the RRSS against Lanqiu is in full steam. This moment marks the beginning of Ruoxi's downfall, which eventually leads to her loss of love and the disintegration of her personal life in almost every aspect. In contrast, Lanqiu escapes to a remote place where there is no Internet connection and phone service is also extremely unstable; but her emotional life is remedied and comes to terms with her life, most importantly gaining love from Shoucheng. Here, the place without the Internet seems to be romanticized as a utopia where human bonds disrupted online get restored; this utopian sense is echoed by *Invisible Killer*, in which, at the end, Fei is shown the last message that Yan has sent to him before she takes her own life: "I will say goodbye to the past in a place where there is no Internet." What is implied here, however, is less a return to a "no-Internet's land" than a return to affection as a possible remedy to the ailment of human alienation of or caused by the Internet, which inevitably results in ethical problems online.

Affection is particularly relevant in our discussion of the RRSS, as one central issue in controversies about the RRSS is privacy, and privacy signals not only a personal right but also an intimate relationship. It is only with those whom one trusts and to whom one has close ties that one shares his or her privacy, and this sharing marks an act of intimacy and affection. The RRSS, on the other hand, breaches this social etiquette of privacy in the name of moral justice and, worse still, with a voyeuristic eye. It violates not only the private sphere that one is entitled to, but also the sense of closeness and intimacy that one shares with significant others. Viewed in this regard, the ethical problem on the Chinese Internet that the RRSS exemplifies does not simply arise from a legal controversy, but is also tied closely to human affection, or a lack thereof.

Moreover, this loss of privacy and intimacy takes place under the pressure of irrational mobs, and harkens back to the Cultural Revolution. This reminds us of the radical elimination of *si* (the individual, the private, and the personal) in the name of ultra-collectivity during that time. For example, "*dousi pixiu*" (fight self-ishness, repudiate revisionism), a guiding principle of the Great Proletariat Cultural Revolution, and "*hen dou si zi yi shannian*" (resolutely fight against selfish thought), a household catchword in *dousi pixiu*, limited the room for any pursuit of individualism or personal affection, and accomplished this restraint through corporeal coercion and punishment. This fight against things private during the Cultural Revolution, ironically, finds its contemporary counterpart on the Chinese Internet, an alternative space that is supposed to be liberal and liberating. This irony, to a great extent, can be traced to the aforementioned paradox of deficiency of communication in hyper-connectivity, as the presumable freedom online, in fact, does not guarantee a real freedom in humanity, but on the contrary oftentimes disrupts a constructive practice of real freedom. Ideological maneuvers, it has been shown, usually conceal the mediality of the Internet and render the Internet in China more a carnivalistic outlaw space than an alternative space of constructive rationality. Affection, in this context, may function as an important index of real and deep communication.

Indeed, these works' "affective" approach to the RRSS is grounded on the generic writing that marks popular entertainment, and is thus subject to the risk of (over)-dramatization and romanticization. This populist approach usually turns to immediate sensationalism, instant venting of emotions, and, worse still, voyeuristic desire. In the case of the RRSS, in which Internet ethics and self-reflectivity are two key issues, this turn to the form of popular entertainment seems particularly problematic because these writers and filmmakers may have weakened their moral messages and created audience passivity by encouraging an "involuntary emotion" in their audience that "is the opposite of reflection and implication" (Aaron 2007: 116). In her study of spectatorship, Michele Aaron (2007: 116) finds that films "that lean most heavily on reinforcing moral processes tend to disable the spectators' capacity to engage their own ethical judgments." The way in which such films achieve what she calls *amoralism*, an "absence of interest in or deference to morality," is, instead, to produce a "spectatorial insulation." This spectatorial insulation, arguably, can be extended to a readership insulation, as the detached stance that a reader adopts when reading books is, in a similar fashion of working through a combination of catharsis and denial, crucial in arriving at amoralism. In this regard, the affective mode in these works may harm the reflective power that is essential to a constructive Internet ethics.

This rather elitist argument, given the nature of the Chinese Internet, should however be balanced by a populist consideration. As Shao Yanjun (2015: 150) convincingly argues, the popularity and effective dissemination of online writings in China are largely based on a fan economy and a "mechanism of pleasure" (*kuaigan jizhi* 快感机制), which help form "affective communities" (*qinggan gongtongti* 情感共同体) among the readership. These affective communities, which may find their predecessors in state practices during the socialist period which popularized national characters of Chinese art and literature by turning primarily to folk culture, today are established based on their members' shared emotional attachment to popular culture (Shao 2014: 70). Genre writing, a dominant form of popular culture, achieves its emotive and affective power by presenting, with its creativity within established models, both "age-long desires" of the humanity and "principal anxieties" of contemporary time (Shao 2015: 148–9). In other words, affection, be it romantic emotion in particular or shared ties among populist readership and spectatorship at large, may play an important role, with its empathetic power, in remedying the disrupted and displaced sense of depth and intimacy, which has been flattened and superficialized by the prevailing hyper-connectivity, and therefore be instrumental to the urgent task of rebuilding a constructive online ethics. After all, development of social ethics as a continuous process of contention and negotiation among various parties involves productive interactions and rational communications among people with disparate opinions so as to reach a degree of agreement.[15] Thus perceived, these works' affective approach, though sometimes bordering on a degree of sentimentalism, may function as an interesting reaction to the ethical lapse on the Chinese Internet.

Coda

The English title of Chen Kaige's film *Caught in the Web*, as in contrast to its original, more neutral Chinese title *Sousuo*, or search, quite obviously expresses the sense of being trapped in the quagmire, physical and spiritual, that human beings are faced with in this age of digital technologies. Indeed, none of the works examined in this chapter seems optimistic about our condition: both *The Human Flesh Search Engine* and *Fatal Searches* seem to end with an assertion of the authority and "sanctity" of the legal system, when an abuse of the system by the use of digital technologies takes place. Yet capital punishments of the "perpetrators," rather than bringing a resolution to the stories, further confound people's ethical perception of the (ab)use of the Internet. *Invisible Killer* presents an even bleaker ending, when rumors continue to spread among and excite the "journalists" even after Yan has paid the price of her life. *Caught in the Web* somehow displaces serious deliberation with its romanticization of Lanqiu's death. *Death on the Internet* displays how the protean and irrational nature of Chinese netizens first contributes to Lanqiu's suicide and later drives Ruoxi to a dead end.

In her study of Internet ethos in China, Shubo Li (2010: 74) observes,

> If we compare the public ethos favoring playful vandalism as currently manifested by popular discourses found in the major forums, to the online public ethos favoring truth-seeking discussion in the early days of the Chinese web, one could argue that a fundamental transition has happened. The transition of the Chinese online public space is characteristic of highly organized centralization and a vibrant proliferation of popular discourses and folk narratives, as well as a narrowing space for rational deliberation.

Indeed, "a narrowing space for rational deliberation," caused ironically by the exponentially broadening space of "liberation," leads to a "playful vandalism" that characterizes the RRSS in particular and the ethos of the Chinese Internet at large. The five works examined in this chapter, in their different ways, showcase the moral problems that confront Chinese netizens in their pursuit of freedom and social justice in the alternative space of the Internet. The ideology of neoliberalism embedded in the Internet enacts the postsocialist condition in China, and shapes netizens' mindset and manners online, as well as offline. Yet, this virgin space presents opportunities and challenges alike, and in the case of the RRSS the law of the jungle often prevails. Abetted by the prevalence of anonymity, the Chinese Internet exhibits an ethical problem of uneven accountability. The moral lapses exhibited in many online activities have raised concerns among intellectuals. Their literary and filmic representations of the RRSS point to the commercial and consumerist ideology that has gripped Chinese society since its postsocialist turn to global capitalism. More interestingly, these literary and filmic works, by themselves a form of media *representation*, seek to bring out the very mediality of the Internet as well as that of other digital technologies, and open up a space for inter-media and meta-media deliberation. In the final analysis, a self-reflective rationality that hopefully is to come about in deep communications, rather than in superficialized hyper-connectivity, is called for to bring about a constructive restructuring of Internet ethics. In this process, a pursuit of affective expressions may help enrich human interactions flattened by the hyper-convenience "blessed" by Internet technologies.

Notes

1 On December 29, 2007, two days after the broadcast of the report, the State Administration of Radio, Film and Television (SARFT) and the Ministry of Information Industry jointly issued "Regulations of Services of Audio and Visual Programs on the Internet," aiming to further control such Internet services.

2 It is generally agreed that the first RRSS case was the online search launched on a Tianya BBS for the real identity of the Internet celebrity "Poison" in February 2006. However, Wang et al. (2010: 46) claim that the very first RRSS event was the search for the real identity of a young woman on Mop.com in 2011. The user who had posted

her photo online claimed her as his girlfriend, but it turned out that she was a minor celebrity.

3 Vincent Capone's (Since 2011) blog website "Human Flesh Search Engine" collects materials related to the RRSS and updates regularly with recent information, development, discussion, and research.

4 Admittedly, legal and moral problems are not the only issues in discussions of the RRSS. In the RRSS case of a Western woman stopping a car driver from entering a bicycle lane in Beijing, for instance, the "wrongdoers," a Chinese car driver, is less judged on the ground of social justice and morality than criticized for humiliating the nation. Obviously, nationalism is a central issue in this case. See Herold (2011b: 134).

5 By "ethical identity," we mean a perception or expression of one's personality with regard to specific ethical values.

6 Tom Downey (2010), in his *New York Time*'s report on the RRSS in China, "China's Cyberposse," mentioned this novel, but did not make any comments on it.

7 This reminds us of the fact that in Internet writings and games in China, many of the latter developed based on the former, and embed, exemplify, and promote the law of the jungle. For instance, the so-called *xiaobai wen* (literally "little idiot writing"), a hugely popular style in Chinese Internet writing, features continuous fighting and conquests, and simply embodies the rule of power (usually on the part of an invincible protagonist). Readers gain their pleasure mainly from an immediate satisfaction of desire and an unreflected endorsement of power. If Internet writing signifies the "core anxiety and value" of an age, as the critic Shao Yanjun argues, then *xiaobai wen*, as well as many other popular genre writings on the Internet, indeed signal a social symptom that is problematic of contemporary China. See Shao (2015: 151).

As a report in *Global Times* goes, "The breakdown in moral values has resulted in a society ruled by the law of the jungle, and the online world cannot be an exception where rationality prevails" (Lu 2010).

8 Xujun Eberlein (2008) writes, "An information expert thinks large-scale human flesh search engines are unique to China, a claim that appears to be true. This is understandable as a consequence of China's ubiquitous manpower and ingrained tradition of 'people's war' tracing back to Mao."

Rebecca MacKinnon (2009) remarks, "Unlike the Red Guards they're [participants of the RRSS] not really being manipulated by one charismatic leader (yet); they're just acting on their own. Like the Red Guards, the intent of today's cyber-vigilantes is idealistic; they believe in their absolute moral righteousness." Comparing the RRSS to the "freedom of speech" during the Cultural Revolution, MacKinnon is more concerned with the lack of institutional changes in both cases that would bring real transformation to a more democratic society in China. She continues to write, as a response to a comment posted below her blog article,

> because people have an expanded ability to speak truth to power thanks to new technology, that doesn't automatically lead to a more just society in the long run unless you have institutional change. I wonder whether people will be so distracted and excited about the ability to use the Internet to speak truth to power that they'll have less interest in such institutional change.

9 Farrell and Herold (2011: 177) have discerned two values determining the anonymity of the Internet in China, as they write:

> The Chinese concept of anonymity is complex and multifaceted. Part of it draws from the traditional Confucian value of collectivism, of the deferment of the individual to the collective interest. However, anonymity now services opposing and more recently ascendant values of libertarianism, privacy and self-determination. It is the more libertarian notions of anonymity that have been evoked in recent public protest against real-name policies, but it may be the collectivist aspect that is more

responsible for the broader default tendencies toward nameless (*wuming*) mediated sociality, today epitomized by the ubiquitous QQ number.

10 Arendt's discussion of thinking was mainly conducted as a reaction to the dark age of totalitarianism in the twentieth century, when people suffered from a severe lack of freedom. But, intriguingly, we find her thoughts, mediated through Rüdiger Safranski, also highly relevant when it comes to an age marked by unprecedented "freedom," where evilness can be prevalent.

11 Shao Yanjun (2012a: 16) calls the age of the Internet a "post-enlightenment" age.

12 The traditional value of filial piety, however, is foregrounded in *Fatal Searches*, as the killer takes those who have shown disrespect for the elderly as his targets. This foregrounding seems to be a response not only to the controversial debates, both in reality and incorporated in the plot of the novel, on the issue of whether young people should offer his or her seat to an elderly person on a bus, but also to the overall moral confusion online and offline. Interestingly, the issue of offering a seat to the elderly is also featured in the plots of Wen Yu's Internet novel, *Death on the Internet*, and Chen Kaige's film adaptation, *Caught in the Web*, both of which will be discussed in detail below.

13 In February 2006, a video in which a woman tortured, crushed, and killed a kitten with her high heel was posted online, and snapshots from this video went viral, causing concerted condemnations of this act online. A human flesh search was immediately launched on Mop.com, and the identities of this woman and the one who recorded this video, as well as their professional and personal information, were soon uncovered and exposed online, which led to the suspension from their jobs and their final resignation.

14 The populist spirit that looms large in the formation of *hongke* in China, and the neoliberalist spirit that is implicitly embedded in the development of the Internet, remind us of what Stuart Hall (1988: 123–46) calls "authoritarian populism," a hegemonic politico-cultural practice in which capitalist elites take advantage of popular supports, assume the role of the voice of the populace, and intriguingly incorporate public interests into their corporate interests. Hall believes that this authoritarian populism plays a decisive role in British neoliberalism. For further elaboration on the term, see Jessop et al. (1984). Wang Weijia (2014: 35–6) makes an interesting connection between authoritarian populism and populism on the Internet, and points out the role that the former plays in the neoliberalist turn of Internet culture.

15 As David Kurt Herold (2011a: 10), in his discussion of Chinese Internet, summarizes Jürgen Habermas's highly influential theory on public sphere: "The continuous rational deliberations of independent individual citizens are seen as leading to the acceptance of shared sets of basic rules for society and the shaping and expression of public wishes for the government of the state."

Bibliography

Aaron, Michele. (2007). *Spectatorship: The Power of Looking On*. London and New York: Wallflower.

Anonymous. (2010). "Wangshi chengwei weiyi ruwei Lu Xun wenxue jiang de wangluo wenxue zuopin" (Death on the Internet becomes the only Internet literary work nominated for the Lu Xun literary awards). *Beijing chenbao*, September 9. http://book.people.com.cn/GB/69360/12681428.html. Last accessed August 31, 2016.

Arendt, Hannah. (1951). *The Origins of Totalitarianism*. New York: Harcourt.

——. (1977). *The Life of the Mind*. Vol. 1. New York: Harcourt Brace Jovanovich.

——. (1982). *Lectures on Kant's Political Philosophy*. Chicago: University of Chicago Press.

Benney, Jonathan. (2015). "'The Corpses Were Emotionally Stable': Agency and Passivity on the Chinese Internet." In *China Online: Locating Society in Online Spaces*, edited by Peter Marolt and David Kurt Herold, 33–48. London and New York: Routledge.

Berry, Chris, Xinyu Lü, and Lisa Rofel, eds. (2010). *The New Chinese Documentary Film Movement: For the Public Record*. Hong Kong: Hong Kong University Press.

Capone, Vincent R. (Since 2011). *Human Flesh Search Engine Blog*. http://humanflesh searchengine.blogspot.com/. Last accessed August 31, 2016.

——. (2013). "Generations Apart: Cultural Revolution Memory and China's Post-80's Generation on the Chinese Internet." MA Thesis. Boston, MA: University of Massachusetts at Boston.

Castells, Manuel. (2000). *The Rise of the Network Society*. 2nd ed. Oxford and Malden, MA: Blackwell Publishers.

Cawelti, John G. (1976). *Adventure, Mystery, and Romance: Formula Stories as Art and Popular Culture*. Chicago: University of Chicago Press.

CCTV. (2007). "It Is Urgent to Clean the Environment on the Internet." *Xinwen lianbo*, December 27. https://www.youtube.com/watch?v=mspuiqlycJA. Last accessed August 31, 2016.

Chao, Chian-Hsueng. (2011). "Reconceptualizing the Mechanism of Internet Human Flesh Search: A Review of the Literature." Paper presented at the 2011 International Conference on Advances in Social Networks Analysis and Mining (ASONAM), July 25–27.

Chen, Rui, and Sushil K. Sharma. (2011). "Human Flesh Search—Facts and Issues." *Journal of Information Privacy & Security* 7, no. 1: 50–71.

Dai Jinhua. (2009). "Rewriting the Red Classics." In *Rethinking Chinese Popular Culture: Cannibalizations of the Canon*, edited by Carlos Rojas and Eileen Cheng-yin Chow, 151–78. London and New York: Routledge.

Downey, Tom. (2010). "China's Cyberposse." *New York Times*, March 3.

Eberlein, Xujun. (2008). "Human Flesh Search: Vigilantes of the Chinese Internet." *New American Media*, April 30. http://news.newamericamedia.org/news/view_article.html? article_id=964203448cbf700c9640912bf9012e05. Last accessed August 31, 2016.

Farrall, Kenneth, and David Kurt Herold. (2011). "Identity vs. Anonymity: Chinese Netizens and Questions of Identifiability." In *Online Society in China: Creating, Celebrating, and Instrumentalising the Online Carnival*, edited by David Kurt Herold and Peter Marolt, 165–83. Abingdon, Oxon and New York: Routledge.

Gong, Haomin. (2016). "Shouji yu richang shenghuo bianqian: Cong *Kouxin* dao *Sousuo*" (Cell phone and changes of our daily lives: from *An oral message* to *Caught in the web*). *Wenhua yanjiu* 24: 81–93.

Hall, Stuart. (1988). *The Hard Road to Renewal: Thatcherism and the Crisis of the Left*. London and New York: Verso.

He Guimei. (2010). *"Xin qimeng" zhishi dang'an: 80 niandai Zhongguo wenhua yanjiu (Knowledge archives of "new enlightenment": Chinese cultural studies in the 80s)*. Beijing: Beijing daxue chubanshe.

He Hanjing. (2012). "Chen Kaige cheng bu na dianying xiang Hu Ge 'gongbao sichou'" (Chen Kaige claims not to revenge himself on Hu Ge with his film). *Dongfang weibao*. http://roll.sohu.com/20120629/n346810453.shtml. Last accessed August 31, 2016.

Herold, David Kurt. (2011a). "Introduction: Noise, Spectacle, Politics: Carnival in Chinese Cyberspace." In *Online Society in China: Creating, Celebrating, and Instrumentalising the Online Carnival*, edited by David Kurt Herold and Peter Marolt, 1–19. Abingdon, Oxon and New York: Routledge.

——. (2011b). "Human Flesh Search Engines: Carnivalesque Riots as Components of a 'Chinese Democracy'." In *Online Society in China: Creating, Celebrating, and Instrumentalising the Online Carnival*, edited by David Kurt Herold and Peter Marolt, 127–45. Abingdon, Oxon and New York: Routledge.

Jessop, Bob, Kevin Bonnett, Simon Bromley, and Tom Ling. (1984). "Authoritarian Populism, Two Nations, and Thatcherism." *New Left Review* 147: 32–60.

Jingxian, Lu. (2010). "Online Viciousness Mirrors Moral Breakdown in Real World." *Global Times*. http://www.globaltimes.cn/content/532614.shtml. Last accessed August 31, 2016.

Li, Hongmei. (2011). "Parody and Resistance on the Chinese Internet." In *Online Society in China: Creating, Celebrating, and Instrumentalising the Online Carnival*, edited by David Kurt Herold and Peter Marolt, 71–88. Abingdon, Oxon and New York: Routledge.

Li, Shubo. (2010). "The Online Public Space and Popular Ethos in China." *Media, Culture & Society* 32, no. 1: 63–83.

MacKinnon, Rebecca. (2009). "From Red Guards to Cyber-Vigilantism to Where Next?" *RConversation*, February 26. http://rconversation.blogs.com/rconversation/2009/02/from-red-guards-to-cyber-vigilantism-to-where-next.html. Last accessed August 31, 2016.

Mai Tian. (2008). " 'Hen huang hen baoli' shijian beihou de wenhua guaitai." (The cultural freak behind the case of 'Very Pornographic and Very Violent'). *Xin jing bao*. http://ent.sina.com.cn/r/m/2008-01-10/09281869404.shtml. Last accessed August 31, 2016.

Martinsen, Joel. (2009). "Harnessing Human Search Engines for Government Use." *Danwei*, February 25. http://www.danwei.org/corruption/lets_find_the_reporter_and_wha.php. Last accessed August 31, 2016.

Moretti, Franco. (1997). *Signs Taken for Wonders: Essays in the Sociology of Literary Forms*. Trans. Susan Fischer, David Forgacs and David Miller. London and New York: Verso.

Nie Wei. (2012). " 'Sousuo' wangluo zhengyi: yi dianying zhi ming?" (Searching for justice online: in the name of the film?). *Dangdai dianying* 8: 30–3.

Ritzer, George, and Nathan Jurgenson. (2010). "Production, Consumption, Prosumption." *Journal of Consumer Culture* 10, no. 1: 13–36.

Rushkoff, Douglas. (2010). *Program or Be Programmed: Ten Commands for a Digital Age*. New York: OR Books.

Safranski, Rüdiger. (1997). *Das Böse oder Das Drama der Freiheit. (Evil or the drama of freedom)*. München ua, Hanser (Munich, Hanser).

Shao Yanjun. (2009). "Chuantong wenxue shengchan jizhi de weiji he xinxing jizhi de shengcheng" (The crisis in the traditional literary production mechanism and the emergence of a new-style mechanism). *Wenyi zhengming* 12: 12–22.

——. (2011). "Miandui wangluo wenxue: xueyuanpai de taidu he fangfa" (Facing Internet literature: attitudes and methods of academics). *Nanfang wentan* 6: 12–18.

——. (2012a). "Wangluo shidai: xin wenxue chuantong de duanlie yu 'zhuliu wenxue' de chongjian" (The age of the Internet: the breakage of the new literary tradition and the reconstruction of 'mainstream literature'). *Nanfang wentan* 6: 14–21.

——. (2012b). "Wangluo shidai, jingying he wei?" (What should elite people do in the age of the Internet?). *Tansuo yu zhengming* 5: 12–14.

——. (2014). "Wangluo wenxue shidai Zhongguo 'zhuliu wenxue' de chongjian" (Reconstruction of Chinese 'mainstream literature' in the age of Internet literature). *Yishu pinglun* 12: 68–74.

——. (2015). "Wangluo wenxue de 'wangluo xing' yu 'jingdian xing'" (The Internet and classical qualities of Internet literature). *Beijing daxue xuebao (zhexue shehui kexue ban)* 52, no. 1: 143–52.

Shao Yanjun, Wang Xiang, Zhuang Yong and Chen Cun. (2012). "Wangluo wenxue: ruhe dingwei yu yanjiu" (Internet literature: how to position and study it). *Renmin ribao*, July 17: 24.

Shao Yanjun, Zhuang Yong and Gao Hanning. (2015). "2014 nian wangluo wenxue: duo-chong boyi xia de bianju" (Internet literature in 2014: negotiations and negotiations). *Wenyi bao*, February 4: 003.

Sina. (2009). "*Wuxing sha* daoyan: xiwang yingpian gei guanzhong dailai shendu sikao" (The director of Invisible Killer: I hope my film will make the audience deliberate seriously). *Xinlang yule*. http://ent.sina.com.cn/m/c/2009–08–27/02202671166.shtml. Last accessed August 31, 2016.

Solove, Daniel J. (2007). *The Future of Reputation: Gossip, Rumor, and Privacy on the Internet*. New Haven, CT: Yale University Press.

Sun Haoyuan. (2008). *Renruo sousuo (The human flesh search engine)*. Chongqing: Chongqing chubanshe.

——. (2010). *Zhiming sousuo (Fatal searches)*. Beijing: Dazhong wenyi chubanshe.

Tang, Lijun, and Syamantak Bhattacharya. (2011). "Power and Resistance: A Case Study of Satire on the Internet." *Sociological Research Online* 16, no. 2. http://www.socreson line.org.uk/16/2/11.html. Last accessed August 31, 2016.

Turkle, Sherry. (2011). *Alone Together: Why We Expect More from Technology and Less from Each Other*. New York: Basic Books.

Wang, Fei-Yue, Daniel Zeng, James A. Hendler, Qingpeng Zhang, Zhuo Feng, Yanqing Gao, Hui Wang, Guanpi Lai. (2010). "A Study of the Human Flesh Search Engine: Crowd-Powered Expansion of Online Knowledge." *Computer (IEEE Computer Society)* 43, no. 8: 45–53.

Wang, Jing. (1996). *High Culture Fever: Politics, Aesthetics, and Ideology in Deng's China*. Berkeley, CA: University of California Press.

Wang Min'an. (2009). "Shouji: shenti yu shehui" (Cell phone: body and society). *Wenyi yanjiu* 7: 100–5.

Wang Weijia. (2014). "Dian xinziyou zhuyi: saibo misi de lishi yu zhengzhi" (Dot-neoliberalism: history and politics of cybermyth). *Jingji daokan* 6: 25–36.

Wen, Yu (Zhang Wenxuan). (2012). *Sousuo (Search)*. Changsha: Hunan renmin chubanshe.

——. (2015). *Mingtian, ni shifou ai wo ru chu (Will you love me tomorrow as you first did)*. Changsha: Hunan renmin chubanshe.

Wu Yue. (2012). "Yingshi gaibian hou, wangluo xiaoshuo haiyou chushu de biyao ma?" (Is it necessary to publish an Internet novel in the book form after it is adapted to a film or a TV drama?). http://book.sina.com.cn/news/c/2012-12-01/0834373542.shtml. Last accessed 11 October 2016.

Zhang, Yingjin. (2006). "My Camera Doesn't Lie? Truth, Subjectivity, and Audience in Chinese Independent Film and Video." In *From Underground to Independent: Alternative Film Culture in Contemporary China*, edited by Paul G. Pickowicz and Yingjin Zhang, 23–45. Lanham, MD: Rowman & Littlefield Publishers.

Zhu Dake. (2015). "Bentu dazhong wenhua de san zhong taishi" (Three forms of indigenous popular culture). *Zhengzhou daxue xuebao (Zhexue shehui kexue ban)* 6: 10–12.

Zhuang Yong. (2014). "Wangluo wenxue de 'zhuliu hua': cong shidai fengxiangbiao dao chuangzuo jizhi pingjing" (Internet literature goes mainstream: from the benchmark of a time to a bottleneck in production mechanism). *Wenxue bao*, June 5: 020.

Postscript
Challenges and prospects

Chinese Internet culture changes at a lightning pace, sometimes so fast that it impacted our research and writing of this book. Events took place that affected some subjects of our research during the very process of our writing, and new developments within Internet ecology and culture never stopped emerging. This constantly changing situation posed many challenges for our project, including some of the changes and new developments below.

First, when we finished our chapter on microfiction in 2013, this new genre was still in its heyday, and writing of microfiction was still conducted on a wide scale by a large number of blog users. However, by 2014, Weibo (the main microblog site) had lost a great many users to Weixin (WeChat 微信), a newer mobile communication app, and as a result, microfiction written on Weibo had lost some of its appeal (Schiavenza 2014). At the same time, a new form of microfiction written on Weixin for Weixin users began to emerge and attracted a growing degree of attention (Liu 2013).[1] Meanwhile, the microfiction genre is undergoing large changes in an effort to regain its lost favor. In June 2016, Sina.com launched its latest annual microfiction contest, but this time the organizer raised the character limit for microfiction works from 140 to 300,000 per piece, in order, as one site manager explained, to "make microfiction a new cultural form that better caters to the new habits and demands of contemporary mobile users" (Sina Reading 2016). By restructuring microfiction, Weibo hoped to find some "Big Gods" (*dashen* 大神) – the term that netizens use for the most prolific and popular online writers – of its own.

Second, in recent years, a large number of online fiction set in the *present day*, in addition to *historical* dramas discussed in Chapter 3, were adapted into TV or net dramas, including *Ode to Joy* (*Huanle song* 欢乐颂, 2015), *My Sunshine* (*Heyi shengxiaomo* 何以笙箫默, 2015), *Remembering Lichuan* (*Yujian Wang Lichuan* 遇见王沥川, 2016), *Yu Zui* (*Yu Zui* 余罪, 2016), to just name a few. These dramas have all caused heated online and offline discussions due to their depictions of contemporary romance or crime, probing into hidden anxieties of class inequality. The online/offline migration of pop web fiction has become a dynamic and lucrative industry. As a result, gendered desires, in cross-media adaptations, have been further highlighted, identified, and commercialized.

Third, originally included in this book was a study of a high-profile, cross-media ethnic event called "I Am from Xinjiang" (*Wo cong Xinjiang lai* 我从新疆来).[2] This event was initiated by the Beijing-based Uyghur photographer Kurbanjan Samat, who, during his tenure with the CCTV, published a photograph book entitled *I Am from Xinjiang* (2014). The book displays disparate lives of 100 Xinjiangers from all walks of life making their living in more prosperous parts of the country, most of whom are Uyghur and other minority ethnicities. Upon its publication, Kurbanjan's book received immediate and extremely positive accolades from official sources. These included a ceremony celebrating the book's first publication held in the Great Hall of the People, a prominent symbol of the central political power, in October 2014, and in December 2014 the author was formally received by Yu Zhengsheng, a member of the CCP's most powerful governing body, the Politburo Standing Committee. A launch ceremony for the English version of the book, supported by the Chinese government, was also held at the BookExpo America 2015 in New York. The author was then sent on a tour to the United States by the Xinjiang Uyghur Autonomous Region government, a provincial-level governing body, to give a series of speeches at seven prestigious American universities, including Harvard and Stanford in September 2015. The tour aimed at showing the world the "harmonious" development in Xinjiang at the historical moment of the sixtieth anniversary of the founding of the Xinjiang Uyghur Autonomous Region. During the tour, several American celebrities, including the former President of the United States Jimmy Carter and his wife, met with Kurbanjan (Li 2015, Wang L. 2015, Wang Z. 2015). Yet, what interests us most is the crowdfunding event that Kurbanjan organized on the Internet aiming at collecting funds for producing a TV documentary series about Xinjiangers. The crowdfunding event was fervently supported and promoted by netizens, and many celebrities participated in promoting it as well. By the time of our writing the last few lines of the chapter on ethnicity, this event was still actively being carried out, so we did not include it in this book.

Fourth, the author of *The Human Flesh Search Engine* and *Fatal Searches*, Sun Haoyuan, published another RRSS-related novel, *The Chinese-Style Search* (*Zhongguo shi sousuo* 中国式搜索), in late 2015, completing his RRSS trilogy. This new novel draws on the "Cat Abuse and Killing" incident (see Chapter 5, note 13) and the notorious "Yao Jiaxin Murder Case," and tells a complicated story of a series of murders caused by RRSS.[3] Again, due to the novel's recent publication date, we could not include it in our study of RRSS.

Despite the fact that we did not have the necessary temporal distance to examine these new cases in our book – arguably one may never be able to catch up with the latest developments on the Internet in a time-consuming academic study – our book in its current form has teased out the cultural-political valence of the Chinese Internet in terms of class, gender, ethnicity, and ethics, of which these cases are newer demonstrations. Sometimes newer cases reaffirm largely existing arguments; other times, they offer new directions to be explored based on the existing arguments.

In the case of *egao*, this cultural phenomenon continues to be relevant today, despite having undergone some changes. Like the case of witty ditties of the 1980s, *egao*, while still maintaining its subcultural edge to some degree in more recent years, has become a part of everyday practice and is easily consumed on Weibo, WeChat, and other forms of social media.[4] It continues to satirize social problems, provide pure fun, and sometimes cause social problems such as the Internet violence described in Chapter 5. It "offers both political criticism and emotional bonding for all participants" (Meng 2011: 35) – a political criticism that, however, fails to turn into activism due to the complicity of political and commercial forces (Yu 2015), as well as an emotional bonding that is formed in its networked socialization (Yang and Jiang 2015).

Micro-narratives also continue to be a significant form of cultural expression online, particularly when the ubiquitous connection to the Internet further individualizes and fragmentizes people's lives, while the authoritarian Party-state increasingly tightens its control of cyberspace. However, micro-narratives have also made huge adjustments in order to survive and prosper in a highly commercialized and competitive space. For instance, Sina microfiction so drastically restructures its form that, while it may hopefully succeed in the so-called *wanghong jingji* (economy of online popularity 网红经济), it risks losing its *microness*, or its symbolic critical thrust, under the condition of large-scale social stratification and class consolidation in contemporary China. How is Sina's effort to "redefine microfiction" to be carried out in order to better fit it into the new ecology of social media and cross-media industry (Sina Reading 2016)? What social, political, and cultural implications will this restructuring have? Answers to these questions are yet to be seen.

Gendered desire remains the focus of the more recent border-crossing adaptations mentioned above. The imagination of contemporary masculinity, femininity, and sexuality, configured in romance or crime thriller, is coupled with a keen awareness of class. *Ode to Joy*, for instance, places five girls from different classes in the same space – a residential building, clearly projecting the social barriers that separate them and their destinies. *Yu Zui* depicts a different kind of masculinity through the figure of the title character, an undercover cop whose name literally means "Yu the crime." A "bad boy" who always cheats his way to win over both his peers and criminals, Yu Zui is a complete subversion of the conventional representation of upright, uptight, and incorruptible police officers and communist spies. Voluntarily or involuntarily, he employs all his street smarts acquired as an underling in the lower stratum of the society to survive in a gang. His double identities are highly metaphorical in that they reflect multiple (masculine) masks people have to wear in a fast-paced and morally ambiguous urban life.

More intriguingly, gendered imagination has been selectively appropriated by the business establishment. Among all the online genre fiction, romances, time-travel stories, and thrillers have been the most welcomed to bigger screens. Boys' love stories, a significant portion of online writings, however, have been largely ignored and remain relatively obscure offline. It thus remains to be seen how marginalized desires will make their way to legitimize a cultural position in the mainstream media dominated by official and commercial rhetorics.

Ethnic self-expression online remains largely shaped by the Party-state's "orthodox" ethnic discourse, whether ethnic groups try to find ways to write counter to this discourse or, unwittingly or even knowingly, are co-opted by it. The crowdfunding event of "I Am from Xinjiang" seems to be an entirely new format for ethnic groups' self-expression of identity. Yet, not unlike the wedding photos or the flash mob performance discussed in Chapter 4, the crowdfunding exemplifies no more than an additional case in which ethnic groups took advantage of recent developments in information technologies as well as cultural fads worldwide in constructing and performing their identity. Beneath these disparate formats of performance, we find the continual work of Party-state-sanctioned ethnic ideologies that come to shape ethnic (self-)imagination.

In the case of "I Am from Xinjiang," despite the use of crowdfunding and intermediality, the production was quickly incorporated into the mainstream ethnic narrative. It is no coincidence that this bottom-up activity emerged and received full top-down support from local and central governments at the moment of some major socio-political shifts within China, including the return of ethnic instability and riots as a thorny social issue in Xinjiang in recent years, as well as the strategically important and much hyped policy of "One Belt and One Road" (*Yidai yilu* 一带一路) being put forward by the Party-state and the "China Dream" propaganda being promoted at full steam nationwide.[5] These socio-political shifts necessitated the emergence of cultural performances that justify and sing praise of relevant official goals, and "I Am from Xinjiang" happened to be such a salient performance. This performance was able to attract the attention of both of the mainstream and popular political and cultural agents because, first, Xinjiang, as an important multiethnic site along the ancient Silk Road, plays a highly symbolic role in China's new developmentalist plans; and more importantly, the entire project signals a modern ethnic *self*-expression that speaks properly to the orthodox ideology and fuels popular imagination of a harmonious yet exotic multiethnic mosaic.

Like many other contemporary online ethnic events, "I Am from Xinjiang" was enabled by the hyper-connectivity made possible by the Internet and other media; yet under the postsocialist condition, this connectivity helps more to circulate politically sanguine and commercially astute messages of self-exoticization than to construct a politically motivated imagined community. Of course, the sense of communal identity – that is, Xinjiangers – is a core idea that holds the entire event together. Yet, this communal identity conveys more a sense of conformity with the state ethnic policy and public imagination, mainly in the form of nostalgic sentimentalism, than a pursuit for an independent ethnic identity. The Xinjiangers depicted are mostly "good" citizens working studiously for a better future; the Xinjiang culture presented almost emits a stereotypically exotic aura in a modern condition. What the Internet has mainly achieved in this case is to create a synchronic and isomorphic nostalgia that is a product of the large-scale demographic migration and social transformation in postsocialist China.

Further, this essentially *regional* identity of Xinjiangers has been perceived almost interchangeably with an *ethnic* identity, mainly owing to the high ethnicization of Xinjiang in the public imagination. While the Xinjiangers depicted in Kurbanjan's book are mostly common ethnic minorities, participants of the online crowdfunding project are much more ethnically varied, and the Xinjiangers that the TV documentary series features most prominently are in fact Han celebrities from Xinjiang, including the well-known film stars Tong Liya and Li Yapeng, both of whom also worked as co-producers of the documentary series.[6] Interestingly, the TV documentary series, as a more popular form, presents, as well as accommodates, more "successful" Xinjiangers (most of whom happen to be Han!) than the book form. How does this speak to ethnic power dynamics on the Internet, and more importantly, about the role that the Internet plays as a mediator between the book and the TV forms? This perhaps only reminds us of the role that neoliberalism, as an apparently "liberating" force, plays in creating a political-economic elite class. The Chinese Internet, shaped by both this neoliberal spirit and the postsocialist political condition, presents a complicated, and sometimes (self-)contradictory, characteristic that will continue to shape ethnic (self-)expression for a long time to come.

Finally, the human flesh search engine, in spite of all the controversies, is still quite widely practiced today, in cases such as disclosing corrupt officials' unknown secrets, finding lost children, and exposing identities of those who are deemed to have violated social morals. Sun Haoyuan's new book, *The Chinese-Style Search*, follows its two predecessors in representing ethical problems involved in RRSS in a new thriller. The book continues to criticize the so-called "square justice" (*guangchang zhengyi* 广场正义) in RRSS, a populist, moralist, and vigilantist virtual practice of "justice" that is in total disregard of the judicial system (Sun 2015: 63). This square justice, in Sun's view, only leads to the formation of a violent mob, which is easily subject to "justice boredom" (*zhengyi pilao* 正义疲劳) – that is, they are easily bored by achieving a sense of justice (Sun 2015: 156). Therefore, they need to be constantly stimulated by newer and more dramatic feelings of justice, which inevitably makes them vulnerable to manipulation. The author attacks the manipulation of netizens in the name of social justice, which he believes causes a collapse in ethical values on the Internet. The most powerful force that manipulates netizens, the author believes, is the all-encompassing commercialization, of which, ironically, the book itself is a product. Although RRSS has become a more normal and less controversial practice today, mainly due to the rise of awareness and the implementation of social regulations and self-regulation, concerns about achieving social justice versus weighing the right to privacy continue to raise questions about the use of RRSS.

Online culture, blurred boundaries, and transnational context

The configuration of class, gender, ethnicity, and ethics in online culture demonstrates the closely intertwined nature of online and offline spaces, the global and the local, and the mainstream and subcultures. As cyberspace is increasingly becoming an integral part of many people's lives, the virtual and the material world has become a critical issue in understanding Internet culture. Most recently, for instance, the location-based reality game, "Pokémon GO," has taken the world by storm. The smartphone game requires players to physically explore various locations in order to catch virtual cartoon monsters. Large crowds of people appear in public spaces, such as city halls, churches, or parks, with lowered heads as they walk around and try to catch the virtual characters. Aside from players potentially alarming the police, the game provides an interesting case regarding the increasingly intertwined nature of virtual and physical spaces. The pursuit of virtual fun leads to physical roaming, and the physical activity in real location, in turn, facilitates the player's online success and psychological gratification. Cyberspace and real space, in this way, connect even closer, fulfilling heterotopic roles of border crossing.

Because of this, we find the newly coined term "virtual civilization" problematic in its conceptualization of cyberspace in relation to reality. Seeing the rapidly developing online textual and new audio-visual culture, the scholar Chen Xiaoming (Shao et al. 2016) claimed, in a roundtable discussion in early 2016, an arrival of the "virtual civilization." Over-optimism aside, "virtual civilization" pits the virtual against the real. As we have discussed throughout the book, cyberspaces that offer imagined empowerment and provide an escapist sanctuary for people to ease their anxieties, voice unrealized fantasies, and express their hidden desires, have already become an integral part of the reality that is deeply ingrained in everyday life. For a fast-growing number of people today, wired computers, smartphones, and tablets have become their new daily necessity. Perhaps WeChat's claim best speaks to this new networked condition – "WeChat is a kind of lifestyle." Indeed, the virtual are portable, mobile, tangible, and, in all, life-changing. Heterotopic in nature, the Internet is simultaneously virtual and real, and abstract and concrete; it destabilizes boundaries and forms new norms, and its very realness is precisely mediated by its virtuality, and vice versa.

In the same roundtable discussion, Shao Yanjun also proudly called Chinese online fiction "a world spectacle" (Shao et al. 2016). Admittedly, this "spectacle" was formed as a result of multiple sociocultural factors. For a period of time in the 1980s, popular genre fiction, due to the elitist status of socially engaged "serious" literature in China, had been kept in a culturally marginalized position. Conventional marketing channels for genre fiction were yet to be fully developed. It was the Internet, Shao remarked, that has opened up an entirely new space that is easily accessible and widely available for both the production and consumption of such genre fiction. The creative energy unleashed in online writing has not been seen at this scale in any other part of the world. Shao's pronouncement seems to be supported by many such cultural "spectacles" in recent years. In December of 2014, for instance, the website "*Wuxiaworld*" (The World of Martial Arts, http://www.wuxiaworld.com/about-wuxiaworld) was launched and quickly rose to the status of the largest Chinese-to-English novel translational platform. Translators are volunteers and dedicated fans of *wuxia* from Hong Kong, the United States,

China, Malaysia, and Singapore. The website works with Chinese online fiction websites such as 17k.com. The novels that have been translated include martial arts and fantasy fiction published online. According to the website's introduction, the website was ranked by Alexa as one of the top 2000 websites in the United States and "has become a brand name in Chinese-to-English novel translation excellence." (Wuxiaworld, undated)

Chinese online popular fiction crossing national and linguistic borders, in Shao's view, could be one form of Chinese "soft power" (Shao et al. 2016). Though it is debatable whether it is the martial arts genre or online fiction per se that has caught the attention of transnational readers, such a website does show that Chinese online fiction has become part of transnational cultural production, consumption, and communication. Different from the state-initiated projects of soft power, such as Confucius Institutes, promotional videos played on Time Square in New York City, or the profit-driven and market-oriented blockbuster production of film and art, these online cultural products are translated and disseminated simply because of the passion, interest, and enthusiasm of fans and volunteers. Fans' free labor has rendered *Nirvana in Fire*, for instance, into English and shared on YouTube, Youku, and Weibo, extending its presence beyond its original language barriers. The fan-initiated transnational online cultural endeavor at the grassroots level, in our eyes, is an intriguing aspect of "soft power" that requires further research.

Online culture has developed at a fast pace, just like the rapidly changing social reality in China in the new millennium. While cyberspace has inevitably received official and commercial endorsement and sponsorship and, as a result, has been manipulated by these forces in one way or another, many other originally subcultural forms also found in the Internet a perfect space for their production, publication, circulation, and consumption. The bottom-up energy, labors of love, and the genuine enthusiasm from netizens in transnational settings have certainly made online creative activities intriguing. These verbal and visual representations have indeed provided an alternative voice to and thus intervened into the otherwise monolithic narratives of identity and community. It is the contestation of different ideologies and mentalities, in both online and offline settings, that have enriched our understanding of the world.

Notes

1 The first Weixin novel is claim to be *I Shake My Cell Phone to Find You, Not Loneliness* (*Yao de shi ni, bushi jimo* 摇的是你, 不是寂寞), written by NBC Second Chief (NBC二当家的). It began serialization on WeChat in 2012.

2 "I Am from Xinjiang" first drew our attention because of a senior capstone project at Macalester College. We would like to thank Ashley Hung for her insight and research on identity issues in this Weibo thread.

3 On the night of October 20, 2010, Yao Jiaxin, then a twenty-one-year-old student of the Xi'an Conservatory of Music, ran down and injured a countrywoman, Zhang Miao, while driving. When Yao saw Zhang trying to memorize his car plate, he stabbed her to death. One controversy during Yao's trial was that Zhang Miao's lawyer Zhang Xian spread the word through several different Weibo and other blog accounts that Yao's father was related to some corrupt high-ranking military officials, which aroused huge

resentment against Yao among netizens. An RRSS was launched for Yao's father. Yao Jiaxin was sentenced to death in 2011. After Yao's execution, Yao's father sued Zhang Xian for spreading rumors and fanning public anger to influence media coverage and the trial. A verdict was made in favor of Yao's father on July 31, 2012.

4 For detailed discussion on the witty ditties in the 1980s, see Jing Wang (1996).

5 "One Belt and One Road," a short term for "The Silk Road Economic Belt and the 21st-century Maritime Silk Road," is a development strategy proposed by the Chinese President Xi Jinping in 2013. By linking China with Central and Western Asia, Southeast Asian countries, Africa, and Europe, it aims at integrating China

> into the world economy and strengthen its influence in these regions. . . . The strategy underlines the government's push to have a bigger say in global economic and political affairs, and to export China's technologies and production capacity in oversupplied areas such as steel manufacturing.
>
> (Caixin 2014)

6 The TV documentary series was broadcast in CCTV Documentary Channel on June 22, 2016, and was available for online viewing on major streaming servers, including Sohu, IQiyi, LeTV, and Tencent.

Bibliography

Caixin (2014). "One Belt, One Road." http://english.caixin.com/2014–12–10/100761304. html. Last accessed August 31, 2016.

Liu Lizhi. (2013). "Weixin xiaoshuo qiaoran xingqi, shichang qianjing bu mingque" (WeChat fiction quietly emerges, and its market is unclear). *Bandao wang*, March 20. http://news.bandao.cn/news_html/201303/20130320/news_20130320_2099814.shtml. Last accessed August 31, 2016.

Li Lulu. (2015). "Kuerbanjiang: wo cong Xinjiang lai" (Kurbanjan: I am from Xinjiang). *Beijing wanbao*, April 14.

Meng, Bingchun. (2011). "From *Steamed Bun* to *Grass Mud Horse*: *E Gao* as Alternative Political Discourse on the Chinese Internet." *Global Media and Communication* 7, no. 1: 33–51.

Samat, Kurbanjan. (2014). *Wo cong Xinjiang lai* (*I am from Xinjiang*). Beijing: Zhongxin chubanshe.

———. (2015). *I Am from Xinjiang on the Silk Road*. New York: New World Press.

Schiavenza, Matt. (2014). "China's Weibo Losing Users." *The Daily Beast*, January 25. http://www.thedailybeast.com/articles/2014/01/25/china-s-weibo-losing-users.html. Last accessed August 31, 2016.

Shao Yanjun, Chen Xiaoming and Li Jingze. (2016). "Yeman shengzhang hou, zhongguo wangluo wenxue yi cheng shijie qiguan" (After a wild growth, Chinese online literature has become a world spectacle). *Zhongguo zuojia wang*. http://www.chinawriter.com.cn/n1/2016/0627/c404027–28488814.html. Last accessed August 31, 2016.

Sina Reading. (2016). "2016 'weixiaoshuo' dasai shangxian, jiemi weibo 'zaoshen jihua'" (2016 microfiction contest starts: deciphering microblog's 'star-making plan'). http://book.sina.com.cn/news/c/2016–06–23/1735810647.shtml. Last accessed August 31, 2016.

Sun Haoyuan. (2015). *Zhongguo shi sousuo* (*The Chinese-style search*). Nanjing: Jiangsu fenghuang wenyi chubanshe.

Wang, Jing. (1996). *High Culture Fever: Politics, Aesthetics, and Ideology in Deng's China*. Berkeley, CA: University of California Press.

Wang Lei. (2015). "English version of 'I am from Xinjiang on the Silk Road' launched in NYC." *Xinhua wang.* http://news.xinhuanet.com/english/photo/2015–05/29/c_13427 9789.htm. Last accessed August 31, 2016.

Wang Zongping. (2015). "Wo cong Xinjiang lai, Meiguo yanjiang hua jiaxiang" (I am from Xinjiang—talking about hometown in the US). *Chenbao*, September 21.

Wuxiaworld. (undated). http://www.wuxiaworld.com/about-wuxiaworld. Last accessed January 8, 2017.

Yang, Guobin, and Min Jiang. (2015). "The Networked Practice of Online Political Satire in China: Between Ritual and Resistance." *The International Communication Gazette* 77, no. 3: 215–31.

Yu, Haiqing. (2015). "After the 'Steamed Bun': E'gao and Its Postsocialist Politics." *Chinese Literature Today* 5, no. 1: 55–64.

Index